Lecture Notes in Computer Science   6606

Commenced Publication in 1973
Founding and Former Series Editors:
Gerhard Goos, Juris Hartmanis, and Jan van Leeuwen

Daniel Berry   Xavier Franch (Eds.)

Requirements Engineering: Foundation for Software Quality

17th International Working Conference, REFSQ 2011
Essen, Germany, March 28-30, 2011
Proceedings

 Springer

Volume Editors

Daniel Berry
University of Waterloo, Cheriton School of Computer Science
200 University Ave. West, Waterloo, Ontario N2L 3G1, Canada
E-mail: dberry@uwaterloo.ca

Xavier Franch
Universitat Politècnica de Catalunya - Campus Nord, Department ESSI - UPC
Omega Building, Room 122, c/Jordi Girona 1-3, 08034 Barcelona, Spain
E-mail: franch@essi.upc.edu

ISSN 0302-9743   e-ISSN 1611-3349
ISBN 978-3-642-19857-1   ISBN 978-3-642-19858-8 (eBook)
DOI 10.1007/978-3-642-19858-8
Springer Heidelberg Dordrecht London New York

Library of Congress Control Number: 2011922663

CR Subject Classification (1998): C.2, C.5.3, D.4, D.2.11, H.3.5, H.4, H.5.4

LNCS Sublibrary: SL 2 – Programming and Software Engineering

Typesetting: Camera-ready by author, data conversion by Scientific Publishing Services, Chennai, India

Printed on acid-free paper

Springer is part of Springer Science+Business Media (www.springer.com)

Preface

This volume of the LNCS contains the papers accepted for presentation at the 17th Working Conference on Requirements Engineering: Foundation for Software Quality (REFSQ 2011), held in Essen, Germany during March 28–31, 2011.

Since the beginning of computing, long before 1994 when the first REFSQ took place, requirements engineering (RE) has always been a major factor determining the quality of software-intensive, computer-based systems and services. From REFSQ's beginnings as a workshop, the REFSQ working conference series has steadily established itself as a leading international forums in which to discuss RE in its many relations to computer-based system quality. REFSQ seeks reports of novel ideas and techniques that enhance RE processes and artifacts as well as reflections on current research and industrial practice about and in RE. Probably the most appreciated characteristic of a REFSQ working conference is its format in which, unlike most conferences and workshops, the discussion following a paper's presentation is as long as the presentation.

A total of 59 papers of all categories were submitted, 2 more than last year, despite the fact that in moving the working conference 4 months earlier, authors had less time to prepare this year. Each paper was subjected to reviews by three different members of the Program Committee. Whenever the reviews for a paper showed any divergence, the reviewers were asked to conduct a discussion electronically with the aim of reaching a consensus. Following the discussions, a few of which ended with the reviewers agreeing to differ, the Program Committee met to resolve these differences and to choose the final set of 19 accepted papers, yielding an overall acceptance rate of 32%. Of the 38 long papers submitted, 10 were accepted, yielding a long-paper acceptance rate of 26%, and of the 21 short papers submitted, 9 were accepted, yielding a short-paper acceptance rate of 43%. The long accepted papers included 7 research papers and 3 experience report papers. The short accepted papers included 7 research preview papers, and 2 problem statement papers.

As in previous years, these proceedings serve not only as the record of one meeting of REFSQ, but also as a snapshot of the state of research and practice about and in RE. Therefore, these proceedings are of interest to the whole RE community, ranging from students beginning their PhD studies, through experienced scholars doing sustained RE research, novice requirements analysts, to experienced practitioners interested in emerging knowledge.

At the time of writing, REFSQ 2011 had not yet happened. Anyone interested in an account of the discussions that took place during the working conference should consult the post-conference summary that we intend to publish, as is usual, in ACM SIGSOFT's *Software Engineering Notes*.

Above all, REFSQ is a collaborative effort. First, we thank Klaus Pohl for his continuing work as General Chair of the working conference. We thank also

Vanessa Stricker, who very ably served as Organization Chair. We thank the Steering Committee, listed here, consisting of Program Committee Chairs and General Chairs of past REFSQ working conferences, for their seasoned advice. The advice of Anne Persson and Roel Wieringa, last year's Progam Committee Chairs, was particularly helpful.

We thank also the organizers of the four workshops held on the day after the conference for their effort and Martin Glinz for managing the workshop selection process. We thank Vincenzo Gervasi and Barbara Paech for organizing the Doctoral Symposium on the day after the working conference. We thank Christof Ebert for organizing the Industry Track on the middle day of the working conference. Planned were industry presentations and workshops on product-line engineering, lean development, domain-specific languages, quality attributes, and requirements management tools. Ebert has set up a novel concept in which challenges, experiences and open questions from industry are presented and discussed with the audience.

REFSQ 2011 saw the innovation of two new events, proposed by Jörg Dörr, in a new Empirical Track. One of these is the Empirical Studies at REFSQ event, organized by Jörg Dörr, in which one proposed study of 11 submitted was selected to be conducted during a session of the first day of the working conference. The second of these is the Empirical Research Fair, organized by Brian Berenbach and Nazim Madhavji. For this Fair, all 12 submitted proposals for empirical research to be done in industrial settings were selected for presentation during one session during the Industry Track day. The hope is that researchers who want to conduct the research can be matched with companies that want to provide the industrial setting and subjects for the research in exchange for first access to the results.

As the Program Committee Co-chairs for REFSQ 2011, we thank especially the members of the Program Committee, listed here, for their careful, thorough, and timely reviews and for their lively consensus e-discussions. We thank in particular those of the Program Committee who attended the Program Committee meeting and those, listed here, who volunteered to serve as shepherds to help improve promising papers. Finally, we thank all the sponsors, also listed, who contributed generously to the smooth running of the working conference itself.

January 2011   Daniel Berry
                                                                     Xavier Franch

Conference Organization

General Chair

Klaus Pohl   University of Duisburg-Essen, Germany

Program Committee Co-chairs

Daniel Berry   University of Waterloo, Canada
Xavier Franch   Technical University of Catalunya, Spain

Organizing Committee

Brian Berenbach   Siemens Corporate Research, USA
Jörg Dörr   Fraunhofer IESE, Germany
Christof Ebert   Vector, Germany
Vincenzo Gervasi   University of Pisa, Italy
Martin Glinz   University of Zurich, Switzerland
Nazim Madhavji   University of Western Ontario, Canada
Barbara Paech   University of Heidelberg, Germany
Vanessa Stricker (Chair)   University of Duisburg-Essen, Germany

Publication Chairs

Daniel Berry   University of Waterloo, Canada
Xavier Franch   Technical University of Catalunya, Spain

Program Committee

Ian Alexander   Scenarioplus, UK
Aybüke Aurum   University New South Wales, Australia
Jürgen Börstler   University of Umeå, Sweden
Sjaak Brinkkemper   Utrecht University, The Netherlands
David Callele   University of Saskatchewan, Canada
Alan Davis   University of Colorado at Colorado Springs, USA
Jörg Dörr   Fraunhofer IESE, Germany
Eric Dubois   CRP Henri Tudor, Luxembourg
Christof Ebert   Vector, Germany
Anthony Finkelstein   University College London, UK
Samuel Fricker   University of Zurich and Fuchs-Informatik AG, Switzerland

Vincenzo Gervasi	University of Pisa, Italy
Martin Glinz	University of Zurich, Switzerland
Tony Gorschek	Blekinge Institute of Technology, Sweden
Olly Gotel	Independent Researcher, USA
Paul Grünbacher	University of Linz, Austria
Peter Haumer	IBM Rational, USA
Patrick Heymans	University of Namur, Belgium
Sara Jones	City University London, UK
Natalia Juristo	Politechnic University of Madrid, Spain
Erik Kamsties	University of Applied Sciences Dortmund, Germany
Kim Lauenroth	University of Duisburg-Essen, Germany
Søren Lauesen	IT-University of Copenhagen, Denmark
Seok-Won Lee	University of North Carolina at Charlotte, USA
Pericles Loucopoulos	Loughborough University, UK
Nazim Madhavji	University of Western Ontario, Canada
Raimundas Matulevičius	University of Tartu, Estonia
Luisa Mich	University of Trento, Italy
Ana Moreira	New University of Lisbon, Portugal
Haralambos Mouratidis	University of East London, UK
John Mylopoulos	University of Toronto, Canada
Cornelius Ncube	Bournemouth University, UK
Andreas Opdahl	University of Bergen, Norway
Barbara Paech	University of Heidelberg, Germany
Oscar Pastor Lopez	Politechnic University of Valencia, Spain
Gilles Perrouin	University of Namur, Belgium
Anne Persson	University of Skövde, Sweden
Jolita Ralyté	University of Geneva, Switzerland
Gil Regev	Federal Polytechnic University of Lausanne, Switzerland
Björn Regnell	Lund University, Sweden
Colette Rolland	University of Paris 1, Panthéon Sorbonne, France
Camille Salinesi	University of Paris 1, Panthéon Sorbonne, France
Kristian Sandahl	Linköping University, Sweden
Peter Sawyer	Lancaster University, UK
Kurt Schneider	University of Hannover, Germany
Norbert Seyff	University of Zurich, Switzerland
Guttorm Sindre	Norwegian University of Science and Technology, Norway
Janis Stirna	Royal Institute of Technology, Sweden
Davor Svetinovic	Masdar Institute of Science and Technology, UAE

Roel Wieringa   University of Twente, The Netherlands
Eric Yu   University of Toronto, Canada
Konstantinos Zachos   City University London, UK
Andrea Zisman   City University London, UK

External Reviewers

Eya Ben Charrada   André Rifaut
Willem Bekkers   Germain Saval
Alexander Delater   Reinhard Stoiber
Remo Ferrari   Vanessa Stricker
Robert Heinrich   Marcus Trapp
André Heuer   Kevin Vlaanderen
Slinger Jansen   Inge van de Weerd
Cédric Jeanneret   Dustin Wüest
Isabel John   Jelena Zdravković
Peter Karpati

Shepherds

Samuel Fricker, Nazim Madhavji, Gilles Perrouin, Anne Persson, Kurt Schneider,
Guttorm Sindre, Roel Wieringa

Steering Committee

Daniel Berry   University of Waterloo, Canada
Daniela Damian   University of Victoria, Canada
Xavier Franch   Technical University of Catalunya, Spain
Vincenzo Gervasi   University of Pisa, Italy
Martin Glinz   University of Zurich, Switzerland
Patrick Heymans (Vice-Chair)   University of Namur, Belgium
Kim Lauenroth   University of Duisburg-Essen, Germany
Andreas Opdahl   University of Bergen, Norway
Barbara Paech   University of Heidelberg, Germany
Anne Persson   University of Skövde, Sweden
Klaus Pohl   University of Duisburg-Essen, Germany
Björn Regnell   Lund University, Sweden
Camille Salinesi   University of Paris 1, Panthéon Sorbonne,
                                   France
Peter Sawyer (Chair)   Lancaster University, UK
Ernst Sikora   Automotive Safety Technologies, Germany
Roel Wieringa   University of Twente, The Netherlands

Sponsors

Platinum Level Sponsors

Gold Level Sponsors

Silver Level Sponsors

evu|t.

e-Spirit

Table of Contents

Session 4: Models

Session 5: Services

Session 6: Embedded and Real-Time Systems

Session 7: Prioritization and Traceability

Delivering Requirements Research into Practice: A Keynote to the REFSQ'2011 Conference

Neil Maiden

City University London
Northampton Square, London, EC1V0HB, UK
N.A.M.Maiden@city.ac.uk

Abstract. Requirements research over the last 25 years has delivered numerous methods, techniques and tools. These methods, techniques and tools have been reported in requirements and software engineering journals and conferences, often with small-scale evaluations based on experiments and controlled studies. Alas few of these methods, techniques and tools have been applied to large-scale requirements problems or transferred to widespread requirements practice. This keynote reviews the challenges that researchers face to apply research solutions to requirements practices. It demonstrates how some of these challenges have been overcome with presentations of cases that show the application of requirements research on large-scale industrial projects, and reflect on how these successes were achieved. The keynote ends with proposals to deliver more requirements research into practice.

Keywords: Requirements engineering, industrial practice, exploitation and dissemination.

1 Introduction

There have been few systematic attempts [12, 13, 14] to review the impact of the requirements engineering research reported in academic journals and conferences on downstream industrial practices. This is because undertaking such reviews is difficult, for at least two reasons. The first is the length of the lapsed time between first reporting a research result and applying that result in a commercial process, technique or software tool. The second is the difficulty of tracing the impact of a reported research result on a concrete solution. The design of one process, technique or tool is often influenced by a range of business trends, feedback from stakeholders and existing processes and techniques, as well as results from academic research.

Whilst systematic reviews across the breadth of the discipline are difficult to undertake, it is possible to highlight examples of requirements solutions based directly on research outcomes. The influence of Jackson's problem frames [2] on the REVEAL requirements method [1] and the KAOS method [10] on the Objectiver software tool both come to mind. Alas, however, these examples are the exception. An informed trawl of the proceedings of the requirements engineering conferences over the last 10 years suggests that most reported research has not impacted directly

D. Berry and X. Franch (Eds.): REFSQ 2011, LNCS 6606, pp. 1–3, 2011.

on commercial requirements solutions, in spite of increasing number of evaluation papers that seek to demonstrate the utility of emerging requirements research on practice. Given that requirements engineering is an applied discipline in a design science, one that cannot be detached from evolving technologies and their uses in domains, there are reasons to be concerned for the future of the discipline.

So why is the transfer of research knowledge to industrial practice not happening? What barriers are inhibiting the effective transfer and update of requirements engineering research results? It is simple to identify many potential barriers, for example the limits of our education system and what is required to obtain a doctorate, the limited scale of funding mechanisms for requirements research, and the inabilities of requirements practitioners to articulate future research directions. In this keynote presentation the author reflects on these barriers and how to overcome them in terms of his own experiences.

One aim of the author's research team over the last twelve years has been to consolidate results from its own requirements engineering research so that large-scale formative and summative evaluations of the research results become the norm rather than the exception, thereby providing feedback and evidence so that the research results can be taken on into pre-competitive then commercial products. Examples of this research and its application include:

- the application of creativity models, techniques and tools to requirements processes for socio-technical systems in domains ranging from air traffic management, policing, food information traceability and reflective learning [3, 6, 7, 8];
- the application of the *i** goal modeling technique to model and analyze socio-technical systems in domains including air traffic management and preventative health [4, 5, 9];
- the application of established information retrieval techniques to enable requirements-based service discovery as early as possible in requirements projects, applied in one automotive domain [11], and;
- the development of linked quality requirement and quality-of-service standards for cloud service selection and adaptation, as part of an international commercial consortium at *www.cloudcommons.com*.

The author uses these experiences to construct important lessons learned that can inform other requirements researchers to transfer their research results to industrial practice.

References

1. Hammond, J., Rawlings, R., Hall, A.: Will It Work? In: Proceedings 5th IEEE International Symposium on Requirements Engineering, pp. 102–109. IEEE Computer Society, Los Alamitos (2001)
2. Jackson, M.A.: Problem Frames: Analysing and Structuring Software Development Problems. Addison-Wesley, Reading (2001)
3. Jones, S.V., Lynch, P., Maiden, N.A.M., Lindstaedt, S.: Use and Influence of Creative Ideas and Requirements for a Work-Integrated Learning System. In: Proceedings 16th IEEE International Conference on Requirements Engineering, pp. 289–294. IEEE Computer Society Press, Los Alamitos (2008)

4. Lockerbie, J., Bush, D., Maiden, N.A.M., Blom, H., Everdij, M.: Using i* Modelling as a Bridge between Air Traffic Management Operational Concepts and Agent-Based Simulation Analysis. In: Proceedings 18th IEEE International Requirements Engineering Conference, pp. 351–356. IEEE Computer Society Press, Los Alamitos (2010)
5. Maiden, N.A.M., Manning, S., Jones, S., Greenwood, J.: Generating Requirements from Systems Models using Patterns: A Case Study. Requirements Engineering Journal 10(4), 276–288 (2005)
6. Maiden, N.A.M., Ncube, C., Robertson, S.: Can Requirements Be Creative? Experiences with an Enhanced Air Space Management System. In: Proceedings 28th International Conference on Software Engineering, pp. 632–641. ACM Press, New York (2007)
7. Maiden, N.A.M., Robertson, S.: Integrated Creativity into Requirements Processes: Experiences with an Air Traffic Management System. In: Proceedings 13th IEEE International Conference on Requirements Engineering, pp. 105–114. IEEE Computer Society Press, Los Alamitos (2005)
8. Maiden, N., Robertson, S., Gizikis, A.: Provoking Creativity: Imagine What Your Requirements Could be Like. IEEE Software 21(5), 68–75 (2004)
9. Maiden, N.A.M., Jones, S., Ncube, C., Lockerbie, J.: Using i* in Requirements Projects: Some Experiences and Lessons. In: Yu, E., Giorgini, P., Maiden, M., Mylopoulos, J. (eds.) Social Modeling for Requirements Engineering, pp. 155–185. MIT Press, Cambridge (2010) ISBN: 978-0-262-24055-0
10. Van Lamsweerde, A.: Requirements Engineering: From System Goals to UML Models to Software Specifications. John Wiley and Sons Inc., Chichester (2008)
11. Zachos, K., Maiden, N.A.M.: Inventing Requirements from Software: An Empirical Investigation with Web Services. In: Proceedings 16th IEEE International Conference on Requirements Engineering, pp. 145–154. IEEE Computer Society Press, Los Alamitos (2008)
12. Davis, A., Hickey, A.: A quantitative assessment of requirements engineering publications – 1963-2008. In: Glinz, M., Heymans, P. (eds.) REFSQ 2009. LNCS, vol. 5512, pp. 175–189. Springer, Heidelberg (2009)
13. Davis, A., Hickey, A., Dieste, O., Juristo, N., Moreno, A.: A quantitative assessment of requirements engineering publications – 1963–2006. In: Sawyer, P., Heymans, P. (eds.) REFSQ 2007. LNCS, vol. 4542, pp. 129–143. Springer, Heidelberg (2007)
14. Hickey, A., Davis, A., Kaiser, D.: Requirements Elicitation Techniques: Analyzing the Gap Between Technology Availability and Technology Use. Comparative Technology Transfer and Society 1(3), 279–302 (2003)

Supporting Requirements Engineers in Recognising Security Issues

Eric Knauss[1], Siv Houmb[2], Kurt Schneider[1],
Shareeful Islam[3], and Jan Jürjens[4],[*]

[1] Software Engineering Group, Leibniz Universität Hannover, Germany
{eric.knauss,kurt.schneider}@inf.uni-hannover.de
[2] SecureNOK Ltd., Norway
sivhoumb@securenok.com
[3] School of Computing, IT and Engineering, University of East London, UK
shareef@daad-alumni.de
[4] Software Engineering, Technische Universität Dortmund and Fraunhofer ISST, Germany
http://jan.jurjens.de

Abstract. Context & motivation: More and more software projects today are security-related in one way or the other. Many environments are initially not considered security-related and no security experts are assigned. Requirements engineers often fail to recognise indicators for security problems. **Question/problem:** Ignoring security issues early in a project is a major source of recurring security problems in practice. Identifying security-relevant requirements is labour-intensive and error-prone. Security may be neglected in order to finish on time and in budget. **Principal ideas/results:** In this paper, we address this problem by presenting a tool-supported method that provides assistance for requirements engineering, with an emphasis on security requirements. We investigate whether security-relevant requirements can be automatically identified using a Bayesian classifier. Our results indicate that this is feasible, in particular if the classifier is trained with domain specific data and documents from previous projects. **Contribution:** We show how the ability to identify security-relevant requirements can be integrated in a workflow of requirements analysis and reuse of experience. In practice, this can increase security awareness within the software development process. We discuss limitations and potential of this approach.

Keywords: secure software engineering, requirements analysis, natural language processing, empirical study.

1 Introduction

IT security requirements increasingly pervade all kinds of software systems, sometimes unexpectedly. Security requirements are often not identified during requirements analysis. Thus, security issues are neglected and can cause substantial security problems later. There are standards and best practices available aimed at guiding developers in building secure systems [1]. Nevertheless, identifying requirements with security implications requires security expertise and experience. Unfortunately, security experts

---

[*] The work is partly supported by the EU project Secure Change (ICT-FET-231101).

D. Berry and X. Franch (Eds.): REFSQ 2011, LNCS 6606, pp. 4–18, 2011.

are not always available. Missing security expertise early in a project is one of the main reasons for security problems.

Security requirements may be implicit, hidden, and spread out over different parts of mostly textual requirements specifications. Any bug in the systems might lead to a security weakness. It is tedious and error-prone to search a document manually or evaluate requirements during elicitation. Resources are usually limited for security analysis.

Therefore, fast and efficient identification of security-relevant statements and requirements is a key skill. Ideally, the identification should follow objective rules and be reproducible (e.g. by being automated or supported by a semi-automatic tool). In this paper, we present a tool-supported approach for identifying security-relevant requirements. It uses experience extracted from previously classified requirements documents. We show that Bayesian classifiers can be used to identify security-relevant requirements (with recall > 0.9 and precision > 0.8 in our evaluation setting). Despite the need for domain specific training these classifiers can support security awareness in software evolution scenarios.

Such a classifier can be integrated into a requirements elicitation tool. It then points out security-relevant issues during interviews. In SecReq [2], this task has been supported by the Heuristic Requirements Assistant (HeRA) [3], based on simple keyword-lists. In this paper, we present Bayesian classifiers as an improvement to the SecReq approach: They are easier to train with new experiences and generate more true findings and fewer false positives.

Section 2 provides an overview of the SecReq approach and how it can be used to simulate the presence of a security expert in requirements elicitation. It outlines how Bayesian classifiers can improve security awareness. Section 3 presents the evaluation for our technical solution. Results are discussed in Section 4. Section 5 outlines related work, and Section 6 concludes the paper by summing up the main results and outlining further directions of work from here.

2 Simulating the Presence of a Security Expert

Our SecReq approach assists in security requirements elicitation. It provides mechanisms to trace security requirements from high-level security statements, such as security goals and objectives, to secure design [2]. We aim at making security best practices and experiences available to developers and designers with no or limited experience with security. SecReq integrates three distinctive techniques (see Figure 1): (1) Common Criteria and its underlying security requirements elicitation and refinement process [1], (2) the HeRA tool with its security-related heuristic rules [3], and (3) the UMLsec approach for security analysis and design [4].

Unfortunately, there are not many security experts, and most security guidelines or "best practices" are written by and for security experts. Also, security best practices such as standards ISO 14508 (Common Criteria), ISO 17799 are static documents that do not account for new and emerging security threats. Security issues can be characterized as known or hidden, generic or domain-specific. Normally, a security expert is absolutely necessary to identify *hidden* security issues, while *known* issues can be identified using security best practices.

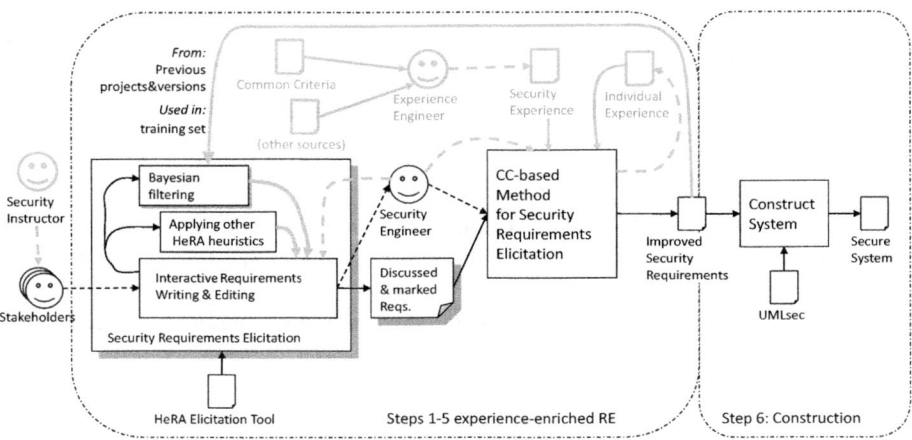

Fig. 1. Overview of SecReq approach. Flow of requirements (black) and experience (grey) is modelled in the FLOW information flow notation [5]. Document symbols and solid arrows indicate documented requirements, experiences, and their flows. Faces symbolise people or groups; direct communication is denoted by dashed lines. Boxes represent activities. The focus of this paper is the activity highlighted by a shadow: Security Requirements Elicitation is refined by applying Bayesian filters. They are trained by reusing documents from earlier projects.

SecReq - and the HeRA tool in particular - guide the translation of these best practices into heuristic rules. They try to make better use of the few security experts around. Rather than having experts do the identification and refinement of all security issues, SecReq reuses their expertise and makes their security knowledge available to non-security experts.

In this paper we describe an improved version of the SecReq approach. We intended to reduce the amount of manual work by making better use of documents and experience from previous projects. Figure 1 shows this improvement as a solid arrow from improved security requirements from previous projects back to the early security requirements elicitation activity (shaded box). We use them to continually train a Bayesian filter. Growing numbers of pre-classified requirements from previous projects will increase the classification ability of that filter. This new experience flow improves the effectiveness and efficiency of the SecReq apporach, because it reduces manual work by leveraging Baysian classifiers. This enables HeRA to address both generic and domain-specific security aspects and to capture experts' tacit knowledge better. Based on this knowledge, heuristic computer-based feedback can simulate the presence of a security expert during security requirements elicitation.

2.1   Classifying Security Requirements

In order to train the Bayesian classifier, we need pre-classified requirements. During expert classification, we encountered three different types of security requirements. We define:

Security requirement: (i) A (quality) requirement describing that a part of the system shall be secure, or *(ii)* a property which, if violated, may threaten the security of a system.

In our context, security requirements are the result of refining security-relevant aspects. Our goal is to support this process.

Security-relevant requirement: (i) A requirement that should be refined into one or more security requirement(s), or *(ii)* a property that is potentially important for assessing the security of the system.
Example: "The card must ensure that the transaction is performed by the same POS device as was used for the purchase being canceled [...]"

During pre-classification, we encountered another type of requirements:

Security-related requirement: (i) A requirement that gives (functional) details of security requirements, or *(ii)* a requirement which arises in the context of security considerations.
Example: "The card and the PSAM must use a public key algorithm for mutual authentication and session key exchange [...]"

To support the identification of hidden security aspects, we need to identify *security-relevant requirements*. It took our experts some training to avoid false classification (e.g. classifying a security requirement or security-related requirement as being security-relevant). Furthermore, each and every functional requirement could be regarded to be *somewhat* security-relevant: Safety and Confidentiality of data should always be ensured. Hence, we need a good classification strategy for manual classification. The *classification question* was very instrumental when classifying a requirement:

Classification Question: Are you willing to spend money to ensure that the system is secure with respect to this requirement? Assume there is only a limited budget for refining requirements to security requirements and that there is a need to prioritize and balance cost and risk.

Outputs from security risk analysis approaches (such as CORAS [6], CRAMM [7], and OCTAVE [8]) can be used to support such evaluations, as these provide lists of threats and their related risk level, including potential consequences. Some approaches also directly consider the potential monetary losses. The question then becomes:

Can you afford to not invest to reduce or remove relevant risks?

2.2 Using Bayesian Classification to Enhance Security Awareness

Machine learning plays an important role in many fields of computer science, especially in practical applications for software engineering [9,10]. It allows for using machines to analyze huge amounts of data. A prominent example is Bayesian classification which proved to be valuable in classifying spam mails [11]. Spam filters help to find the few important mails between all that annoying spam mails. We think that the technology in these Spam filters is applicable for identifying among all requirements those that need refinement since they are security-relevant. Our rationale is:

- Bayesian classifiers are superior to simple keyword lists, as they do not only consider keywords indicating security relevance, but also keywords that indicate innocence (i.e., security irrelevance) of a requirement.
- For Spam filtering, good results could be reached with only small training sets. A part of a single specification may be sufficient for training.
- Bayesian classifiers can be trained while being used (e.g. by re-classifying false positives). This immediate feedback can support elicitation of tacit security experience.

Bayesian classifiers use statistical methods for classification. In our case, we want to compute the probability $P(\sec_r)$ that a requirement r is security relevant. A classic technique to do this is the *Naive Bayesian Classification*, a mix of stochastic methods and pragmatic assumptions. Our approach is based on Paul Grahams seminal article, one of the most popular descriptions of such a classifier [11]. Basically, we need to compute weights for distinctive features of our requirements (i.e. the words they are composed of), combine the weights of all features, and finally compare this value with a threshold.

Naive Bayesian Classification has some drawbacks and limitations. Rennie et al. discuss technical limitations as well as strategies to overcome them [12]. Accordingly, Naive Bayesian Classifiers are widespread because they are easy to implement and efficient. This makes them a good choice for our evaluation, despite the known drawbacks. Bayesian classifiers are only as good as their training. It is considerably more difficult for humans to identify security-relevant requirements than identifying spam-mail. In this paper, we evaluate whether machine learning could be used for identification of security-related requirements.

Assessing the Security-Relatedness of a Single Word. For computing the weights of the distinctive features of a requirement r, we need to compute $P(\sec_r|w)$: The probability of r being security-relevant under the condition that it contains the word w. The Bayesian rule allows to compute this as follows [13]:

$$P(\sec_r|w) = \frac{P(w|\sec_r) \cdot P(\sec)}{P(w)} \tag{1}$$

$P(\sec)$ is the probability of encountering security-relevant requirements in real-world specifications. We do not know this value. Therefore, we assume $P(\sec) = 0.5$ as suggested by Graham [11]. $P(w|\sec_r)$ is the probability that we encounter the word w under the condition that r is security-relevant. We can compute this value based on the training set of classified requirements. Let sec_w be the number of security-relevant requirements that contain w and sec_{total} the number of all security-relevant requirements in the training set. Then the following equation gives us an approximation of $P(w|\sec_r)$:

$$P(w|\sec_r) = \frac{sec_w}{sec_{total}} \tag{2}$$

$P(w)$ is the probability to encounter the word w in a requirement. Based on our training set and the theorem of total probability, this value is computed by the following equation ($P(\text{nonsec})$ and $P(w|\text{nonsec}_r)$ are computed analogues to the sec variants):

$$P(w) = P(\text{sec}) \cdot P(w|\text{sec}_r) + P(\text{nonsec}) \cdot P(w|\text{nonsec}_r) \tag{3}$$

With the assumption of $P(\text{sec}) = P(\text{nonsec}) = 0.5$ the equations (1) and (2) result in the following equation for $P(\text{sec}_r|w)$:

$$P(\text{sec}_r|w) = \frac{\frac{\text{sec}_w}{\text{sec}_{\text{total}}}}{\frac{\text{sec}_w}{\text{sec}_{\text{total}}} + \frac{\text{nonsec}_w}{\text{nonsec}_{\text{total}}}} \tag{4}$$

Weight Combination: All words of a Requirement. $P(\text{sec}_r|w)$ gives the probability of a requirement r being security-relevant under the condition that it contains the word w. Thus, every word in a requirement is a witness for r being security-relevant. Now, we need to combine the evidence given by each witness. Again, we have only limited knowledge and borrow some "naive" assumptions from Bayesian spam filtering:

a) $P(\text{sec}_r|w)$ is pairwise independent for each word w.
b) There is a symmetry between the results $P(\text{sec}_r|w)$ and $P(\text{nonsec}_r|w)$:
$P(\text{nonsec}_r|w) = 1 - P(\text{sec}_r|w)$.

In English, the probability of finding an adjective is affected by the probability of finding a noun. Assumption (a) does not hold for natural languages. Nevertheless, Spam-filters work under these assumptions, which allow us to derive the following equation from Bayes' theorem: Let $P(\text{sec}_r|w_i)$ be the probability of r being security-relevant under the condition that it contains the word w_i. Let $w_i, 1 \le i \le n$ be the n words contained in r.

$$P(\text{sec}_r) = \frac{\prod P(\text{sec}_r|w_i)}{\prod P(\text{sec}_r|w_i) + \prod (1 - P(\text{sec}_r|w_i))} \tag{5}$$

For classification, we compare $P(\text{sec}_r)$ with a threshold. Based on Graham's article, we classify the requirement r as being security-relevant, if $P(\text{sec}_r) > 0.9$ [11]. The approach we described is called *Naive Bayesian Classification*, due to its simplifying assumptions. This technique works in spam filters. Although improved solutions exist, we chose the classic variant to investigate whether even this simple variant would work in security requirements identification.

3 Evaluation of Bayesian Classifiers

This section discusses the quality of classifiers and how they can be used to assist in security requirements elicitation. First, we define our evaluation goals in Section 3.1. Then we describe our strategy to reach these goals and the general process of evaluation in Section 3.2). Finally, we show and discuss the results for each evaluation goal in Sections 3.3, 3.4, and 3.5.

3.1 Evaluation Goals

In order to evaluate our Bayesian classifiers, we define three evaluation goals:

(G1). Evaluate accuracy of classifiers for security-relevant requirements.
(G2). Evaluate if trained filters can be transferred to other domains.
(G3). Evaluate how useful practitioners consider automatically identifying security requirements.

For the goals (G1) and (G2) we used expert evaluation and data mining to create meaningful test data, as described in Section 2. Subsets of this test data were used to train and evaluate the Bayesian Classifiers. Our evaluation strategy had to ensure that training and evaluation sets were kept disjoint. In the context of this paper, goal (G3) is informally evaluated by asking experts for their opinions about classification results. See Section 4.3 for the implications of our results on industrial practice. A more formal evaluation remains future work.

3.2 Evaluation Strategy

Assessing the quality of machine learning algorithms is not trivial:

- *Use disjoint training and evaluation data.* We must not use the same requirements for training and evaluation.
- *Select training data systematically.* For reproducible and representative results, we need to systematically choose the requirements we use for training.
- *Avoid overfitting.* We need to show that our approach is not limited to the specific test data used. Overfitting happens when the Bayesian classifier adjusts to the specific training data.

Typically, *k-fold cross validation* is used to deal with these concerns [9,14]. This validation method ensures that statistics are not biased for a small set of data [15]. The dataset is randomly sorted and then split into k parts of equal size. $k - 1$ of the parts are concatenated and used for training. The trained classifier is then run on the remaining part for evaluation. This procedure is carried out iteratively with a different part being held back for classification each time. The classification performances averaged over all k parts characterizes the classifier. According to [9], we used $k = 10$: With larger k, the parts would be too small and might not even contain a single security-relevant requirement.

We used standard metrics from information retrieval to measure the performance of Bayesian classifiers: precision, recall, and f-measure [16]. Based on the data reported in [14], we consider f-measures over 0.7 to be good. For our purpose, high recall is considered more important than high precision. A classifier is regarded useful in our SecReq approach if precision is at least 0.6, and recall is at least 0.7.

We used three industrial requirements documents for evaluation; the Common Electronic Purse Specification (ePurse) [17], the Customer Premises Network specification (CPN) [18], and the Global Platform Specification (GP) [19]. As described in detail below, we experimented with various different training sets applied to each of the three real-world specifications.

Table 1 provides an overview of the three specifications we used for evaluation of our classifiers: For each specification (left column), we list the total number of requirements they contain (2nd. column) and the number of requirements considered security-relevant (3rd. column). We used either experts (see Sect. 2) or existing databases for identifying security-relevant requirements (last column).

Table 1. Industrial requirements specifications used for evaluation

Document	total reqs.	security-relevant reqs.	security-relevance determined by
Common Electronic Purse (ePurse)	124	83	expert
Customer Premises Network (CPN)	210	41	database
Global Platform Spec. (GP)	176	63	expert

3.3 Accuracy of Security Classifiers: G1

To test the accuracy of the Bayesian classifier, we use 10-fold cross validation on each of our classified specifications. In Figure 2 we also show the results for smaller training sets. *Training size* gives the number of parts in the 10-fold cross validation considered for training. The trend shown in Figure 2 helps to evaluate whether the training set is sufficient. Results exceed the above-mentioned thresholds for recall and precision. Hence, we consider the classifier useful.

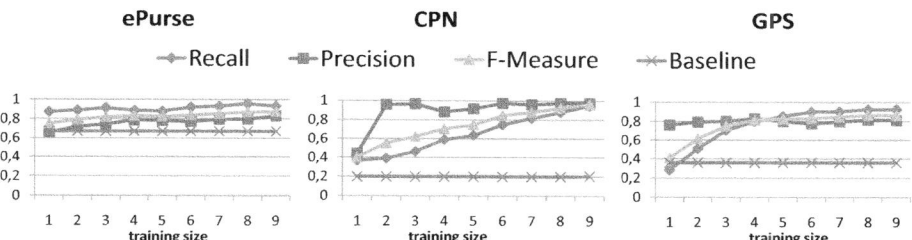

Fig. 2. Results of 10-fold cross validation using only one specification. Baseline is the precision we get when classifying all req. to be security-relevant.

3.4 Transferability of Classifiers Trained in a Single Domain: G2.a

Classifying industrial specifications manually was very time-consuming. It was needed for training the classifiers. Reuse of trained classifiers could reduce that effort. Therefore, we evaluated the quality of classification when we applied a trained classifier to specifications from different projects - without additional training. In order to produce comparative results, we used 10-fold cross validation in all cases, but varied the specifications used for training and for applying the classifiers.

Table 2 shows our results. The first column indicates which specification was used for training. We list the quality criteria (recall, precision, and f-m.) when applying the respective classifier to each of the three industrial specifications in the last three columns. Values on the main diagonal are set in italics: they represent the special case of (G1) reported above, where the *same* specification was used for training and for testing. Even

Table 2. Training classifier with one specification, applying it to another

Training	Applying to:	ePurse	CPN	GP
ePurse	recall	**0.93**	0.54	0.85
	precis	**0.83**	0.23	0.43
	f-measure	**0.88**	0.33	0.57
CPN	recall	0.33	**0.95**	0.19
	precis	0.99	**0.98**	0.29
	f-measure	0.47	**0.96**	0.23
GP	recall	0.48	0.65	**0.92**
	precis	0.72	0.29	**0.81**
	f-measure	0.58	0.4	**0.86**

in those cases, the 10-fold cross validation ensured that we never used the same requirements for training and evaluation.

The results in Table 2 are surprisingly clear: f-measures on the diagonal are 0.86 and higher (same specification for training and test). All other f-measures are far below 0.7: whenever we used different specifications for training and evaluation, transferability is very limited. A filter cannot easily be used in a different context.

3.5   Transferability of Classifiers Trained in Multiple Domains: G2.b

If we apply a Bayesian classifier trained with a specification from one domain to a different domain, we get poor results (see G2.a). This could either point to the fact that we cannot transfer classifiers to other domains or that we used a bad training set. To investigate this, we carried out a third evaluation run where the classifier was trained with values from a mix of specifications. For this, we join the requirements from two or three specifications as input for the 10-fold cross validation. The results in Table 3 show: When we used more than one specification for training, the filter became more

Table 3. Training with more than one specification

Training	Applied to:	cross-eval	ePurse	CPN	GP
ePurse + CPN	recall	0.93	0.95	0.85	0.56
	precis	0.81	0.80	1	0.51
	f-m.	0.87	0.87	0.92	0.53
ePurse + GP	recall	0.96	0.98	0.85	0.85
	precis	0.80	0.78	0.26	0.8
	f-m.	0.87	0.87	0.40	0.82
CPN + GP	recall	0.87	0.31	0.75	0.88
	precis	0.82	0.84	0.88	0.81
	f-m.	0.85	0.46	0.81	0.84
ePurse + CPN	recall	0.91	0.95	0.85	0.88
+ GP	precis	0.79	0.80	0.94	0.78
	f-m.	0.84	0.87	0.89	0.83

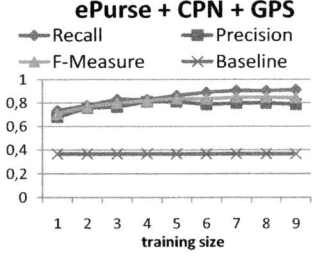

Fig. 3. 10-fold cross validation, multiple training

generally applicable. If we used two specifications in training, the evaluation for the third specification delivered better results than after a single-specification training (G2.a).

Combination of different specifications in training made the classifier more generally applicable. Obviously, classification quality is not only based on domain-specific terms - which would not occur in the second training specification. Thus, a good domain-independent classifier can be created with a sufficiently large training set.

The bottom entry in Table 3 shows the results when we combined all three specifications for training. Now we got good results for all three specifications included in the evaluation. Figure 3 shows the learning curve, by giving the results when using less than 9 parts for training. The learning curve grows not as fast as in the Figure 2, probably because the classifier cannot leverage the domain specific concepts. Nevertheless, we get a recall of 91 %, a precision of 79 %, and a f-measure of 84 % - results that clearly show that the trained classifier is suitable to support security requirements elicitation in all of the three domains used for training.

4   Discussion and Implications on Industrial Practice

In Section 3 we described the process of evaluating our concepts. It is important to note that for evaluation purposes we did not use the Bayesian classifier in the way it was designed for (compare Section 2.2):

- *For evaluation* we used a complete specification. Parts of the specifications were used for training, other parts were used for evaluation of recall and precision.
- *In practice* we suggest to use the Bayesian Classifier in an Elicitation tool. Each requirement is classified immediately after it has been written down.

This feedback can be used during an elicitation meeting for immediate clarification on how to proceed with security-relevant requirements. Later, it could be used to generate a list of security-relevant requirements to discuss with security experts. In our SecReq approach, we trigger a refinement wizard that allows laymen to start with the refinement themselves.

In this section we discuss whether the observed results are sufficient for employing the filter in practice at its current status. Then we take a look at the validity of our evaluation of the Bayesian classifier filter. Finally, we summarise the discussion with practitioners and describe how they perceive the implications of the filter in practice, meaning their development projects.

4.1   Interpretation of Evaluation Results

As shown in Section 3 we achieved very good results in cases where the classifier is applied to the requirements from the same source as it was trained with. We also observed poor results in cases where the classifier was applied to a different requirements specification than the one it was trained with. We also observed that the combination of training sets from different sources produces a classifier that works well with requirements from all sources. This shows that a general classifier for security relevance can be created with larger training sets and specifications from more domains.

To summarise, in its current status the classifier is indeed a very valuable addition for example in the context of software evolution or product lines. I.e., the classifier could be trained using the last version of the requirements specification and than offer precious help in developing the new software version. Typically, subsequent specifications resemble their predecessor in large parts and add only small new parts. Evaluation of this situation is covered by k-fold cross validation, as large $(k-1)$ parts of a specification are used for training and applied to a small held-out part. Therefore, the results in Figure 2 apply to this situation. In other situations, the learning curve in Figure 3 and tests with systematic training with falsely classified requirements show that the classifier quickly adopts to new domains.

4.2   Discussion on Validity

Wohlin et al. define types of threats to validity for empirical studies [20]. We consider threats to construct, internal, external, and conclusion validity to be relevant to our evaluation.

Construct Validity. In our case, the assumptions made on the classification question and our interpretation of what comprises a good result is critical to determining the goodness of the evaluation. When it comes to the classification question there are many alternative ways to define security-relevance. However, our classification was an effective choice in practice as it helped us to adjust our classification in a way that our security experts could agree on the majority of requirements. Next it is important to consider whether it was sound to apply the classifier on final versions of requirements during the evaluation. This depends on the level of abstraction on which the functional information is presented. In practice the requirements are regularly refined from high level functional requirements to low-level descriptions of security-related aspects.

Internal Validity. We used k-fold cross validation and avoided using identical requirements in training and evaluation, as well as overfitting. Randomly choosing requirements for training is not the best way to produce a good filter. Ideally, we would train the filter systematically with false positives and false negatives, until it produces good results. Preliminary tests show that this even increases the performance of the classifier with very small training sets.

External Validity. External validity addresses the level of generalisability of the results observed. We used three real-world requirement specifications from different domains and authors. We have no reason to doubt the applicability of our approach on different specifications.

Conclusion Validity. We used specifications from two different domains in our evaluation. Therefore, we cannot guarantee that our results would hold for a third domain. To leverage this threat, we share our evaluation tool, classified data sets, and databases of learned words at http://www.se.uni-hannover.de/en/re/secreq. We invite others to replicate our experiment, or use our results.

4.3   Implications on Industrial Practice (G3)

In practice, there will rarely be budget to tackle all relevant security aspects. Some of them may even conflict. Hence, developers need to get the right security. For this reason, the classification question (see Section 2) focuses on money (which includes costs, schedule, effort, resources, etc.), where money covers both development costs but also the cost associated with the lack of a critical security feature in the end-product. When it comes to techniques and tools for security elicitation support, such a tool needs to help a developer getting security right, including being able to separate out the important and prioritised security aspects and hidden security requirements that are somehow concerned with potential business and money consequences (loss and gain). Furthermore, such support must be integrated in a natural way such that the tool supports the way the developer work in the security requirements elicitation process and not the other way around. In practice, spending money on something that is not going to end up in the final system is considered a waste of time and effort. This is a sad reality in industrial development.

The Bayesian classification as an addition to SecReq not only contributes to a more effective and focused security elicitation process, but also in separating important from not so important security-relevant aspects. In particular, the Bayesian classification and security expert simulation in HeRA, with its ability to train the classification to be system and project specific, directly enables effective reuse of earlier experience, as well as prioritising and company specific security-related focus areas or policies. The ability to first train the classification engine to understand how to separate important security-relevant aspects from not so important, and then use this newly gained knowledge to traverse functional descriptions and already specified security requirements have a promising potential to contribute in a better control of security spending in development projects.

5   Related Work

Security Requirements. A significant amount of work has been carried out on security requirements engineering in particular relating to tools support in security requirement engineering process, cf. e.g. [21,22,23,24,25]. However, this work does not usually employ techniques from natural language processing to detect security requirements, as we do here.

Processing of Natural Language in Requirements. Requirements are often specified using natural language, if only as an intermediate solution before formal modelling. As natural language is inherently ambiguous [26], several approaches have been proposed to automatically analyse natural language requirements in order to support requirements engineers in creating good requirements specifications [27,28,9,29]. Kof, Lee et al. work on extracting semantics from natural language texts [27,28] by focusing on the semi automatic extraction of an ontology from a requirements document. Their focus is on identifying ambiguities in requirements specifications. It would be interesting to compare our results to the performance of security specific adoptions of these approaches. A comparable methodical approach is proposed by Kiyavitskaya et al. [29] for extracting requirements from regulations. These methodical and semi-automatic approaches resemble our SecReq approach, the results in this paper describe a supportive technique needed in such a method. Chantree et al. describe how to detect nocuous ambiguities in natural language requirements [9] by using word distribution in requirements to train heuristic classifiers (i.e. how to interpret the conjunctions *and/or* in natural language). The process of creating the dataset is very similar to our work: collection and classification of realistic samples based on the judge of multiple experts to enhance the quality of the dataset. The reported results (recall = 0.587, precision = 0.71) are useful in the described context, but are too low for the SecReq approach.

6   Conclusion

In this paper, we addressed the problem that security becomes increasingly important in environments where there may not be any security experts available to assist in requirements activities. This situation leads to the risk that requirements engineers may fail to identify, or otherwise neglect, early indicators for security problems. We presented a tool-supported method that provides assistance for the labour-intensive and error-prone first round of security requirements identification and analysis. The tool support makes use of a trained Bayesian classifier in order to heuristically categorise requirements statements as *security-relevant* resp. *less security-relevant*. We also showed how HeRA, our heuristic requirements assistant tool can be used to integrate that filter mechanism into a secure software development process. Note, that the approach is not restricted to HeRA, and can be used in other elicitation tools.

We evaluated this approach using several industrial requirements documents; ePurse, CPN, and GP. Our experiences with this "real-life" validation was overall positive: According to the numerical results, the approach succeeds in assisting requirements engineers in their task of identifying security-relevant requirements, in that it reliably identifies the majority of the security-relevant requirements (recall > 0.9) with only few false positives (precision > 0.8) in software evolution scenarios. Our evaluation of different training strategies shows that the classifier can quickly be adopted to a new domain when no previous versions of requirements specifications are available for training. This could be done by a security expert during a first interview.

Our approach does not aim at completeness in a strict logical sense. There is no 100% guarantee that all security-relevant requirements are found, nor that no non-security-relevant requirements are falsely reported. This is, however, a limitation that is directly imposed by the current limitations from computational linguistics (essentially, the fact that a true automated text understanding is currently not available). In general, security experts cannot give such a guarantee, either. Therefore, we believe that the approach provides useful assistance in that it supports requirements engineers to identify security-relevant requirements, when no security expert is present. Even if security experts are present, our approach helps them to focus on already identified requirements and thereby efficiently use their limited time. Moreover, since this selection process is supported by automated tools, its execution is easy to document and it is repeatable and thus well auditable. This adds another level of trustworthiness to the process, compared to an entirely manual assessment.

Based on our work we see two main topics for future research. On the one hand, it would be interesting, if the approach could be applied to other types of cross-cutting quality requirements (e.g. safety or usability). On the other hand, the application in industrial practice will show the efficiency of our approach.

References

1. International Standardization Organization. ISO 15408:2007 Common Criteria for Information Technology Security Evaluation, Version 3.1, Revision 2, CCMB-2007-09-001, CCMB-2007-09-002 and CCMB-2007-09-003 (September 2007)
2. Houmb, S.H., Islam, S., Knauss, E., Jürens, J., Schneider, K.: Eliciting Security Requirements and Tracing them to Design: An Integration of Common Criteria, Heuristics, and UMLsec. Requirements Engineering Journal 15(1), 63–93 (2010)
3. Knauss, E., Lübke, D., Meyer, S.: Feedback-Driven Requirements Engineering: The Heuristic Requirements Assistant. In: International Conference on Software Engineering (ICSE 2009), Formal Research Demonstrations Track, Vancouver, Canada, pp. 587–590 (2009)
4. Jürjens, J.: Secure Systems Development with UML. Springer, Heidelberg (2005)
5. Schneider, K., Stapel, K., Knauss, E.: Beyond Documents: Visualizing Informal Communication. In: Proceedings of Third International Workshop on Requirements Engineering Visualization (REV 2008), Barcelona, Spain (2008)
6. den Braber, F., Hogganvik, I., Lund, M., Stølen, K., Vraalsen, F.: Model-based security analysis in seven steps - a guided tour to the CORAS method. BT Technology Journal 25(1), 101–117 (2007)
7. Barber, B., Davey, J.: The use of the CCTA risk-analysis and management methodology [CRAMM] in health information systems. In: Degoulet, P., Lun, K., Piemme, T., Rienhoff, O. (eds.) MEDINFO 1992, pp. 1589–1593. Elsevier, North-Holland (1992)
8. Alberts, C., Dorofee, A.: Managing Information Security Risks: The OCTAVE (TM) Approach. Addison-Wesley, New York (2002)
9. Chantree, F., Nuseibeh, B., de Roeck, A., Willis, A.: Identifying Nocuous Ambiguities in Natural Language Requirements. In: Proceedings of the 14th IEEE International Requirements Engineering Conference, Minneapolis, USA, pp. 56–65. IEEE Computer Society, Los Alamitos (2006)
10. Kiyavitskaya, N., Zeni, N., Mich, L., Berry, D.M.: Requirements for tools for ambiguity identification and measurement in natural language requirements specifications. Requirements Engineering Journal 13(3), 207–239 (2008)
11. Graham, P.: A Plan for Spam (2002) Web (January 2011), http://www.paulgraham.com/spam.html
12. Rennie, J.D.M., Shih, L., Teevan, J., Karger, D.R.: Tackling the Poor Assumptions of Naive Bayes Text Classifiers. In: Proceedings of the Twentieth International Conference on Machine Learning (ICML 2003), Washington, DC (2003)
13. Russell, S., Norvig, P.: Artificial Intelligence: a Modern Approach. Prentice Hall, New Jersey (1995)
14. Ireson, N., Ciravegna, F., Califf, M.E., Freitag, D., Kushmerick, N., Lavelli, A.: Evaluating machine learning for information extraction. In: ICML 2005: Proceedings of the 22nd International Conference on Machine Learning, Bonn, Germany, pp. 345–352. ACM, New York (2005)
15. Weiss, S.M., Kulikowski, C.A.: Computer systems that learn: classification and prediction methods from statistics, neural nets, machine learning, and expert systems. M. Kaufmann Publishers, San Mateo (1991)
16. Baeza-Yates, R., Ribeiro-Neto, B.: Modern Information Retrieval. ACM Press, Addison Wesley (1999)
17. CEPSCO: Common Electronic Purse Specification (ePurse), http://web.archive.org/web/, http://www.cepsco.com (accessed April 2007)

18. TISPAN, ETSI: Telecommunications and Internet converged Services and Protocols for Advanced Networking (TISPAN); Services requirements and capabilities for customer networks connected to TISPAN NGN. Technical report, European Telecommunications Standards Institute
19. GlobalPlatform: Global Platform Specification (GPS), http://www.globalplatform.org (accessed August 2010)
20. Wohlin, C., Runeson, P., Höst, M., Ohlsson, M.C., Regnell, B., Wesslén, A.: Experimentation In Software Engineering: An Introduction. Kluwer Academic Publishers, Boston (2000)
21. Chung, L.: Dealing with Security Requirements During the Development of Information Systems. In: Rolland, C., Cauvet, C., Bodart, F. (eds.) CAiSE 1993. LNCS, vol. 685, pp. 234–251. Springer, Heidelberg (1993)
22. Dubois, E., Wu, S.: A framework for dealing with and specifying security requirements in information systems. In: Katsikas, S.K., Gritzalis, D. (eds.) SEC. IFIP Conference Proceedings, vol. 54, pp. 88–99. Chapman & Hall, Boca Raton (1996)
23. Lin, L., Nuseibeh, B., Ince, D.C., Jackson, M., Moffett, J.D.: Introducing Abuse Frames for Analysing Security Requirements. In: RE, pp. 371–372. IEEE Computer Society, Los Alamitos (2003)
24. Giorgini, P., Massacci, F., Mylopoulos, J.: Requirement engineering meets security: A case study on modelling secure electronic transactions by VISA and mastercard. In: Song, I.-Y., Liddle, S.W., Ling, T.-W., Scheuermann, P. (eds.) ER 2003. LNCS, vol. 2813, pp. 263–276. Springer, Heidelberg (2003)
25. Heitmeyer, C.L., Archer, M., Leonard, E.I., McLean, J.: Applying Formal Methods to a Certifiably Secure Software System. IEEE Trans. Software Eng. 34(1), 82–98 (2008)
26. Berry, D., Kamsties, E.: 2. Ambiguity in Requirements Specification. In: Perspectives on Requirements Engineering, pp. 7–44. Kluwer, Dordrecht (2004)
27. Kof, L.: Text Analysis for Requirements Engineering. PhD thesis, Technische Universität München, München (2005)
28. Lee, S.W., Muthurajan, D., Gandhi, R.A., Yavagal, D.S., Ahn, G.J.: Building Decision Support Problem Domain Ontology from Natural Language Requirements for Software Assurance. International Journal of Software Engineering and Knowledge Engineering 16(6), 851–884 (2006)
29. Kiyavitskaya, N., Zeni, N., Breaux, T.D., Antón, A.I., Cordy, J.R., Mich, L., Mylopoulos, J.: Automating the extraction of rights and obligations for regulatory compliance. In: Li, Q., Spaccapietra, S., Yu, E., Olivé, A. (eds.) ER 2008. LNCS, vol. 5231, pp. 154–168. Springer, Heidelberg (2008)

Discovering Sustainability Requirements:
An Experience Report

Martin Mahaux, Patrick Heymans, and Germain Saval

PReCISE Research Centre
University of Namur, Belgium
{martin.mahaux,patrick.heymans,germain.saval}@fundp.ac.be

Abstract. Sustainability has become one of the "grand challenges" of our civilization. Because of their pervasiveness, the way we design, and consequently use, software-intensive systems has a significant impact on sustainability. This gives software requirements engineering an important role to play in society. However, there is currently no specific support for handling sustainability requirements, while such support exists and has proved useful for other quality requirements like security or usability. This paper reports on a software project in which sustainability requirements were treated as first class quality requirements, and as such systematically elicited, analysed and documented. The authors intended to assess how current techniques support these activities. Beyond raising awareness on the importance of sustainability concerns in requirements engineering, this experience report suggests that, while a lot of work remains to be done, small and easy steps may already lead us to more sustainable systems. It also contributes to the agenda of requirements engineering researchers concerned with sustainability.

1 Introduction

Achieving sustainability is recognized by many as one of the "grand challenges" of our society. Although there is a lot of debate surrounding this endeavour (e.g., as to its justifications, the means to achieve it, etc.), we leave the controversy aside from this article. Here, we take the pragmatic stance of adhering to one of the common definitions of sustainable development.

The United Nations' Brundtland commission defines *sustainable development* as "development that meets the needs of the present without compromising the ability of future generations to meet their own needs" [12]. It is traditionally considered that sustainable development involves three major "pillars": social, environmental and economic sustainability. In this paper, we only focus on environmental sustainability. We also adhere to the common thesis that *environmental sustainability* (simply called *sustainability* henceforth) is threatened by a number of practices such as depletion of non-renewable resources, production of non-recyclable or toxic substances, etc.

Over the last decades, information technology (IT) has become one of the leading industries worldwide. Its effects on the environment are considerable. Its most obvious effects result from the production, operation, maintenance and disposal of IT infrastructure, roughly hardware. This is what the majority of "green IT" initiatives have been concerned with up to now.

D. Berry and X. Franch (Eds.): REFSQ 2011, LNCS 6606, pp. 19–33, 2011.

Yet, there is another important manner in which IT affects the environment: IT changes individual and organisational behaviour. Think of how the Internet, office automation, mobile phones, route planners and many other applications have affected the way we act (e.g., work, travel) and communicate, which in turn affects our environment.

At the heart of IT lies software. The way software is designed (e.g., what functions it supports, which parts of its environment it interacts with, which IT infrastructure it uses and how) can have a major influence on the sustainability of the human activities involved. Such fundamental decisions are typically made during Requirements Engineering (RE), and finally expressed as requirements. In this paper, we are concerned with how to discover requirements that help minimize the negative environmental impacts of (the activities supported by) the software under construction.

More precisely, *our goal is to (i) get an insight on how sustainability requirements can be discovered, (ii) what existing tools and techniques facilitate this task, and (iii) what their limitations are in this respect.* Our aim is not to produce strong evidence that some technique is more efficient than another, but rather to perform a first exploration of ways to deal with such requirements.

After a brief presentation of related work (Section 2), this paper reports on the experience gained during a real project. Its settings are described in Section 3 whereas Section 4 gives a more complete account of its execution. Section 5 summarizes its main results. Finally, lessons learned are presented in Section 6 whereas Section 7 lists a number of contributions to the research agenda and concludes this paper.

2   Related Work

A search on the DBLP Computer Science Bibliography database [7] for articles with the prefixes "sustainab-" OR "ecolog-" OR "environmental-" in the title returns (in January 2010) over 3000 results. The venue "Environmental Modelling and Software" provides a third of these. Interestingly, filtering on important software and RE related venues leads to as few as 11 results, which are shown in Table 1. After checking their content, it turns out that only one of these entries [4] is concerned with providing support for handling sustainability requirements. This tends to show that RE research is far behind other computer science disciplines in this domain, and in fact has not really started yet. This paper is consequently more of an exploratory nature, which we believe makes sense in this context.

Cabot *et al.* [4] advocate usage of a sustainability taxonomy combined with goal-oriented techniques. In their proof of concept, they used the $i*$ framework to model the stakeholders and their respective goals. Goals are then operationalized through tasks that help or hurt the satisfaction of the sustainability goals. The authors point out that there is no standard definition of sustainability and its related concepts, and thus proposed a taxonomy that is limited to the particular example used in the paper.

As far as we can consider sustainability as a quality requirement, much of the literature on quality and non-functional requirements might be considered as related work (see, for example, the related work section of [6]). In particular, safety and security are related to sustainability in the sense that in all cases one tries to avoid harming

Table 1. Articles with *"sustainab-"* or *"ecolog-"* or *"environmental-"*

ICSE International Conference on Software Engineering	3
IEEE Software Journal	2
CAiSE International Conference on Advanced Information Systems Engineering	2
CAiSE Forum	1
ICSE Companion	1
IEEE Transactions on Software Engineering	1
RE International Requirements Engineering Conference	1
ER International Conference on Conceptual Modeling	0
REFSQ International Working Conference on Requirements Engineering: Foundation for Software Quality	0

the environment. Hence, we argue that best practices from these subdisciplines should be considered for dealing with sustainability requirements (possibly undergoing some adaptation). We make some attempts at this in the study described later in this paper.

Literature and techniques from the environmental sciences (e.g. Life Cycle Analysis [2] and Environmental Impact Assessment [1]) could also be adapted to our specific RE context. We have not attempted this yet in this study, but we add it to the proposed research agenda.

3 The Yellow Project

3.1 The Company and the Requirements Engineer's Mission

Yellow Events is a seven employees Belgian company that creates, organises and manages events for individuals, companies and administrations. Upon request from a customer, they design a tailor-made offer by coordinating activities, transport, catering, in various places, with various service providers. If the offer is accepted, they organise everything so that the event can take place. On the day of the event, they are on site to manage it. Typical events include wedding animations, team building events, corporate events and big city festivals. Throughout the lifecycle of the event, the best effort is made to minimise its environmental impact.

In the future, Yellow Events plans to be in charge of larger events, which gives them a strong motivation to enhance their efficiency, consistency and team communication. A second objective is to remain the reference in sustainable events in Belgium, so Yellow Events is constantly looking for ways to make their business greener and to communicate about it to their potential customers.

The authors' mission consisted in discovering, analysing and documenting the requirements for a software tool supporting Yellow's business while minimising the negative environmental impact of its activities.

3.2   Research Method

This experiment was managed by the first author of this article, in the double role of requirements engineer for the project side, and observer for the empirical research side. We thus used the participant-observer technique, with a very basic qualitative analysis: the first author simply kept recording observations about the efficiency of his RE tasks, and adapted some techniques on the fly where needed.

Given this lightweight empirical research method (as compared, for example, with a full scale controlled experiment [9]), limited conclusions could be formally drawn. The assessment of efficiency is based on a comparison between this experiment and the authors' experience (five years) as requirements engineer on non-sustainability focused projects. Another indicator is the researchers' and stakeholders' perception of the quality of the deliverables, and of the relative degree of sustainability achieved. As mentioned earlier, the point is not to make a strong argument for or against the efficiency of some technique but rather report on observations and insights. We hope that those can be useful to other practitioners and researchers working on sustainability requirements.

3.3   Tasks and Deliverables

The first task was to design the requirements process, mainly made of a selection and adaptation of methods and techniques presented in the book *Discovering Requirements*, from Alexander and Beus-Dukic [3]. As illustrated in the timeline on Figure 1, we ran a series of meetings, that were typically separated by 3 to 4 weeks. After each meeting, the requirements engineer spent 4 to 12 working days on analysis and documentation. The total duration of the requirements phase was 8 months. In more details, we had:

- 7 interview sessions where we iteratively elicited and validated the following requirements elements: stakeholders, goals, scope, use cases, scenarios, data elements and requirements with their input priorities[1]. We proceeded iteratively, going into more details as we progressed;
- 2 team workshops for information and goal modeling respectively;
- 3 solution meetings with IT designers, where we decided on buy vs. build, technological options and their consequences, budgets, and finally defining output priorities and selecting a solution provider.

The authors soon realized that the scope was too big to fit one project phase. Consequently, the project was split in various functional modules, which would be specified and implemented in turn. This experience report covers the high level analysis for the full scope, and detailed analysis for two of these modules: the central "Event Manager" module (creation and follow up of events) and the "Suppliers" module (custom supplier search and repository).

The list of deliverables, compiled in a comprehensive requirements document, includes the following, appearing in chronological order of their initial creation:

---

[1] In [3], the authors distinguish the input and output priorities in the following way: input priority is made of what stakeholders find more valuable, while output priority reflects what will effectively be implemented first, considering the input priority and the technical and budgetary constraints.

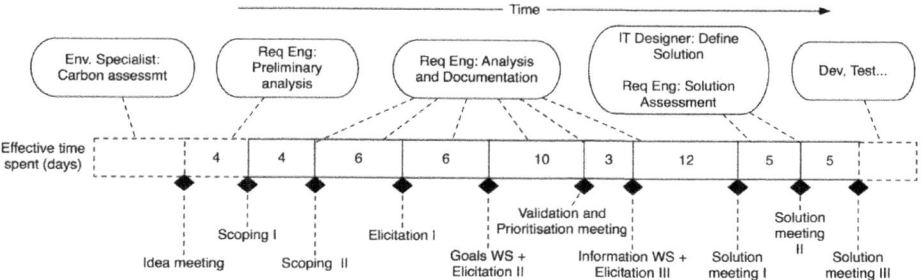

Fig. 1. Timeline

- Full scope artifacts:
  - an adapted stakeholders checklist, augmented with environment related roles,
  - a stakeholders list,
  - a "rich picture"-style context model representing Yellow's business,
  - a decomposition of the solution space in various functional modules,
  - a high level use case diagram representing the high level use cases for the full solution (21 high-level use cases),
  - a generic goal model for environmental sustainability,
  - an instantiation of this generic goal model for Yellow,
  - a goal model rooted at Yellow's strategic goals,
  - a glossary of the main concepts of interest in Yellow's domain,
  - a class diagram representing the data of interest in Yellow's domain.
- Detailed artifacts (linked to module 1 and/or 2):
  - a business process diagram representing the lifecycle of an event,
  - a state diagram representing the lifecycle of an event,
  - a lower level use case diagram representing the use cases for the central event management module (15 use cases),
  - a use case description for the two main use cases, with scenarios,
  - a misuse case sheet, describing possible environmental misuses and mitigation,
  - a "lo-fi" prototype made of a dozen screen sketches,
  - a list of 51 detailed requirements, with satisfaction and dissatisfaction indicators.

Some of these will be presented in this paper as illustrations or where they are related to sustainability concerns. For confidentiality reasons, the whole requirements documents may not be disclosed. The budget for the development effort of modules 1 and 2 was estimated at around 80 man-days (average of the 3 bids received).

4   Discovering Sustainability Requirements

This section goes through some of the RE activities performed: stakeholders analysis, context and scope definition, use case analysis and goal modelling. It presents the resulting models, discusses how they were realised, and how they helped in discovering sustainability requirements. Figure 2 provides an overview of these, and highlights the sustainability-specific part of each activity.

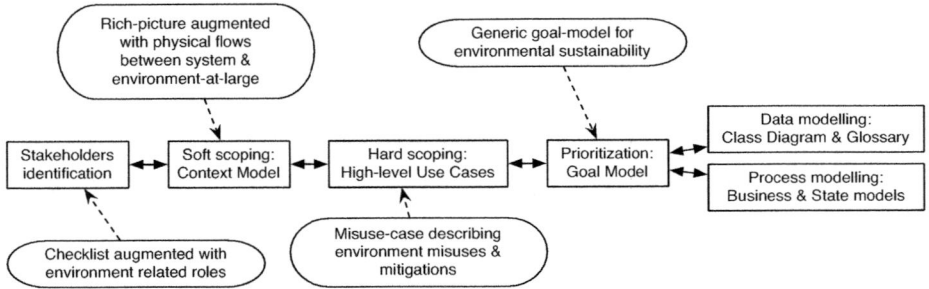

Fig. 2. Overview of requirements activities and their sustainability-specific parts

4.1   Stakeholders

The stakeholders analysis was supported by the *Volere* checklist [11]. The role "Environmental Specialist" *was* in this checklist, and this was our main sustainability-specific stakeholder. Our environment specialist is a Yellow employee (HR Manager) who has received a specific 5-days training in analysing the environmental impact of human activities. Prior to the study, he already analyzed the "carbon footprint" of some important events.

Some specific "green thinking" and "anti-green thinking" actors were added to represent typical Yellow clients and event participants. This enabled us to imagine desired and undesired customer-oriented scenarios focusing on the sustainability aspect.

In the rest of the process, the list of stakeholders identified at this stage turned out to be sufficient. But we could have thought of more sustainability-specific stakeholders. In fact, most of the classical roles could have a "green" counterpart, as illustrated in figure 3, inspired by [3].

4.2   Soft Scoping and Context Discovery

For defining the scope and context of the system and product[2], the authors used a combination of "softer" and "harder" techniques, as suggested by [3].

Figure 4 is a "rich picture"-style Context Model, showing context using an informal but intuitive pictorial syntax. This model was created during in one interview session, and completed after a review by the stakeholders. It helped a lot in understanding the problem, including the important environmental dimension. This model shifted the focus from the product to its wider environment and helped the authors consider where the impacts on sustainability might be. Indeed, the environmental impacts are in and around the system, not in the product itself. This wider environment might be called the "environment-at-large", as opposed to the immediate environment of the software product.

---

[2] As suggested by [3], we use the word "product" for the result of the development work, i.e. a piece of software, and the word "system" for the network of entities that, by operating the product (and maybe other products), provide a value to some functional beneficiaries.

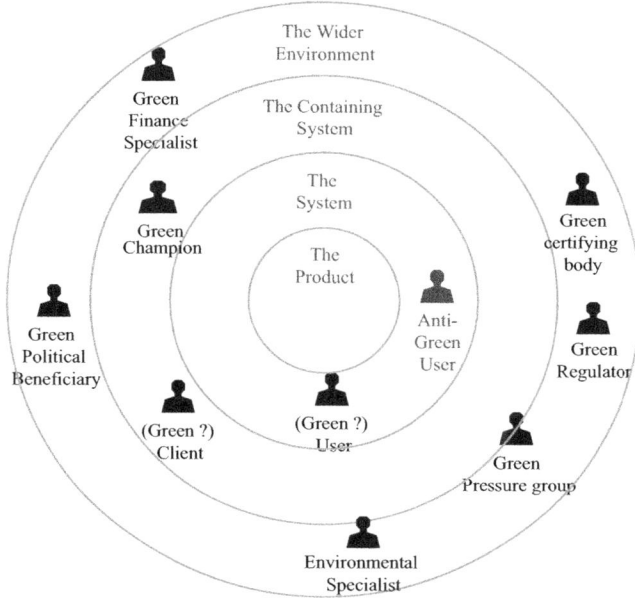

Fig. 3. "Green onion" diagram

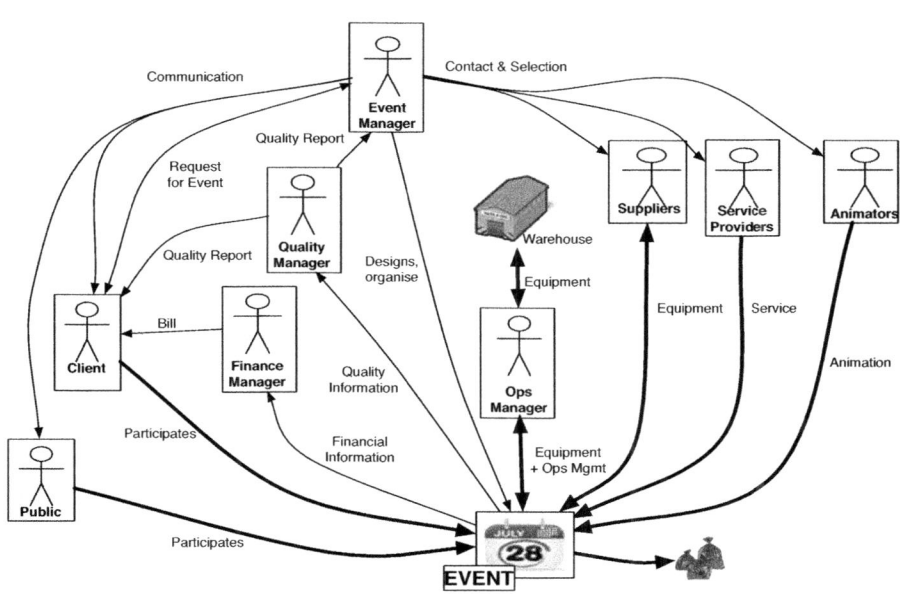

Fig. 4. A "rich picture"-style context model

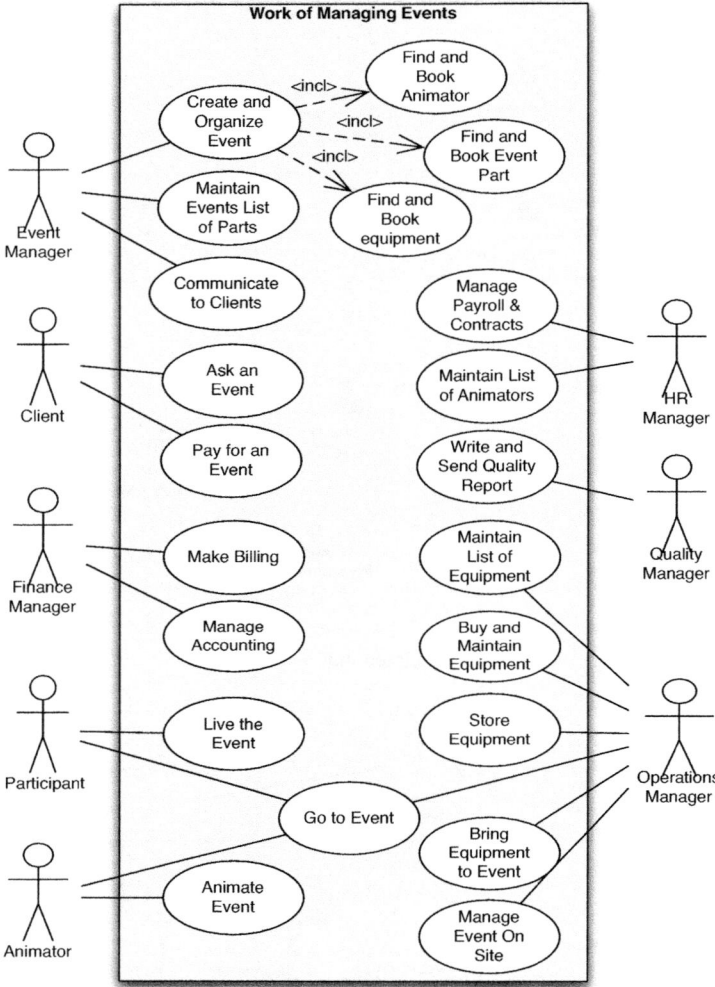

Fig. 5. System Level Use Case Diagram

To highlight the environmental content of this model, the authors drew bold arrows for the interactions that involve physical artifacts. They are of interest to the sustainability analysis, in the sense that (i) all transports must be minimised, and (ii) these arrows represent inputs and outputs that will have to be taken into account in the environmental calculations.

In the rest of the RE process, the rich picture could be used as a checklist of the issues we had to tackle to lower the environmental impact of Yellow Events. The environment specialist could easily follow each diagram item (an object on the diagram or an arrow between two objects) and comment on the current situation, the importance of the impact, his solution ideas. He found this model to be useful and clear for this purpose,

Use Case	Threat (MUC)	Mitigating UC	Descriptions
Go To Event	Emit CO2 through using personal car	Manage Carpooling	The system shall enable people to place carpooling demands and offers, and provide the needed information to help them organize carpooling efficiently for a specific event.
		Find Events Parts	The system shall help the Event Manager to select optimal event parts locations so as to minimize distances. The system shall compute optimal places, optimal service providers, optimal animators... depending on clients' location.
Live the Event	Emit CO2 through energy use or through emitting activities	Find Events Parts	The system shall enable the Event Manager to select Event Parts that require low energy and emit low CO2 amounts.
	Waste Food	Communicate Participation	The system shall help reduce food waste through letting participants inform of their (non) participation
	Act irresponsibly	Animate event	Animators shall be trained to raise awareness of participants on acting responsibly

Fig. 6. Misuse Cases

and it helped him complete his analysis of Yellow's environmental impacts. It played a crucial role in facilitating the communication of these impacts to all stakeholders.

At this point in time, the collaboration with the environment specialist was of a great help, as we were able to sort out the various impacts by their importance in terms of CO2 equivalent. His ranking of the most impacting parts of the business is the following:

1. Transport of participants to the events
2. Transport of material and staff to the events
3. Warehouse: use of land
4. Warehouse: use of energy
5. Event: use of equipment
6. Event: use of energy

Items 1, 2 and 5 above are clearly represented by arrows on the rich picture. Items 3, 4 and 6 do not appear explicitly on the picture, but were elicited by discussing around the 'Event' and 'Warehouse' objects of the picture.

4.3   Harder Scoping

Based on the rich picture and a first understanding of the business problems, the requirements engineer could create a Use Case Diagram for the system and imagine a high level solution. The latter consists of various functional modules and allowed to phase the project. Each module was described in terms of the use cases it would support, but also its main objectives in doing so, and in particular if there were any environmental concerns. Figure 5 shows the system-level use case diagram.

In order to push the environmental analysis further, we achieved a misuse case analysis [10]. We inspected each previously obtained use case asking the question: "What is (or might be) harmful to the environment here?". The results were mostly the same

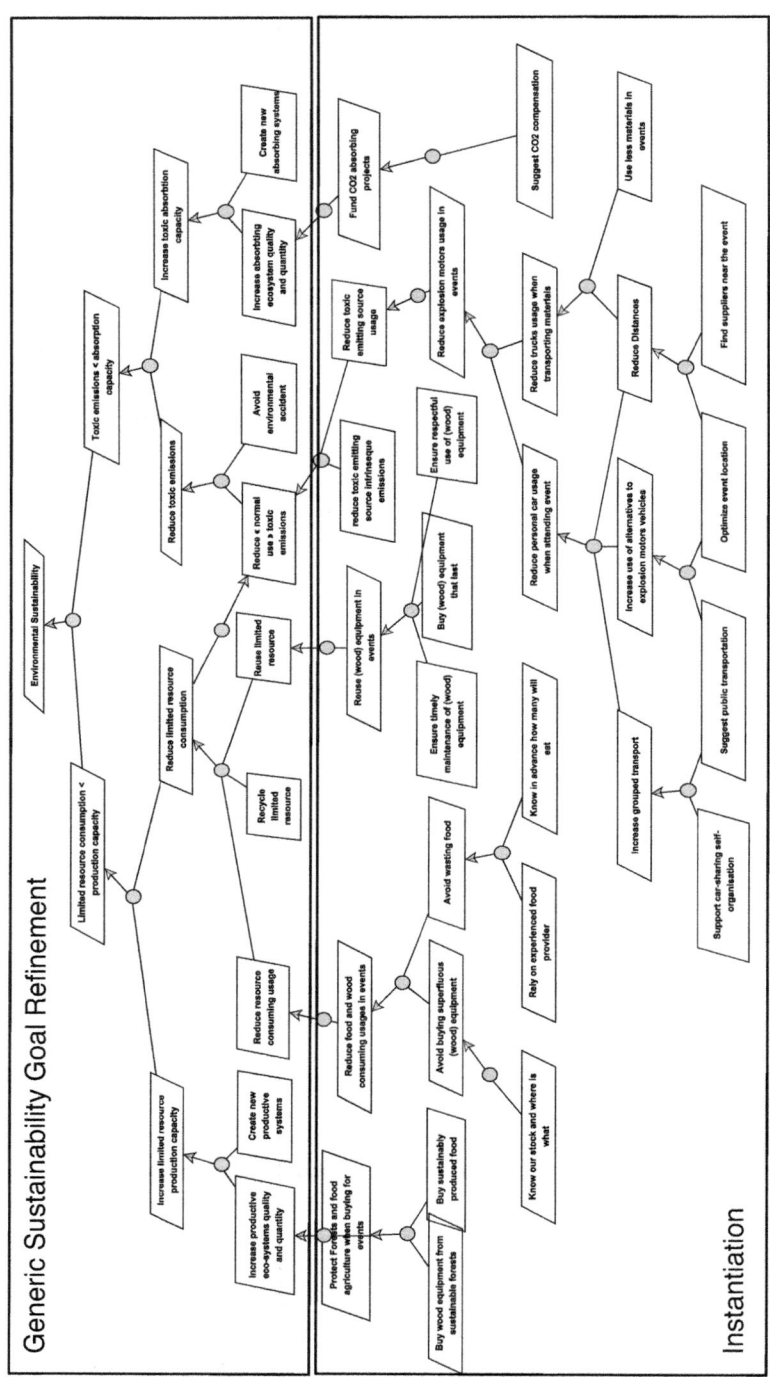

Fig. 7. Generic goal refinement for environmental sustainability and its instantiation

as elicited from the rich picture, adding some new ideas coming from specific negative scenarios (like a participant acting irresponsibly towards the environment during
an event). Also, the question of the possible ways to mitigate the identified harm (typically a new detailed use case or a modification to an existing one) brought the project
one step further towards the design of a solution.

Figure 6 shows part of the analysis that was made on the system (i.e., high-level)
Use Cases. It shows the threats to the environment related to our system and possible
mitigation actions.

4.4 Goal Modelling

In order to determine priorities and complete our analysis, we achieved a goal analysis.
In [3], a simple and intuitive goal notation is used (essentially a simplified version
of KAOS). High level goals are placed above and are then refined into lower level
sub-goals.

As in [4], we used a generic sustainability goal refinement, that we had previously
defined. This generic refinement can be considered as our taxonomy for sustainability
requirements, similarly to what was done in [4], but aiming at some more independence
from the specific targeted case. Figure 7 shows the generic refinement (four higher
layers) and its instantiation (layers below). This helped defining more precisely what
sustainability meant for Yellow, to complete the list of impacts and possible means of
action. Some new insights were found, like the possible contribution to compensation
programs, leading to new requirements (e.g., the need to compute the total amount of
$CO2$ of an event).

This goal model then needed to be integrated with the other (non sustainability related) objectives of Yellow. So, while we used the first goal model to brainstorm on
sustainable requirements, we built a second goal model (not shown here for lack of
space), which roots are Yellow's strategic objectives.

4.5 Other Elements

An information model (a class diagram of 30 classes) and a glossary (of 50 entries) were
then created. The analysis of the lifecycle of an event led to a Business Process Model
and a State Model. Finally, detailed requirements were written and linked to Business
Processes and Goals.

During this part of the work, which focuses on detailed specification rather
than discovering new sustainability requirements, we felt no need for treating sustainability aspects in a specific way. Hence, no particular technique was applied here for
sustainability.

5 Results

Although the description above may render the idea of a sequential process, we proceeded iteratively. Each artifact thus influenced the others in some way. Since the origin
of requirements was not recorded, we cannot determine exactly what kind of requirements were produced by which technique, or which technique was most successful.

However, to give an idea of the results of the global process, here is an excerpt of the major sustainability-related system functionalities retained:

- The system shall provide the Event Manager with the possibility to find the most optimal locations, suppliers, animators for the event, and do so depending on geographical criteria (minimize motorized personal transportation), and a "green score" representing other green criteria. The green score is assigned by the Event Manager to each relevant entity.
- The system shall be able to show what equipment is available, where it is located and in which state. This will avoid buying superfluous equipment, and maximize the expected lifetime of equipment by doing maintenance when needed.
- The system shall help the equipment manager to collect the complete and correct equipment for an event, in order to avoid superfluous transportation (typically by truck).
- The system shall support the quality manager in efficiently assessing the sustainability of an event, in order to enhance Yellow's practices. The system shall make selected results presentable to clients, comparing Yellow's results with other typical events, or with previous events of the same customer.
- The system shall support the creation of an event-specific website, where participants will be able to see public transportation possibilities to go to the event, and to place on-line carpooling offers and consult carpooling demands.
- The system shall enable participants to register for (parts of) an event, in order to organize the catering so as to reduce waste.

When the list of requirements was completed and validated, the team became convinced to have made the maximum towards sustainability in their business. They estimated that the solution would bring the company a significant competitive advantage in this domain and at the same time meet the other initial objectives.

6   Lessons Learned

Sustainability requires specific attention. At least, we encourage requirements engineers to add sustainability to their quality requirements checklist, and consider it as they do with other quality requirements. It was our experience that dealing with this new type of quality requirement was in many respects similar to dealing with other quality requirements. In essence, it represents one more criterion for trade-offs, one more goal to achieve in a system, and in this sense it is just one more "-ility" that has to be dealt with.

Sustainability is clearly raising more and more interest, and will consequently (we hope) gain more and more importance in software projects. In these cases where sustainability is deemed important, it is needed to tailor the tools and techniques during the requirements process. For example, as a first easy step, one can consider those little adaptations to existing techniques that the authors themselves found useful to achieve a more sustainable system:

- for stakeholder analysis, one could augment the checklists with environment related roles;

– for context modelling, one could chose a model that will enable to think about the system as a whole in its environment-at-large, and show the physical flows, not only the information flows, coming to or from the product;
– for use case analysis, one could investigate risks and mitigations through misuse cases directed at sustainability threats;
– for goal modelling, one could prepare and instantiate a generic sustainability goal model.

Beyond this, requirements engineers can collaborate with environment specialists, who will assess the existing system, drive priorities, and help design the most effective mitigations of environmental threats. The authors were lucky to have such an expert at hand, and were able to integrate his inputs into the RE process, sometimes leading to the small adaptations in the aforementioned techniques. We also found that some of our RE tools and techniques could help the environment specialist refine and complete his analysis. There was thus an interesting two-way communication and mutual learning. Systematic use of RE artifacts like Context Models to make the link between the environmental impact analysis and the system model is a practice we found to be useful.

Considering the importance of the environment specialist, and the fact that few projects will have such a stakeholder readily available, we suspect it would be necessary for requirements engineers to acquire a minimum of expertise in environmental analysis, and probably that some toolkit could help the requirements engineer take sustainability-related decisions. This toolkit would include, for example, simple tools for comparing various alternatives in terms of environmental impact (e.g., "Is the impact from air fret bigger than road fret?"). A really generic and solid ontology for sustainability should also be part of this toolbox.

6.1   Inputs and Outputs

When modeling the system with Context Models, we faced the question of how deep we should go in modeling environmentally significant system inputs and outputs. For example, since energy consumption is a major component of a system's environmental impact, should we have modeled the energy flows on this picture?

Independently from this question, and because the environmental impacts are not exerted in the software product itself but in the (possibly many) physical entities that surround it, system-at-large Context Models are useful. In order to be used for systematic exploration of environmental impacts, Context Models should show physical entities and interactions between them as clearly as possible. Whatever style is used, requirements engineers should make sure that Context Models contain this information, and adapt them in case they do not. For example, a typical Data Flow Diagram like the one used in [8] should be augmented with these interactions, as they usually show only information flows and omit physical flows.

6.2   Generic Goal Refinement

The most relevant related work we found [4] mostly exploits the goal dimension for finding sustainability requirements. In this article, Cabot *et al.* report on using the *i**
goal-oriented RE framework to reason about environmental sustainability requirements

and consider them when making design decisions. By working on the '*Conference organization*' case study, they found that the *i** model facilitated the exploration, understanding and comparison of sustainability measures, allowing for better informed decisions. We explicitly reused the idea of a generic goal refinement for sustainability. It can be used as a checklist for sustainability requirements, and we share the observation that it was useful to its purpose. Yet, Cabot *et al.* recognized the limited genericity of their refinement. Since we wanted to apply their technique on our project, we proposed a new one. The suggestion we made, shown in the four top layers of Figure 7, is only tentative. This is a topic that requires more research in the future.

7   Conclusion

In this experience report, we performed an exploratory study of various means to handle sustainability during RE. Its main outcomes are a number of insights and lessons learned. Additionally, it allowed us to identify a number of topics to be added to the research agenda for sustainability-related RE:

- We need a "sustainability toolbox" for the requirements engineer, including a generic ontology (for example, under the form of a generic goal model).
- We need to study further the collaboration between requirements engineers and environment experts (similarly to what Firesmith suggested for safety concerns [5]).
- We need to investigate the results of environmental sciences, checking how techniques like Life Cycle Analysis (LCA, [2]) and Environmental Impact Assessment (EIA, [1]) could be applied in the RE context.
- There is a need to explore the suitability of other RE techniques to sustainability requirements. This report covers only a very limited number of techniques presented in the book *Discovering Requirements* [3], which is in turn a small fraction of all methods and techniques available to requirements engineers.
- There is a need to broaden the scope from environmental sustainability to the two other companions, social and economic sustainability, aiming at a holistic approach to sustainability.
- We need more, and more systematic, empirical studies on sustainability in RE.

Acknowledgements

This work was funded by the the Walloon Region under the European Regional Development Fund (ERDF). It is also partly supported by the Interuniversity Attraction Poles Programme of the Belgian State, Belgian Science Policy under the MoVES project, the BNB National Bank of Belgium and the FNRS.

References

1. Principles of Environmental Impact Assessment Best Practice. International Association for Impact Assessment (1999)
2. ISO 14040:2006 Environmental Management - Life Cycle Assessment - Principles and Framework. American National Standards Institute (2006)

3. Alexander, I., Beus-Dukic, L.: Discovering Requirements. Wiley, Chichester (2009)
4. Cabot, J., Easterbrook, S.M., Horkoff, J., Lessard, L., Liaskos, S., Mazón, J.N.: Integrating sustainability in decision-making processes: A modelling strategy. In: ICSE Companion, pp. 207–210. IEEE, Los Alamitos (2009)
5. Firesmith, D.: Engineering safety and security related requirements for software intensive systems. In: ICSE Companion, p. 169. IEEE Computer Society, Los Alamitos (2007)
6. Herrmann, A., Paech, B.: MOQARE: Misuse-Oriented Quality Requirements Engineering. Requirements Engineering Journal 13(1), 73–86 (2008)
7. Ley, M., Bast, H.: http://dblp.mpi-inf.mpg.de/dblp-mirror/index.php
8. Robertson, S., Robertson, J.: Mastering the Requirements Process. Addison-Wesley, ACM Press Books (1999)
9. Shull, F., Singer, J., Sjøberg, D.I.K. (eds.): Guide to Advanced Empirical Software Engineering. Springer-Verlag London Limited, London (2008)
10. Sindre, G.: A look at misuse cases for safety concerns. In: Ralyté, J., Brinkkemper, S., Henderson-Sellers, B. (eds.) Situational Method Engineering. IFIP, vol. 244, pp. 252–266. Springer, Heidelberg (2007)
11. The Atlantic Systems Guild: Volere Requirements Template. Volere, http://www.volere.co.uk
12. United Nations. World Commission on Environment and Development: Our Common Future. Oxford Univ. Press, Oxford (1987), http://www.un-documents.net/wced-ocf.htm

Requirements Engineering Process Improvement: An Industrial Case Study

Georgi A. Markov[1], Anne Hoffmann[2], and Oliver Creighton[2]

[1] Siemens AG, CT T DE TC4, San-Carlos-Str. 7,
91058 Erlangen, Germany
[2] Siemens AG, CT T DE IT2, Otto-Hahn-Ring 6,
81739 Munich, Germany
{georgi.markov,anne.hoffmann,oliver.creighton}@siemens.com

Abstract. [**Context and motivation**] This paper reports the results and lessons learned of a requirements engineering improvement project conducted in a Siemens business unit. [**Question/problem**] In particular, the project addressed the following major problems: (i) communication gap between marketing and development, resulting in misbalance between technology-driven and market-driven requirements; (ii) limited value of monolithic requirements specifications, resulting in inconsistencies across product versions; (iii) requirements overloading, resulting in cumbersome and time consuming descoping; (iv) insufficient traceability, resulting in poor or missing impact analysis, regression testing and other traceability errors; (v) intransparent mapping between a non-hierarchical topology of problem space artifacts to hierarchically structured solution space artifacts; (vi) missing support for platform variant management and reuse, resulting in long release cycles; (vii) waterfall process, resulting in inability to effectively handle change in requirements or design. [**Principal ideas/results**] The paper describes the situation at the business unit before the process improvement project, gives a short overview on how the project was implemented and the techniques applied to solve the various problems the organization was facing. The paper wraps up with a comparison between the initial and the final state of the requirements engineering process in the organization and finally, a lessons learned section discusses some of the highlights and pitfalls encountered during the project. [**Contribution**] The paper can be used as an initial point of reference to other practitioners and organizations facing similar problems and/or involved in similar improvement projects.

Keywords: Requirements Engineering Process Improvement, Feature Modeling, Model-based Requirements Engineering, Goal-oriented Requirements Engineering.

1 Introduction

In this paper, we present the approach and lessons learned from an industrial requirement engineering process improvement project at a software development

D. Berry and X. Franch (Eds.): REFSQ 2011, LNCS 6606, pp. 34–47, 2011.

organization. The main business of this organization is the development, maintenance, and enhancement of a software platform providing core assets to developers of other organizations. However, there is a second, smaller group, which, similarly to developers from other organizations, is using the platform to integrate (business) applications and sell them to end customers. Because of this difficult set-up, features for new releases are the result of the agreement between the developers from different organizations using the platform for their applications and the end-customers.

The initial trigger for the project was a recent reorganization at the customer's side, as a result of which two development departments were merged and therefore needed to consolidate existing processes, methods, and infrastructure. An initial effort on the customer's side to achieve this has increased the awareness of problems and issues connected to requirements engineering and of the high costs associated with errors resulting from those problems (see [1], [2], [3] for more information on the cost and significance of requirements engineering errors).

From project initiation to project completion, the improvement effort took almost two years and was supported by a team of requirements engineering experts.

The remainder of this paper is organized as follows: Section 2 gives a short overview on the concepts used during the improvement activities. The approach used for the improvement is described in section 3. The project results and lessons learned are presented and discussed in sections 4 and 5, respectively. An outline of our future work concludes the paper in section 6.

2 Literature Review and Recommendations

To develop the improvement approach, several concepts were taken from results of recent research in the domain of requirements engineering, product-line engineering and business and process improvement and integrated together. These concepts as well as their application in the project will be briefly introduced here.

2.1 The Requirements Engineering Reference Model

Reference models provide views on relevant information and are often used as points of reference, a standard basis for comparison, or as a source of ideas for good practices to support such improvement efforts as described in this paper. Accordingly, over the years many models have emerged, which describe best RE practices for an organization. A few examples of such models are: Gorschek and Wohlin's Requirements abstraction model [4], Volere's requirements knowledge model [5], IEEE's Requirements specification standard, the requirements engineering related aspects of RUP, CMMI, and others [6], [7].

For our improvement project, the requirements engineering reference model (REM) [8] was introduced as the one to best map to the organization's business domain and desired practices. REM provides a framework for a model-based requirements engineering artifact model, which defines a core set of requirements artifacts and their dependencies and thus guides the establishment, tailoring and maintenance of RE processes [9]. It supports iterative processes, and includes a tailoring concept that allows its adaptation to different projects. In our concrete case study it served as an input for creating the renewed information model, which captured the information flow in the process, the responsibilities of the stakeholders in terms of authorship and guided us during the definition of the review and change management-relevant aspects of the 'to-be process'.

2.2   Goal-Oriented Requirements Engineering

In recent years, requirements engineering researchers have recognized the role of goals in the requirements engineering process and have spent much effort on developing techniques on goal modeling and goal specification for different RE-relevant purposes (requirements elicitation, impact analysis, etc.) [10], [11], [12]. One of the main reasons behind this is the inability of traditional system approaches to capture the rationale behind the development or manufacturing process, making it difficult to understand high-level concerns in the problem domain [13]. The use of goals, on the other hand, offers a precise criterion for feature pertinence and support for validation and prioritization of different alternatives and therefore provides a solid basis for conflict management [10].

2.3   The Requirements Pyramid

Traceability provides a relationship between the different artifacts and their respective abstraction levels in the system. The requirements pyramid, as suggested in [14], is a model that puts artifacts on a certain abstraction level according to their detail and formality. This allows the artifact from the next level to be derived, in a traceable manner, from the level above. This relationship is maintained through traceability links.

2.4   Feature-Driven Development and Scrum

Feature-driven development (FDD) and Scrum are both iterative and incremental software development methodologies based on agile principles [15]. FDD is a model-driven approach, which makes features the center of concern. It advocates the specification of systems in terms of integrated features. These features are based on a common system core, providing the basic functionality. It consists of five sequential processes, during which the design and build of the system is carried out: 1) Develop overall model; 2) Build feature list; 3) Plan by feature; 4) Design by feature and 5) Build by feature.

Scrum concentrates on the management aspects of software development and on how team members should collaborate in a constantly changing environment, which makes the development process unpredictable and complex. It divides development in short iterations and closely controls and monitors the progress in daily Scrum meetings. The backlog is the central management tool of Scrum and defines all open issues for the system being developed [16].

In our concrete case FDD was primarily concentrated on the development and implementation side at a lower level, while Scrum was used to cover the project management. Additionally, FDD provided well-defined milestones for progress tracking, which were missing in Scrum.

2.5   Feature Modeling

A feature model is a tree-like model consisting of all end-user relevant system characteristics and constraints on their combination toward instantiating end-products. There are different conventions used to describe these constraints. During the project, we identified (and evaluated) the following different conventions: FODA [17], FORM [17], FODAcom [15], FeatuRSEB [18], GP [19], FOPLE [20], FORE [21], CONSUL [22], PLUSS [8], etc. As a result of this, evaluation of the identified approaches on a set of predefined criteria, gathered through several expert workshops, was performed and the CONSUL approach was selected in our use case.

2.6   Component Family Modeling

Nuseibeh [23] argues that although the conceptual differences between requirements and architectural design are well understood, the process of moving from problem space to solution space is still a problem for many organizations. This is even more the case when dealing with platforms, where often complex configuration rules between problem and solution space need to be expressed. Our way to deal with this problem is to use a hierarchical structure for representing the solution space as a composition of configurable sets of functionalities defined by logical components. This approach for mapping between the problem and solution space was first proposed in [22] and called CCFM (CONSUL Component Family Modeling). CCFM was used as it provided a formal relationship between the solution space (component family model) and problem space (feature model). In addition, this mapping supported the derivation of single solutions by creating feature configurations.

2.7   Model-Based Requirements Engineering

The integration of conventional requirements engineering techniques with model based software development techniques like Feature and Family modeling, as it was the case in our project, is referred to as model-based requirements engineering [24]. In our case, this integration had the following positive side effects: Traces between requirements and other artifacts from later development phases (such as architecture) became visible. Additionally, this aided in management of crosscutting concerns such as non-functional requirements (an effect that is also described in [9]).

2.8   Summary

An overview of how the entities from the different, introduced concepts relate to each other is shown in a meta-model in Figure 1.

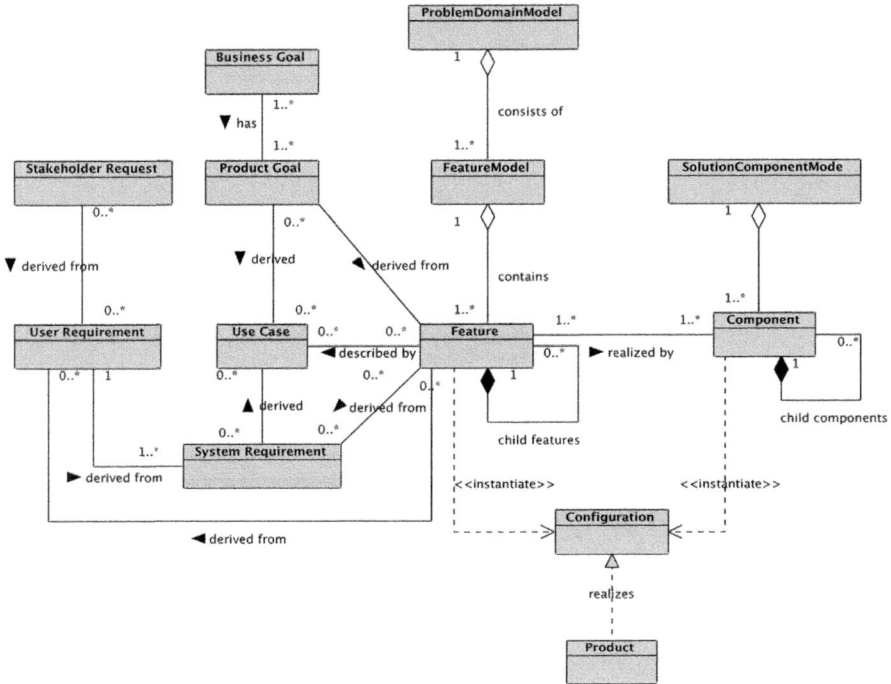

Fig. 1. Requirements Engineering metamodel describing the main entities of the RE process and the relationship among them

3   "Methodical" Approach

Process improvement approaches can be classified in two categories: (i) capability-based and (ii) problem-based.

The capability-based approaches are aimed at improving the company's processes and effectiveness by increasing the processes maturity [25]. To do so, these approaches usually use some more abstract generic model like CMMI, CMM or similar. Consequently, according improvement projects follow the same pattern of first analyzing the current state of the process by measuring key output characteristics against the chosen model, before finally identifying the reasons for variation within the process and either reducing or eliminating them.

The problem-based approaches on the other side are focused on understanding the problems by collecting and analyzing data about its causes and using this information to develop a solution that solves the underlying problems.

Both approaches have their advantages and their disadvantages, and there is a certain amount of overlap in the things that can be achieved with them. However, there are also ways in which they differ significantly.

The project we are describing and discussing in this paper used a problem-based approach, which was extended by elements from the capability-based approach and aimed at correcting problems from earlier projects by anticipating and preventing problems in the future and by adopting best practices. In particular, interview questions, based on different process improvement methodologies were used to guide the initial data collection period.

The adopted approach involved the following steps, which are described below:

- Phase 1: Project preparation and initiation
- Phase 2: Data collection and analysis
- Phase 3: 'To-Be' process definition
- Phase 4: Tool selection
- Phase 5: Pilot project
- Phase 6: Training and coaching

3.1 Preparations and Initiation

This step refers to all activities that need to be completed before the actual project kick-off. This involves understanding the organizational environment, defining scope and boundaries for the project, defining and negotiating project goals, outlining a project plan and engaging with the management to understand their vision of the project and to secure their support. This is necessary as process improvements projects usually involve organizational change and for this to be successful, the project set up requires the support of middle and senior management [26]. The make-up of the project team and the establishment of roles and responsibilities involved the establishing of a project task force to carry out the work on the project without disturbing the ongoing business of the company. The project task force consisted of key stakeholders, including several product managers from the client organization forming the core project team, which was complemented with external technical consultants. The main responsibilities of the later were to guide the core team toward defining the improved process, by providing experience and expertise in the area of focus, and ensuring the standard and quality of the work produced by the team. All members of the team were given dedicated time, authority, and hence responsibility to fully execute the project.

The different Software Development Life Cycle (SDLC) processes are tightly integrated together and work in balance. Process improvement projects, however, are often carried out as if the to-be-improved process was independent and changes to this process won't have any impact on other SDLC processes [27]. To avoid this frequent mistake, special care was taken during the project team make up to actively involve representatives from all areas contributing to, or affected by, the project. This in particular led to including architecture, tooling, and other experts to the project team and dedicating time to ensuring consistency between the processes in order to utilize possible synergies.

3.2 Data Collection and Analysis

The data collection and analysis step involved conducting several informal structured interviews and surveys, and reviewing historical information in order to identify the problems and their roots. For the interviews we developed (in collaboration with the Coburg university of applied sciences, in the form of joint supervision of a master's thesis [28]) a questionnaire based on questions from different process improvement methodologies, and a framework for assessing the capability of an organization's process from the data elicited through the interviews. The framework was based on two dimensions - on the one side, an idealized picture of a Requirements Engineering process, derived from thorough literature study and used to evaluate the organization against, and on the other side a number of hierarchically structured criteria used as indicators to judge the success of the organization's process by measuring both the process itself as well as it's observable outcomes. The structure included the identification of several process dimensions, representing the major areas of concern and interest, each further broken down in so called key process areas (KPAs), which as defined in the CMMI context represent collections of practices with common purposes and goals. Further for each KPA critical attributes or characteristics, called parameters were identified, and finally each parameter was subdivided in so called indicators, which represent the directly ascertainable facts on which the questions mainly focused [28]. The following figure 2 graphically represents the dependencies between the different structural elements, while figure 3, further down, shows an excerpt of the developed structure, to exemplify, how it was applied in the context of the case study.

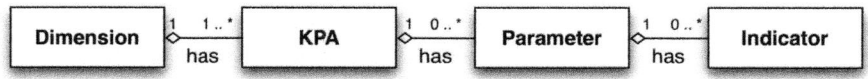

Fig. 2. Structural elements of the assessment framework [28]

The information, gathered in such a way, was further visualized using use-case and activity diagrams. This activity supported the verification, understanding, summarization, and served as a guide toward the identification of unmentioned information sinks and other gaps that were initially overlooked. It also assisted the capturing of common vocabulary (glossary), and the prioritization and reorganization of issues and actions toward achieving consensus on a final list of problems. It was performed in groups of different stakeholders, as this allowed a higher degree of participation and involvement and ensured different perspectives. This contributed that the process itself was also perceived as very valuable for the team, as it was the first time some of the members could see how the work processes really flowed.

The final results of the data collection and analysis phase revealed that the business unit was facing several challenges and was receiving greater pressure to come up with suitable responses for such issues as:

- Communication gap between marketing and development, resulting in misbalance between technology-driven and market-driven requirements.
- A lack of platform configurability and long release cycles, caused by the missing support for reuse.

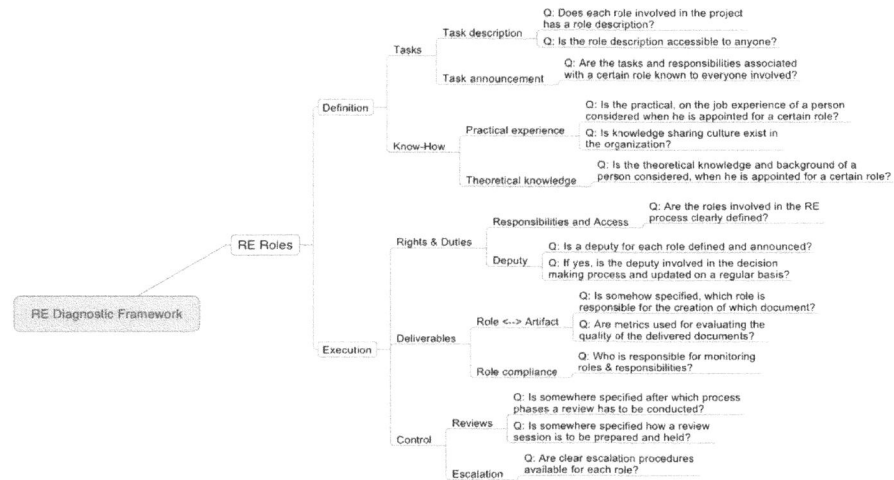

Fig. 3. Hierarchical structure of the evaluation criteria [28]

- A limited value of requirements specifications and inconsistencies across different product versions, stemming from the varying quality, abstraction level, and nature of the incoming requests.
- Missing requirements prioritization process and constant requirements overload. As a result, requirements creep was prevalent throughout the development life cycle. A larger number of features were initially committed in contrast to what was delivered. Such initial over-commitment, combined with a poor change impact analysis, led to the necessity of cumbersome and time-consuming descoping and negotiation sessions, frequent schedule overruns, dropped functionality, and complicated the release planning process.
- Insufficient traceability, resulting in difficult impact and risk analysis, traceability errors and increased effort for requirements authors.
- Intransparent mapping between a non-hierarchical topology of problem space artifacts to a hierarchically structured solution space artifacts [29].
- A Waterfall-oriented process, which fails to provide the necessary flexibility to handle change in requirements and design and agility to respond to today's rapidly changing environment.

3.3 To-Be Process Definition

After the improvement areas have been identified, it is important to determine the appropriate order in which the improvement steps shall be completed. Often practical restrictions exist, which make one particular order more appropriate than another. Therefore a prioritization of the identified problems might be necessary in order to resolve or bundle the dependencies between them in the most meaningful way and to determine the best order to pursue the necessary improvements [30]. In the project under discussion this led to the formation of three different working groups focusing on three main topics:

- Definition of an optimized, organization-wide meta-model and artifact model (based on the abovementioned REM [7] and the requirements pyramid [2]). These have the purpose of revealing all possible artifacts and their dependencies for all phases of an information systems development, from analysis through deployment in order to enable the creation of a traceability strategy [9].
- Definition of a feature model and family model to support variant management and reuse and to provide a bridge between requirements and their architectural realization and architectural component descriptions [31].
- Definition of an improved requirements engineering process, that considers results produced by the other two working groups.

The following figure 4 shows the structure of the project with its 3 work packages (WP) and the contributing partners.

Supported by the described concepts, the requirements engineering process was tailored to best address the current challenges. The resulting approach has the following characteristics:

- A goal model to capture and structure business and product goals and product drivers.
- A feature model to capture and structure common and variable system elements, relevant to the user. All top-level features are motivated by and linked to elements of the goal model.

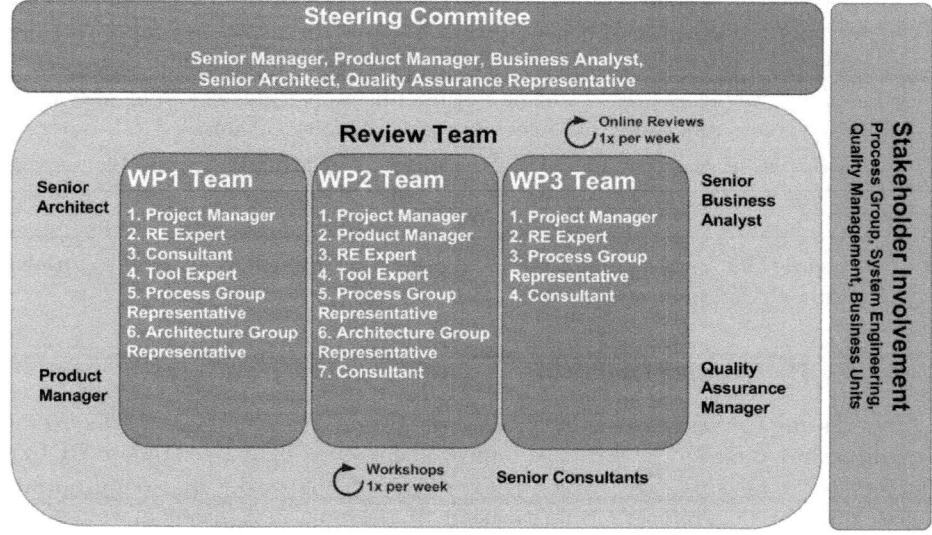

Fig. 4. Project structure

- Several levels of textual requirements with the top-level derived from the feature model and each subsequent level derived in a hierarchical manner from the level above.
- Version and change management of single requirements artifacts.
- Information model based on the REM-model to capture the internal and external information flows, the responsibilities of the stakeholders in terms of authorship and to guide the definition of the review and change management-relevant aspects of the process.
- Component family model to provide a mapping between problem space and solution space.
- Improved end-to-end traceability model.
- Iterative approach to better describes the step-wise nature of this process and to improve flexibility.
- Tightly integrated tool-chain to automate key-processes and support information flow in the entire development life cycle and the cooperation across departments.

3.4   Tool Selection

Requirements engineering tools can help to systematize the requirements engineering process, to support its organization-wide implementation and is a necessary prerequisite for semi-automating it.

A tool evaluation was performed to find how, the different off-the-shelf tools available for the different life-cycle processes, can be best be integrated with each other, and to explore possibly existing synergies that can simplify development, traceability or requirements maintenance. The evaluation process included gathering tool evaluation criteria in several expert workshops before finally evaluating several tools against these criteria. After completion of the evaluation process, the tool vendors of the most appealing tools were invited for an in-house tool demonstration. The result of this step was the selection and integration of the different tools in the process in order to provide the best coverage and efficiency.

3.5   Pilot Project

In order to ensure the feasibility of the new approach in a real-life situation, we performed a small pilot project. We used the newly selected tools to create initial goal and feature models and create an initial mapping between them. Then we selected three features from the feature model, which we developed and refined through the entire requirements engineering life-cycle and further until they were mapped to the component family model. This enabled us to introduce suggested changes in a limited way and create an integrated showcase providing a promotional tool for the new approach.

3.6   Training and Coaching

After a pilot is successfully applied, the changes need to be deployed and other people need to adopt them. Before the project is completed, it has to be ensured that the people, at the customer organization, are able to use the acquired experience on their own "in particular with respect to the future development of the technology (tailorability, etc.)" [32]. To achieve that, adequate training and clear guidance for all people affected by the changed RE-approach is essential, and according to [32] if overlooked could become the cause of failure.

For our case study, we reused the deliverables from the pilot project to develop an integrated example, which was later on expanded to a self-training guide and exercise program.

4 Project Results (Outcomes) and Project Success

In general, the overall success of a project can be measured on two levels: the first level refers to the agreed-upon project deliverables and the second level refers to the actual business benefits for the company adopting the improved process.

Table 1. Cornerstones

Challenge	Solution	Benefit
Misbalance between technology-driven and market-driven requirements.	Features traced to product drivers and business goals.	Ensure effectiveness of requirements management.
Missing requirements prioritization process and constant requirements overload.	Workflow driven Feature Model with sellable units and sufficient granularity.	Efficient requirements elicitation and negotiation, ensure common product view
Insufficient traceability.	Simplified tracing by hierarchical relationships between requirement artifacts.	Less effort for requirement authors by simplified structure, avoidance of tracing errors.
Intransparent mapping between problem and solution space.	"Feature Model" to "Family Model" mapping. Clear hierarchy of requirement objects.	Early impact analysis and estimations, support of project management.
Inefficient review of detailed specs upfront.	Optimized review concept, (review of solution specs at feature completion).	Saving of review effort by consideration of iterative changes to specifications.
Waterfall approach, many handoffs, work in progress, missing feedback loops.	Introduction of MVP, priority based iterative, "just-in-time" preparation of feature specs.	Avoidance of waste, flexibility to react on changes, risk reduction.
Specification based RE, possibility of inconsistencies across product versions.	Administration of single requirement artifacts (CM for RE objects)	Version and change mgmt. for requirement artifacts, enabling shorter release cycles.
No proactive variant management and no support for reuse.	Modeling of feature variability upfront.	Easy generation of variants, support of R&D platform strategy.

While the second level appears to be easier to quantify, it is difficult to measure as there are many important effects that cannot be convincingly put into a €-measure. Additionally, we believe that many of the improvements will become more effective only once the new process has reached some threshold level of maturity. For this reason we have not tried to estimate the economic effects of the project.

Based on the agreed upon deliverables table 1 summarizes the technological benefits of the improved requirements engineering approach.

5   Lessons Learned

In retrospect, we can summarize our key learnings from this improvement project.

By involving experienced RE consultants that demonstrated an exceptional background in all RE topics, a broad spectrum of possible improvement areas and approaches were considered.

The feature modeling and variability management technology was instrumental for solving the complex challenges that the development organization has to face.

The complex interaction of mapping problem and solution spaces needs high expertise in setting up. A common terminological base from start to finish is essential.

If in any way possible, one should minimize separation of phases and work streams. Otherwise, intermediate results may not be accepted between teams. Key deciders should be present in all teams, while at the same time; too "personal" identification of some stakeholders with the technical results should be prevented (separate the people from the problem).

Between consulting and executing organizations, a trustful relationship is necessary to reduce contractual complexities.

6   Future Work

The elicitation process at the customer's organization is a very complex endeavor, happening on two levels: the third-developer organization side and our customer. Additionally it required much negotiation and dispute resolution between the many involved stakeholders. A potential solution to these problems is the use of storytelling as an elicitation technique. The few documented studies on the use of storytelling in working groups show that stories are vitally important to support a sense of vision, shared values and purpose as they allow people to get to know each other better, and to understand why other people feel how they feel. This shows the potential of storytelling in conflict resolution, which is an important part of our customer's elicitation process. Its use as an elicitation technique, however, still requires further research.

References

1. Boehm, B.W.: Software Engineering Economics. Prentice-Hall PTR, Englewood Cliffs (1981)
2. Rainer, S., Hall, A., Beecham, T.: Requirements problems in twelve software companies: an empirical analysis. IEEE Proceedings Software 149 (2002)
3. Software process improvement on the right road with espiti - the espiti european survey results (1996)
4. Gorschek, T., Wohlin, C.: Requirements abstraction model. Requirements Engineering Journal 11, 79–101 (2006)
5. Robertson, J., Robertson, S.: Requirements-Led Project Management. Addison-Wesley, Reading (2005)
6. Kroll, P., Kruchten, P.: The Rational Unified Process made easy: A practitioner's guide to the RUP. Addison-Wesley Professional, Boston (2003)
7. Geisberger, E., Broy, M., Berenbach, B., Kazmeier, J., Paulish, D., Rudorfer, A.: Requirements Engineering Reference Model (REM). Technical report, Technischer Bericht, Technische Universitart Muenchen (2006)
8. Eriksson, M., Brstler, J., Borg, K.: Software product line modeling made practical. Communications of the ACM 49, 49–54 (2006)
9. Berenbach, B., Paulish, D.J., Kazmeier, J., Rudorfer, A.: Software & Systems Requirements Engineering: In Practice. The McGraw-Hill Companies, New York (2009)
10. van Lamsweerde, A.: Goal-oriented requirements engineering: a guided tour. In: Proceedings of the Fifth IEEE International Symposium on Requirements Engineering, pp. 249–262 (2001)
11. Jarke, M., Pohl, K.: Vision-Driven Requirements Engineering. In: Proc. IFIP WG8. 1 Working Conference on Information System Development Process, pp. 3–22
12. Dardenne, A., Fickas, S., van Lamsweerde, A.: Goal-directed concept acquisition in requirements elicitation. In: IWSSD 1991: Proceedings of the 6th International Workshop on Software Specification and Design, pp. 14–21. IEEE Computer Society Press, Los Alamitos (1991)
13. Lapouchnian, A.: Goal-oriented requirements engineering: An overview of the current research. Technical report, University of Toronto (2005)
14. Hoffmann, A.: Requirements Pyramid. In: EuroPLop 2010, Irsee, Germany, July 7 (2010) (accepted)
15. Vici, A.D., Argentieri, N., Mansour, A., d' Alessandro, M., Favaro, J.: Fodacom: An experience with domain analysis in the italian telecom industry. In: Proceedings of the Fifth International Conference on Software Reuse 1998, pp. 166–175 (2004)
16. Schwaber, K., Beedle, M.: Agile Software Development with Scrum. Prentice Hall PTR, Englewood Cliffs (2001)
17. Kang, K.C., Kim, S., Lee, J., Kim, K., Shin, E., Huh, M.: Form: A feature-oriented reuse method with domain-specific reference architectures. Annals of Software Engineering 5, 143–168 (1998)
18. Griss, M.L., Favaro, J., d' Alessandro, M.: Integrating feature modeling with the rseb. In: ICSR 1998: Proceedings of the 5th International Conference on Software Reuse, p. 76. IEEE Computer Society, Washington, DC, USA (1998)
19. Krzysztof, C., Eisenecker, U.: Generative Programming: Methods, Tools, and Applications (2000)
20. Kang, P., Jaejoon, K.C., Donohoe, L.: Feature-oriented product line engineering. IEEE Software 19, 58–65 (2002)

21. Streitferdt, D.: Family-oriented requirements engineering. PhD thesis, Technical University Ilmenau (2004)
22. Beuche, D.: Composition and Construction of Embedded Software Families. PhD thesis, University of Magdeburg (2003)
23. Nuseibeh, B.: Weaving together requirements and architectures. IEEE Xplore 34, 115–119 (2001)
24. Broy, M., Slotosch, O.: From requirements to validated embedded systems. In: Henzinger, T.A., Kirsch, C.M. (eds.) EMSOFT 2001. LNCS, vol. 2211, pp. 51–65. Springer, Heidelberg (2001)
25. Brinkkemper, S., van de Weerd, I., Saeki, M., Versendaal, J.: Process improvement in requirements management: A method engineering approach. In: Rolland, C. (ed.) REFSQ 2008. LNCS, vol. 5025, pp. 6–22. Springer, Heidelberg (2008)
26. Damian, D., Zowghi, D., Vaidyanathasamy, L., Pal, Y.: An industrial study of immediate benefits of requirements engineering process improvement at the australian center for unisys software. Empirical Software Engineering 9, 45–75 (2004)
27. Palyagar, B.: A framework for validating process improvement in requirements engineering. In: First International Workshop on Requirements Engineering Visualization, REV 2006 (2006)
28. Hemmer, S.: Identifikation von Schwächen im Requirements-Engineering-Prozess anhand eines Bewertungsmodels (unpublished master's thesis). Fakultaet Elektrotechnik/Informatik, Hochschule Coburg (available through the faculty archive) (2010)
29. Loy, P.H.: A comparison of object-oriented and structured development methods. ACM SIGSOFT Software Engineering Notes 15, 44–48 (1990)
30. Pettersson, F., Ivarsson, M., Gorschek, T., Ohman, P.: A practitioner's guide to light weight software process assessment and improvement planning. Journal of Systems and Software 81(6), 972–995 (2008)
31. Savolainen, J., Vehkomaki, T., Mannion, M.: An Integrated Model for Requirements Structuring and Architecture Design. In: Proceedings of the Seventh Australian Workshop on Requirements Engineering, Melbourne. Citeseer (2002)
32. Bodker, S.: Creating conditions for participation: Conflicts and resources in systems development. Human-Computer Interaction 11, 215–236 (1996)

Requirements for a Nutrition Education Demonstrator*

Ing Widya[1], Richard Bults[1], Rene de Wijk[2], Ben Loke[3], Nicole Koenderink[2],
Ricardo Batista[1], Val Jones[1], and Hermie Hermens[1]

[1] Remote Monitoring & Treatment group, University of Twente, The Netherlands
[2] Wageningen University & Research, Food & Biobased Research, The Netherlands
[3] Noldus Information Technology BV, The Netherlands
widya@ewi.utwente.nl

Abstract. **[Context and Motivation]** Development of innovative ICT-based applications is a complex process involving collaboration of all relevant disciplines. This complexity arises due to differences in terminology, knowledge and often also the ways of working between developers in the disciplines involved. **[Question/problem]** Advances in each discipline bring a rich design environment of theories, models, methods and techniques. Making a selection from these makes the development of distributed applications very challenging, often requiring a holistic approach to address the needs of the disciplines involved. This paper describes early stage requirements acquisition of a mobile nutrition education demonstrator which supports overweight persons in adopting healthier dietary behaviour. **[Principal idea/results]** We present a novel way to combine and use known requirements acquisition methods involving a two stage user needs analysis based on scenarios which apply a theory-based model of behavioural change and are constructed in two phases. The first phase scenarios specify an indicative description reflecting the use of the transtheoretical model of behavioural change. In the second phase, a handshake protocol adds elements of optative system-oriented descriptions to the scenarios such that the intended system can support the indicative description. **[Contribution]** The holistic and phased approach separates design concerns to which each of the disciplines contributes with their own expertise and domain principles. It preserves the applied domain principles in the design and it bridges gaps in terminology, knowledge and ways of working.

Keywords: requirements acquisition, nutrition education, scenario-based design, transtheoretical model of behavioural change.

1 Introduction

Exposure to plentifully available food in today's 24/7 economy, together with our increasingly sedentary behaviour, are blamed for causing an epidemic of overweight and obesity in many countries [1]. In this context, nutrition education is receiving increasing attention in the drive to improve public health. We define nutrition

* This work is funded by the Dutch Ministry of Economic Affairs & the Province of Gelderland under Pilot Gebiedsbericht Innovatiebeleid programme in FOVEA (www.project-fovea.org).

D. Berry and X. Franch (Eds.): REFSQ 2011, LNCS 6606, pp. 48–53, 2011.
© Springer-Verlag Berlin Heidelberg 2011

education as "any combination of educational strategies, accompanied by environmental supports, designed to facilitate voluntary adoption of food choices and other food- and nutrition-related behaviors conducive to health" ([2], p. 15). Studies report that nutrition education interventions which aim at behavioural change have significant effect in improving dietary practices [2].

One challenge is to investigate how Information and Communication Technology (ICT) based systems can facilitate nutrition education processes by re-engineering the environment of individuals to support them in dealing with unhealthy food temptations. In the multidisciplinary FOVEA project, food scientists and ICT engineers collaborate in the development of a mobile peer-to-peer demonstrator which facilitates overweight persons in adopting healthier dietary behaviour by making healthy food choices which balance energy intake and energy expenditure.

This paper reports on the early stage requirements acquisition of the demonstrator; later stage requirements related to common look and feel of device interfaces are not in the scope of this paper. To our knowledge, we present a novel way to combine and use known requirements acquisition methods in a collaboration process between the disciplines. The process specifies scenarios in two phases such that the acquired requirements align to the application's underlying principles and are feasible to implement.

This work has been inspired by requirements engineering and nutrition education literature. Scenario-based user needs analysis has been discussed in many articles, including [3, 4]. Development of scenarios that reflect medical guidelines and envisioned healthcare interventions has been proposed in [5]. Nutrition education interventions often adopt healthcare models. In this domain, the determinants and need for a healthier food choice and the relevance of behaviour change theories and models (e.g. [6]) have been discussed in [1, 2].

2 Nutrition Education Intervention

This section discusses food choice factors and a model for behavioural change.

Food factors. Many factors influence food choices and dietary behaviour of individuals; for example, biologically determined preferences such as sensory factors (e.g. sweet, salt and hunger), experience or familiarity with food, cultural norms and individual beliefs (e.g. green is healthy), environmental factors (e.g. availability and price) or social structure influences [2]. Food choice therefore depends on the individual, but some influencing factors are common to a community. Dietary strategies may make use of these common factors to manage desirable food choices but need also to take account of the individual's food factor profile, for example for weighing risk and enjoyment of unhealthy food.

Our work uses food factors to specify levels of unhealthy food temptations so as to instrument the demonstrator with ICT-support that engineers an augmented reality environment such that individuals can better deal with these temptations.

Transtheoretical model. Nutrition education adopts socio-psychological models of behavioural change. The transtheoretical model (TTM) is an intentional change model focusing on decisions of the individual [6]. In this model, behavioural change occurs gradually and dynamically throughout a series of five stages: Precontemplation (individuals are not interested in changing behaviour), Contemplation (individuals are considering changing behaviour but weigh the cost and benefit which often proves a barrier to progress to the next stage), Preparation (individuals are motivated and intend to change), Action (individuals have taken first steps to change; e.g. have learned to cope with some food cues but need action-oriented support to improve self efficacy), Maintenance (individuals adopt a new learned behaviour but have to exert effort to prevent relapse).

Typical in TTM is that factual and procedural knowledge necessary for change are considered insufficient for individuals in the preparation stage to take action to change their behaviour. These individuals need support to set action plans and goals. They have to be facilitated to make deliberate decisions, enabling them to weigh benefits and effort of intended actions. These supports bridge the intention to action gap between the preparation and action stages. Support for self-efficacy is furthermore essential in behavioural models in general.

TTM identifies ten mechanisms enabling individuals to progress through stages, for example stimulus control (to manage unhealthy food cues) and helping relationships (to get external help to change).

Feedback mechanisms. Feedback is an important instrument in nutrition education to facilitate self-efficacy. Feedback may be used to advise individuals to avoid unhealthy food cues (cue avoidance) or to notify them for cues to be managed (cue control).

Feedback is also needed to improve awareness of eating (mindful eating) to reduce the risk of overeating. In mindful eating, feedback can be used to slow down the speed of eating such that food intake is better synchronized with the delayed feeling of satiation. Feedback types (e.g. positive or negative), modalities, frequency and content depend on the context and objective of the feedback.

3   Requirements Acquisition Methodology

The early stage requirements acquisition methodology applies a waterfall model which consists of two stages; the first stage consists of two phases.

In the first phase, domain experts bring in their theories, models or guidelines into the envisioned intervention specified as an indicative description by scenarios [4, 5, 7]. These scenarios are expressed in terms of PACT [8], which stands for People (i.e. actors in the scenario), Activities (e.g. intervention relevant activities of the actors), Context (i.e. the environmental circumstance of the actors and activities) and Technologies (i.e. essential technologies for the intervention).

Activities specified in the PACT scenarios may be expressed independently from the need for ICT support or the way the intended system eventually mediates those of them which do require ICT support. An analysis of the activities which require ICT support determines the required functionality of the intended system.

In the second phase, ICT engineers with experience in systems development propose to augment the PACT scenarios with FICS elements [8], including the user-system interactions needed to realize PACT activities that need ICT support. Adapted to our nutrition education context, FICS stands for Functions (i.e. functionality of the intended system which is capable to realize actor's activities), Interactions (i.e. user-system or system-component interactions mediating actor's activities), Content (i.e. variables of the interactions) and Services (i.e. types of the interactions, e.g. unidirectional data streaming service or reliable messaging service). FICS elements describe how the intended system mediates actors' activities and therefore form an optative (i.e. wished) service description of the intended system [7].

If the domain experts believe that the proposed interactions indeed mediate the PACT activities and are aligned with their intentions, they acknowledge the proposal and augment the PACT scenarios with these interactions, resulting in combined PACT-FICS scenarios. This procedure therefore implements a two-way handshake communication protocol in which scenarios become the common discourse of the collaborating disciplines; therefore, reducing the risk of misinterpretation.

In the second stage, the ICT engineers become the lead designers and further analyze user needs given the agreed-upon PACT-FICS scenarios. These engineers may apply requirements engineering methods, techniques and tools without preoccupation of application domain theories or models applied.

Augmented methods. Cross-disciplinary studies further reduce the risk of misinterpretation mentioned earlier; so the ICT engineers studied literature on behavioural change models and nutrition education. The knowledge gained made collaboration in a multidisciplinary setting easier and more effective. Task analysis was used to complement the scenario development and analysis. Goal analysis may also reveal design alternatives, but was marginally used in the current exercise.

4 Development Trajectory

This section addresses some of the design choices, rationale and results of the use of the methodology in the development of the nutrition education demonstrator.

Design choices and rationale. The envisioned nutrition education intervention applies TTM to change the dietary behaviour of an overweight inclined abstainer who also is typified as an external eater. An inclined abstainer knows the risk of unhealthy food choices and is motivated to adopt a healthier dietary behaviour, but experiences difficulties in moving forward from having intentions to taking action. As an external eater, this abstainer is easily tempted by external unhealthy food cues; therefore, progresses and relapses between the TTM preparation, action and maintenance stages. An augmented reality environment re-engineered by means of a mobile nutrition education demonstrator may help this abstainer to control unhealthy food cues.

PACT scenarios are considered suitable to express the envisioned nutrition education intervention. They specify activities of the abstainer (People and Activities) to manage external food cues (Context) by using a mobile application (Technology). Thereafter, the implementation aspects can be addressed using FICS elements.

Results. Dietary behavioural interventions are not only based on food choice control at eating moments. Energy intake and expenditure need to be balanced over longer periods; for example at a daily or weekly basis. Accordingly, a comprehensive set of scenarios which cover daily and weekly activities were developed under responsibility of the food scientists in the project. These scenarios result in eighteen small PACT and FICS requirements tables specifying indicative activities (i.e. not all activities need to be mediated by the intended system) and optative interactions (i.e. required to realize the activities which need the system's mediation), respectively. Besides activities or interactions, the tables describe the actors, the intentions or goals (e.g. cue control or avoidance), and the functionality or resource components needed.

The lunch scenario of the abstainer at the Restaurant of the Future (RoF) [9] was selected for further elaboration towards the demonstrator. The RoF is a company restaurant which also acts as a field laboratory, enabling close observation of people during selection of food items and during eating and drinking. Extensive discussions and five iterations result in a detailed lunch scenario which complies with the comprehensive scenarios. This scenario focuses on food choice aspects as well as mindful eating aspects. Moreover, it incorporates both cue avoidance and cue control.

A time-sequence diagram of interactions of the abstainer with the intended system has been derived from the lunch scenario. From this diagram, a state diagram of user-system and system component interactions has been derived and expressed in UML. Further, an associated service-oriented state diagram has been specified describing state change conditions and the interactions observable at the user-system interface of the mobile component of the intended system. This last mentioned state diagram is expressed by a screen mock-up for abstainer's mobile device, which acts as input device of the abstainer and which outputs informative or feedback actions initiated internally by the mobile component or externally by the RoF's peer component.

5   Discussion and Conclusions

This paper discusses the acquisition of requirements of a dietary intervention for supporting healthier behaviour, despite external temptations of unhealthy food, implemented as a mobile demonstrator. The acquisition process followed known pathways of requirements engineering once the combined PACT-FICS scenarios have been derived. A task analysis complemented the acquisition process further. The elaborated lunch scenario and the screen mock-up, representing the service level state diagram at the mobile device, have been validated by food scientists and were presented at a stakeholder workshop of the project.

The PACT and FICS notions and their use in the development process were found to separate the application domain from the system support concerns effectively. Under responsibility of the food scientists, the envisioned intervention was defined without much burden of implementation issues. These food scientists have sufficient background in the basic principles which underlie the dietary intervention. ICT engineers bring in their system development experience in the second phase. The use of scenarios as a common discourse is considered effective to reduce misinterpretation and was found to bridge the terminology and knowledge gaps between the collaborating disciplines, but the process needed several iterations despite the fact that the ICT engineers studied nutrition education (including TTM).

However, the study may have caused a technological push affecting the first phase PACT scenarios, which turned out to contain more FICS elements than desired. But these FICS elements could have been implied by the focus on cue control which re-engineered the abstainer's environment.

Due to pragmatic reasons decided during the second requirements acquisition stage, cue control and avoidance feedback were not implemented directly at RoF food counters but provided indirectly by emoticons on the abstainer's mobile device. This latter is a valid helping relationship in TTM, but from a design perspective it is a design deficiency because the design starting point was to use stimulus control only.

Experience also showed that incorporation of domain principles in scenarios is a necessity, otherwise scenario activities may become aimless. Analysis of such activities does not easily lead to befitting FICS elements or to implementation alternatives. Moreover, incorporation of TTM and feedback in the developed PACT scenarios was not easy due to the state of the art in applying these theories in practice. Furthermore, experience in applying these theories in nutrition education intervention was felt missing in the project. Particularly, a dietician should be involved in the project, amongst others because it was difficult to determine the type of feedback to apply in mindful eating (e.g. positive feedback to acquire the skill or negative feedback for prolonged learning it?). These are topics for future work.

References

1. Crawford, D., Ball, K.: Behavioural determinants of the obesity epidemic. Asia Pacific J. Clin. Nutr. 11(suppl.), 718–721 (2002)
2. Contento, I.R.: Nutrition Educations: Linking Research, Theory and Practice. Jones and Bartlett Publ., Sudbury (2007)
3. Van Helvert, J., Fowler, C.: Scenario-based User Needs Analysis. Chimera Working Paper 2003-02, Colchester, University of Essex (2003)
4. Widya, I., Bults, R.G.A., Huis in 't Veld, R.M.H.A., Vollenbroek-Hutten, M.M.R.: Scenario-based Requirements Elicitation in a Pain-teletreatment Application. In: Proc. of the 4th. Int. Conf. on Software and Data Technologies (ICSOFT), pp. 406–413 (2009)
5. Huis in 't Veld, R.M.H.A., Widya, I., Bults, R.G.A., Sandsjö, L., Hermens, H.J., Vollenbroek-Hutten, M.M.R.: A scenario guideline for designing new teletreatments: a multidisciplinary approach. Journal of Telemedicine and Telecare 16, 302–307 (2010)
6. Velicer, W.F., Prochaska, J.O., Fava, J.L., Norman, G.J., Redding, C.A.: Smoking cessation and stress management: Applications of the Transtheoretical Model of behavior change. Homeostasis 38, 216–233 (1998)
7. Jackson, M.: The meaning of requirements. Ann. of Software Engineering 3, 5–21 (1997)
8. Benyon, D., Macaulay, C.: Scenarios and the HCI-SE design problem. Interacting with Computers 14, 397–405 (2002)
9. Restaurant of the Future, Wageningen UR centre, http://www.restaurantofthefuture.nl

Scaling Up Requirements Engineering – Exploring the Challenges of Increasing Size and Complexity in Market-Driven Software Development

Krzysztof Wnuk[1], Björn Regnell[1], and Brian Berenbach[2]

[1] Department of Computer Science, Lund University, Sweden,
Box 118, SE-221 00 Lund
{Krzysztof.Wnuk,Bjorn.Rehnell}cs.lth.se
[2] Siemens Corporate Research, Inc, USA
Brian.Berenbach@Siemens.com

Abstract. [Context & motivation] Growing software companies with increasing product complexity face the issue of how to scale up their Requirements Engineering (RE) practices. In market-driven requirements engineering, release planning and scoping decisions are increasingly challenging as the size and complexity increases. [Problem] This paper presents initial results of an on-going exploratory, qualitative investigation of three market-driven, industrial cases with the objective of increasing our understanding of challenges in scaling up requirements engineering and how these challenges are addressed by the studied companies. [Results] Through 13 interviews in three companies, requirements engineering scalability issues are explored related to scoping and the structure of RE artifacts. [Contribution] The main contribution are findings related to increasing RE scale based on interpretations of the experienced interviewees' views.

Keywords: scalability, case study, requirements challenges, market-driven requirements engineering, very large-scale requirements engineering.

1 Introduction

When large organizations develop systems for large markets, the size and complexity of the work products of requirements engineering impose critical challenges [1],[2],[8]. Several studies report on experiences applying RE methods in industrial practice [2],[6] while other report on facing challenges in engineering and managing requirements in industrial practice [3],[4],[5]. On the other hand, the scalability of requirements engineering techniques and processes is neither exhaustively reported when proposing these techniques, nor empirically evaluated [6]. In this paper, we focus on the scalability of RE by analyzing challenges that are reported by advisers in three organizations that differ in size and domain but all acknowledge the need to address the scaling up of their RE practices.

D. Berry and X. Franch (Eds.): REFSQ 2011, LNCS 6606, pp. 54–59, 2011.

2   Case Company Descriptions

Three companies have been involved in this study. All companies produce software intense products in a market-driven context [5]. The characteristics of the involved companies are depicted in Table 1.

Table 1. Characteristics of the companies involved in the study

	Company A	Company B	Company C
Domain	Embedded devices	Embedded devices	Medical care and infrastructure
Size (number of employees)	~5000	~110	~400000
Size of the typical project	Hundreds of market features linked to thousands of system requirements	5-15 persons, 15 man years effort , around 30 features per project	Hundreds of features, several thousands of contract requirements
Length of a typical project	2 years	6 months to 1 year	2-6 years

Company A is a large company in the embedded systems domain that is using a product line approach. Company B provides solutions which enable fast and reliable transmission of handwritten text into a digital format. Company C is a large provider of embedded devices in several different domains, including the energy, transportation and medical sectors.

3   Methodology

The research was conducted using a two-phase qualitative research approach [7]. We used semi-structured interviews with a high degree of discussion between the interviewer and the interviewee [9]. Two interview instruments have been used and can be accessed at [10],[11]. Previous research in large-scale requirements engineering [8][13], related surveys [5][6] and our previous efforts in understanding and supporting scoping [12] have helped to shape the interview instruments. Several aspects were discussed, such as: background and context, tasks related to requirements management, requirements types and representations, issues and challenges. The data from the transcripts was analyzed by using the content analysis technique [7] with respect to the interview instruments. Each chunk of text that was categorized and marked by a corresponding code. Categorized chunks of the text were then grouped into current situation, challenges and improvements.

4   Results

Two challenges among findings have exhibited a potential relation to scaling up of RE practices, namely: *scoping and structure of RE artifacts* (the latter is related to the term *requirements artifact structure* as defined in [13]). These challenges are summarized in Table 2. For each challenge or issue the ID of the advisor who mentioned it is provided, often augmented by a direct quote.

Table 2. The summary of two selected challenges related to scale

Challenge	Company A	Company B	Company C
Scoping	- Satisfy all project stakeholders vs. producing a balanced scope. - Scope reductions are difficult. - Wasting effort on de-scoped features. - Hard to get an overview or see the "big picture". - Requires deep knowledge of people and system.	- Hard to get an overview or see the "big picture". - Acquire enough knowledge to be able to make the decision.	- Difficult to avoid late scoping decisions. - Hard to satisfy all needs.
Req. artifact structure	- Unclear req. - Too complicated to understand. - Uncontrolled changes. - Information cannot be trusted.	- Too complicated to understand. - Unable to reuse the req.	- Unclear req. - Difficult to make relevant grouping.

4.1 Scoping

Responders from both Company A and B experience challenges related to scoping. In the case of Company C, the scoping was reported as partly non-challenging due to the nature of some of the projects discussed (in one case the project was regulated by a contract while in the other case the scope of the project was limited to the core set of features required to launch the product). Five out of seven responders from Company A have mentioned that it was challenging to solve the trade-off between having a balanced scope of the project and satisfying all project's stakeholders. Similarly, responder C2 mentioned that *"sometimes marketing wants it all"*. This situation is frustrating for some of the interviewees, as described by responder A2: *"Yes, and that is a problem because I love the technology, that is why it took this [job], so I love all the features that are proposed and I would love to see them in our products but on the same time I need to take on the bad guy"*. Responder A4 mentioned that sometimes hard decisions have to be made due to the fact that it is not possible to please everyone with given limited implementation resources *"we had to do a very drastic scope reduction cutting down hundreds of features"*. On the other hand, analyzed but removed feature is an extra cost for the company (responder A2).

Surprisingly, responders at Company C did not experience much of scoping reductions stating that *"it was actually less than you can expect from the project of this size"*, responder C2. As explained by responder C1, avoiding scoping decisions was an effect of spending a lot of time on understanding the core set of features and customer needs. Moreover, leaving some *"space for late negotiations"* and *"effort reserved for maintenance"* was also mentioned by responder C1 as a workaround for over-scoping (including more features to the scope of the project than the available resources [12]). Finally, as the date of the product release was critical, the management   limited the functionality to the minimum required for the product to be working, avoiding the *"over-engineering"* issue which was mentioned in case of Company A.

In the case of Company A investigations took much more time comparing to small projects and decisions required more advanced negotiations, as pointed out by responder A1: *"there is a lot of work goes into actually coordinating and understanding different perspectives and getting that into one picture ... so it takes a lot of time to reach that consensus"*. These negotiations are often impeded by previously made commitments that may influence the decision (responder A4). As responder A2 describes it in a suggestive way: *"there are many stakeholders and everybody is screaming that they want their stuff to be done and we are sitting kind of in the middle of this..."*. On the other hand, although responders B2 and B3 mentioned that scope changes require extensive technical knowledge and sometimes time-consuming negotiations with customers, the scoping decisions were made by one person (utilizing a *"dictatorship model"*), which was reported to work well at their scale of the project. However, the challenge mentioned here is the knowledge needed to make the decision; the bigger and the more diverse the project is the more knowledge is required and one person may simply not be capable of storing all this knowledge. Responders C2 and C3 reported that the change process for scoping is rather sophisticated and often standardized. As a result the impact analysis and negotiations with the customer have to be thoroughly performed. Finally, the limited number of scope changes in case of responder C3 was caused by the fact that the project was initiated from a contract written by the customer.

4.2 Structure of RE Artifacts

With the structure of RE artifacts we include the following general aspects in the analysis of responses: (1) requirements entities such as features, system requirements, detailed requirements, quality requirements, etc. and their relationships; (2) the information structure (meta-model) of requirements entities including (a) attribute types of entities, and (b) the relationship types including different types of dependencies to other entities; (2) the evolution of the information structure and its scalability as the number of entities increase and the inter-related set of entities gets more complex.

The structure of requirements is considered to be *"too complicated to extract the information because it passed the limit where it is understandable for the user"* and *"we have little too complicated structure, naturally there is a balance, sure but I think we have driven little bit too far on the complication side"* (responder A4). On the other hand, we noticed problems due to the fact that each new project is coming up with new attributes and change proposals to the ordinary structure of requirements (responders A4 and A5). This problem is partly caused by the differences in requirements management tool policies between the various sites of the company (responder A4) and lack of change control board for handling changes into the requirements management tool structure. This makes searching for information and quality assessment more difficult. Moreover, the result of the mentioned issues may be for example, a problem while doing impact analysis of how many customers a certain de-scoping decision will affect, as pointed out by responder A4. Moreover, Responder A4 expressed the previous fact as a constant problem since *"there are too many trees to see the forest"*. Due to the overload of attributes in the requirements database, there is a lot of redundant information and information whose reliability can be questioned. Moreover, a challenging trade-off between the complexity and the cohesion of the requirements structure was expressed. According to our responders, the more effort is put on documenting a detailed level the less coherent and understandable the structure becomes on the high level. As a result it can be hard to see the full holistic view of a large project (responder A4). Finally responder C3 mentioned that the real problem with the requirements information is a human problem of keeping the information up to date: *"Once you force people to insert and update correct data the information will be maintained automatically"*, says (responder C3).

Responder B3 mentioned that producing a detailed specification with low coupling turned out to be counterproductive for its reuse, understandability and comprehension aspects. As a result, the specification had to be written from the beginning each time a new project starts. All responders from Company B and one from Company C graded understandability (B1, B2, B3 and C3) and extensibility (B3) as important quality aspects of requirements structure. Responder B2 mentioned that grouping and tagging are efficient ways of reducing the complexity and improving the impact analysis. Grouping and creating abstraction layers was also mentioned by responder C1 as an effective workaround of the complexity problem. Responder C3 stressed that finding the best grouping solution depends on the project specifics and can be challenging. For example, grouping by technical areas, or subcomponents of the system does neither refer to marketing requirements, nor to quality attributes. Moreover, it is questionable if quality requirements should be grouped in a separated module or attached to adjacent functional aspect of the system. Adding non-functional requirements on a low level creates a risk of rapidly growing number of duplicates, when the system grows, which is partly cause by the cross-cutting nature of non-functional requirements (Responder C3). Responder B2 mentioned that having a standardized requirements structure is a scalable solution, which is required starting from medium size projects (not necessary for smaller projects). Regarding the abstraction level of requirements and the number of requirements, responder C3 mentioned that the number of requirements is dependent on the process used (naturally the more rigorous process will produce a more detailed specification, in the case of Company B may be counterproductive.

5   Conclusion

In this paper, we report two challenge areas related to the scalability issues of requirements engineering, namely: *scoping and structure of RE artifacts*. The results of this study are aimed at informing further research into the nature of scalability in industrial, market-driven RE. Discovered challenges in scoping call for more research effort in providing a better overview of the size and dynamics of scope changes [12]. Moreover, our results imply a need for revisiting current methods of prioritizing requirements [1] for the purpose of assessment of their scalability and usefulness in multiple-customer environments where decisions have to be re-evaluated and adjusted. More research is required to assess the scalability breakpoints of various scoping models, such as the centralized *"dictatorship model"* reported in case of Company B. Finally, our study reveals a need to provide a scalable method of knowledge management and exchange that can speed up complex investigations. We further explore research opportunities defined in [8] and stress the importance of designing a scalable requirements architecture that can be easy to understand, extend and modify in a controlled way. Our study has confirmed that in large and very-large projects addressing the issues related to the structure of requirements artifacts is important for efficient management of requirements.

Acknowledgments. This work is supported by VINNOVA (Swedish Agency for Innovation Systems) and Siemens Corporate Research Inc. Special thanks to the anonymous informants for their valuable time and knowledge.

References

[1] Aurum, A., Wohlin, C.: Engineering and Managing Software Requirements. Springer, New York (2005)

[2] Berenbach, B., Paulish, D.J., Kazmeier, J., Rudorfer, A.: Software & Systems Requirements Engineering In Practice. McGraw-Hill, New York (2009)

[3] Damian, D.E., Zowghi, D.: The impact of stakeholders' geographical distribution on managing requirements in a multi-site organization. In: IEEE Joint International Conference on Requirements Engineering, pp. 319–328. IEEE Press, New York (2002)

[4] Hall, T., Beecham, S., Rainer, A.: Requirements problems in twelve software companies: an empirical analysis. IEEE Soft. 149, 153–160 (2002)

[5] Karlsson, L., Dahlstedt, s.G., Regnell, B., Natt och Dag, J., Persson, A.: Requirements engineering challenges in market-driven software development - An interview study with practitioners. Inf. Softw. Technol. 49, 588–604 (2007)

[6] Maccari, A.: The challenges of requirements engineering in mobile telephones industry. In: Proc. of Tenth International Workshop on Database and Expert Systems Applications, pp. 336–339 (1999)

[7] Patton Quinn, M.: Qualitative Research & Evaluation Methods, 3rd edn. Sage Publication Ltd., London (2002)

[8] Regnell, B., Svensson, R.B., Wnuk, K.: Can We Beat the Complexity of Very Large-Scale Requirements Engineering? In: Rolland, C. (ed.) REFSQ 2008. LNCS, vol. 5025, pp. 123–128. Springer, Heidelberg (2008)

[9] Robson, C.: Real World Research. Blackwell Publishing, Malden (2002)

[10] The interview instrument for the first part of the study (Company A) can be accessed at, `http://www.cs.lth.se/home/Krzysztof_Wnuk/REFSQ11/Req_Arch_Interview_Guide.pdf`

[11] The interview instrument for the second part of the study (Companies B and C) can be accessed at, `http://www.cs.lth.se/home/Krzysztof_Wnuk/REFSQ11/Scalling_up.pdf`

[12] Wnuk, K., Regnell, B., Karlsson, L.: What Happened to Our Features? Visualization and Understanding of Scope Change Dynamics in a Large-Scale Industrial Setting. In: 17th IEEE International Requirements Engineering Conference, pp. 89–98. IEEE Computer Society, Washington DC (2009)

[13] Wnuk, K., Regnell, B., Schrewelius, C.: Architecting and coordinating thousands of requirements – an industrial case study. In: Glinz, M., Heymans, P. (eds.) REFSQ 2009. LNCS, vol. 5512, pp. 118–123. Springer, Heidelberg (2009)

Towards a New Understanding of Small and Medium Sized Enterprises in Requirements Engineering Research

Thorsten Merten[1], Kim Lauenroth[2], and Simone Bürsner[1]

[1] Bonn-Rhine-Sieg University of Applied Sciences
53757 Sankt Augustin, Germany
{thorsten.merten,simone.buersner}@h-brs.de
[2] University of Duisburg-Essen
45127 Essen, Germany
kim.lauenroth@paluno.uni-due.de

Abstract. **[Context and motivation]** Almost worldwide the software industry mainly consists of small and medium software enterprises. From a requirements engineering perspective these companies are poorly researched. **[Problem]** Though RE research is discovering SMEs as an interesting field, it is difficult to categorize and distinguish these companies sufficiently. This leads to *a)* weakly classified results of observational studies as well as field studies and empirical research and *b)* insufficient mappings between methodical improvements and the companies they can be applied to. Therefore, it is hard for researchers and enterprises to adopt RE state of the art to an enterprises environment. **[Principal ideas]** After defining the problem, initial ideas for attributes classifying SMEs are presented and a way for improving and clustering these attributes is shown. **[Contribution]** This paper raises an important problem statement for RE research and shows an initial way towards solving this problem.

Keywords: SME, RE, requirements engineering in SMEs, empirical study.

1 Introduction

In software industry Small and Medium Sized Enterprises (SMEs[1]) constitute a large proportion of software engineering companies (about 99% of the data processing companies are SMEs and employ approximately 70% of the personnel within that area) [1]. Usually they are very successful, flexible, agile, and open minded for innovations. Furthermore, people in SMEs are acknowledged for their knowledge and their advanced software engineering competence [2, 3].

However, when it comes to requirements engineering in SMEs there is an intensive discussion among academics and in industry regarding requirements engineering approaches and techniques [4, pp. 136]. Though the results of RE research are substantial (e.g. they contribute to standardization) the field of SMEs is still widely undiscovered. We believe that this situation originates in a heterogeneous understanding

---

[1] The term SME and small company will be used as synonym within this article, whereupon we focus on small companies.

D. Berry and X. Franch (Eds.): REFSQ 2011, LNCS 6606, pp. 60–65, 2011.

Table 1. European definition of company sizes. [10]

Enterprise Category	Headcount	Annual Turnover	or	Annual Balance Sheet Total
Medium-Sized	< 250	≤ € 50 million		≤ € 43 million
Small	< 50	≤ € 10 million		≤ € 10 million
Micro	< 10	≤ € 2 million		≤ € 2 million

of what SMEs really are. In addition, today's categories for SMEs as for example in the EU definition (Table 1), seem to be insufficient for RE research.

Within these categories, literature, which shows contradictory results, does not paint a coherent picture of SMEs. The next section in this paper will present the related work regarding RE in SMEs. Section 3 then deduces the problem statement from related work and section 4 outlines a way to cope with the problem.

2 Related Work on RE in SMEs

Related work in the literature can be structured as follows:

1. *Observational studies* exploring requirements engineering in SMEs in general
2. *RE Process models* or *Software Process improvement (SPI) methods*, developed to support requirements engineering in SMEs.

2.1 Studies

Four *observational studies* about RE and SMEs can be found in related work. Aranda et al. show that in seven small companies RE is done differently and in a way that is not described in any of the textbooks. Still they find that RE in every company functions well, due to a strong cultural cohesion and highly skilled software development professionals [2]. Nikula et al. [5] report similar findings in a different light, saying that even 'standard topics in RE' are unknown to many of the twelve companies they observed. Their study also shows that most of the companies have a need to improve RE practices but do not know how to start efforts to improve the RE process. Kamsties et al. [6] also highlight a huge demand for know-how transfer regarding RE in the 10 companies they brought together in a workshop. In contrast to the studies above, they do not report of highly skilled professionals, instead they talk about a maturity level in software engineering, which is very low. Jantunen [7] discovers similar findings to Aranda et al. and adds that companies relying on 'processes' instead of working in a collaboration based environment that depends on common (tacit) knowledge, they start to lose many of their abilities to be adaptive and agile.

Most studies show that most small companies follow agile techniques like Extreme Programming in an evolutionary approach and/or specify requirements by the use of 'stories'. On the other hand, similar companies of roughly the same size can have a software development process similar to RUP with a detailed discovery phase and a detailed specification describing every screen and business rule [2].

Similar to our experience, the studies presented above recognize that a light organization and unconventional RE work better for many of these companies than researchers might think today, though there is still room for improvement.

2.2 RE Process Models and Software Process Improvement

Olsson et al. present a pragmatic framework for RE in SMEs [7]. The framework itself has been created to choose concrete practices for RE in a SME. They state that the selection of RE techniques is a central problem in all aspects of process improvement. Therefore the list of techniques in the framework needs to grow further in the long term.

REDEST [8] intends to develop new and innovative RE techniques and tools in the embedded systems domain as best practices for 14 independent software development companies from different areas of Europe. However, even in the same domain, the solutions for each enterprise differ significantly. This implies that the RE problems are specific for each company and cannot be generally applied for the whole domain.

There is a comprehensive list of other *Software Processes Improvement* (SPI) models compiled by Pino et al. [9]. The systematic review includes mainly SPI methods based on the standards established by the Software Engineering Institute (SEI) or the International Organization for Standardization (ISO). Pino et al. found that SPI models from SEI or ISO are difficult to apply for SME because the complexity of their recommendations. This requires a lot of time and resources, which some SMEs cannot afford.

Additionally, their review states, that in SPI "many authors agree that the special characteristics of small companies mean that process improvement programmes must be applied in a way that is particular to them and visibly different from how this is done in the large organizations" [9, p. 238].

2.3 EU Definition

The EU defines company sizes for small companies according to their annual turnover or annual balance sheet total and the number of heads [10].

3 Stating the Problem

What is the size of a SME and how can small companies be categorized? Today's answer to both questions is the number of employees. We state that this number – as any other single measurement – is insufficient for categorization. Furthermore it is an insufficient unit for measuring size [11].

This results in further problems: The results of observational studies are subsumed in the category SME, i.e. the distribution of team member roles may be shown for different companies from 4 to over 150 people [6] or "SME" is used as a general term without further specification. Additionally, when observing SMEs, it is impossible to categorize the results of these observations. This insufficient categorization produces contradicting results. Because of this, the understanding why some RE techniques can be applied in certain SMEs only is limited. Obviously attributes like the type of software developed by the SME limit the application of certain RE techniques. However, the impact of less trivial attributes and their combinations has not been examined, yet.

As described in the sections 2.1 and 2.2 several findings about small software companies are documented [1, 2, 3, 5, 6, 9, 11]. However, the findings lack a reliable set of criteria defining the kind of SME they are referring to. This implies that

Table 2. SME definitions and SME characterizing attributes

Literature	SME definition	Additional attributes used to describe companies, except size and money
Kamsties et. al [6]	None	- market-driven vs. customer-specific (bespoken) systems - degree of adaptability: user-configurable vs. vendor-configured systems - software development: in-house vs. subcontracting
Nikula [4]	EU	- company age - type of business (software, hardware, services, consultation) - application domain - processes (internally accepted, informal, audited quality model) - project size and duration - project type - software development paradigms, lifecycle models and roles, if known
Aranda [2, 11]	Small companies, less than 50 employees	- cultural cohesion - tacit understanding (based on shared vocabulary) - work environment (e.g. possibility to use shared rooms) - longevity - type of offering / customer types - project length or release cycle - team member roles
Jantunen [3]	EU	- collaboration based (oral) vs. process based RE

solutions like RE Process Models, SPI, best practices, etc. are developed, but the targets of which cannot exactly be defined. Concerning this problem Olsson et al. say that the process of choosing the 'right' techniques for a SME has to be done by requirements specialists, because there is not enough empirical data to support the decision [7]. Hence, frameworks or SPI methods cannot be applied by a SME without external support.

Since most SMEs are rather price sensitive [6], they seldom request external support. RE research should enable those companies to catch up with the state of the art and also make use of innovative RE techniques according to their RE practice without external help.

The literature uses additional attributes to describe the SMEs of interest (Table 2). However, results are not presented in reference to these attributes. We state that specific parameter values of these attributes combined with others will categorize a certain type of SME. Using such a categorization, researchers will be able to develop solutions for a certain type of SME and SMEs will be able to categorize themselves to choose SPI strategies or RE techniques developed for their type of company.

4   Outlook

As argued above, single criteria cannot be used to define SMEs. Therefore, it is necessary to identify additional criteria influencing RE practice. Afterwards these criteria need to be categorized.

4.1 Defining Criteria

We will investigate in combinations of the criteria from Table 2 for categorizing SMEs and their bearing on RE practice as well as – if possible – RE problems.

Additionally, we are going to research additional soft factors such as domain knowledge as an important parameter for RE [12] and the grade of domain specialization of a company, which has a high impact on the use of tacit knowledge in a company and downsizes the use of processes [3]. In summary: These soft factors influence the amount of RE, that has to be done in a written form.

4.2 Questionnaire

After defining a sufficient set of attributes we will develop a questionnaire and distribute it to as many small companies as possible. This first questionnaire will be exploratory and will intend to correlate sets of parameter values within the attributes with RE practices used in the companies. From this initial clustering first results may be derived and precise hypothesis can be formulated.

More reliable categories of small companies and their RE situation, will enable more purposeful RE techniques for certain company types and a more efficient categorization of new findings about small companies.

References

1. Fayad, M., Laitinen, M., Ward, R.: Software Engineering in the Small. Communications of the ACM 43(3), 115–118 (2000)
2. Aranda, J., Easterbrook, S.M., Wilson, G.: Requirements in the wild: How small companies do it. In: Proceedings of the 15th IEEE International Requirements Engineering Conference (RE 2007), Delhi, India (2007)
3. Jantunen, S.: The benefit of being small: Exploring market-driven requirements engineering practices in five organizations. In: Proceedings of the 1st Workshop on RE in Small Companies (RESC), [4], pp. 131–140 (2010)
4. Bürsner, S., Dörr, J., Gehlert, A., Herrmann, A., Herzwurm, G., Janzen, D., Merten, T., Pietsch, W., Schmid, K., Schneider, K., Thurimella, A.K. (eds.): 16th International Working Conference on Requirements Engineering: Foundation for Software Quality. Proceedings of the Workshops CreaRE, PLREQ, RePriCo and RESC 2010. ICB Research Report 40, University of Duisburg-Essen (2010)
5. Nikula, U., Sajeniemi, J., Kalvianen, H.: A state-of-the-practice survey on requirements engineering in small- and medium-sized enterprises. Telecom business research center lappeenranta research report 1, Lappeenrata University of Technology (2000)
6. Kamsties, E., Hörmann, K., Schlich, M.: Requirements engineering in small and medium enterprises. Requirements Engineering 3, 84–90 (1998)
7. Olsson, T., Dörr, J., König, T., Ehresmann, M.: A flexible and pragmatic requirements engineering framework for SME. In: Proceedings: Methods, Techniques and Tools to Support Situation-Specific Requirements Engineering Processes, pp. 1–12 (2005)
8. Hardiman, S.: Redest – 14 best practice SME experiments with innovative requirements gathering techniques. In: Proceedings of the 10th IEEE Joint International Conference on Requirements Engineering, p. 191. IEEE Computer Society, Los Alamitos (2002)

9. Pino, F.J., García, F., Piattini, M.: Software process improvement in small and medium software enterprises: a systematic review. Software Quality Journal 16(2), 237–261 (2008)
10. European Commission. The new SME definition. User guide and model declaration, pp. 1–52 (2008), `http://www.ec.europa.eu/enterprise/enterprise_policy/sme_definition/sme_user_guide.pdf`
11. Aranda, J.: Playing to the strengths of small organizations. In: Proceedings of the 1st Workshop on RE in Small Companies (RESC), [4], pp. 141–144 (2010)
12. IEEE Computer Society. Software Engineering Body of Knowledge (SWEBOK). Angela Burgess, EUA (2004)

Research Preview: Supporting End-User Requirements Elicitation Using Product Line Variability Models

Deepak Dhungana[1], Norbert Seyff[2], and Florian Graf[3]

[1] Siemens AG Österreich, Vienna, Austria
deepak.dhungana@siemens.com
[2] University of Zurich
Binzmuehlestrasse 14, 8050, Zurich, Switzerland
seyff@ifi.uzh.ch
[3] Johannes Kepler University Linz, Austria
florian.graf1@gmail.com

Abstract. **[Context and motivation]** Product line variability models have been primarily used for product configuration purposes. We suggest that such models contain information that is relevant for early software engineering activities too. **[Question/Problem]** So far, the knowledge contained in variability models has not been used to improve requirements elicitation activities. State-of-the-art requirements elicitation approaches furthermore do not focus on the cost-effective identification of individual end-user needs, which, for example, is highly relevant for the customization of service-oriented systems. **[Principal idea/results]** The planned research will investigate how end-users can be empowered to document their individual needs themselves. We propose a tentative solution which facilitates end-users requirements elicitation by providing contextual information codified in software product line variability models. **[Contribution]** We present the idea of a "smart" tool for end-users allowing them to specify their needs and to customize, for example, a service-oriented system based on contextual information in variability models.

1 Introduction and Motivation

Novel software engineering paradigms such as service-oriented computing promote the reuse of available functionality and allow the cost- and time-effective composition of tailored software systems [1]. With such developments, we need to adapt traditional Requirements Engineering (RE) approaches to strengthen end-user involvement in software engineering activities. We foresee that end-users will be directly involved in customizing and tailoring applications to immediately get software fulfilling their needs [2]. This vision has to consider technical, social and methodological constraints and has significant implications for RE research and practice.

In traditional software engineering, it is the *requirements analyst* who facilitates requirements gathering and who abstracts technical details away from end-users. However, requirements analysts are typically not involved in the daily lives of end-users and therefore they usually do not support them in specifying requirements descriptions in situ. Research is needed to explore how end-users can be supported in documenting their needs themselves.

D. Berry and X. Franch (Eds.): REFSQ 2011, LNCS 6606, pp. 66–71, 2011.

The goal of our research is to *explore how contextual knowledge (in models) can support end-users in specifying individual needs and self-customizing service-oriented solutions.* We present a preview of an approach for end-user requirements elicitation using the knowledge "codified" in software product line variability models. We foresee that our approach will enable end-users to specify their needs using natural language text, thereby being supported by tools that are aware of the domain and different variants of customizable products. Particularly, end-users are asked questions about missing details regarding their needs. Our approach is deliberately not fully automated, because human intervention promotes thinking about the results, making it less likely to oversee subtle hints in natural language requirements. We consider our approach to be different to existing product customization based on wizards. In the case of wizards the user already knows which product he would like to have and it is the tailoring of the product to individual needs which is the focus. We envision our approach to be used in situations where the end-user has a need for software support but is not sure which kind of software can support his or her "user story".

We consider our approach to be relevant for the development of software-systems, which can be cost-effectively tailored to end-users needs. This for example includes service-based systems. We therefore have chosen software services to be a key technology for our envisioned research.

2 Research Preview

The aim of the planned research is to build tools and techniques that enable end-users in gathering requirements and consequently customizing, for example a service-based application. We foresee that product line variability models represent the "knowledge base" containing contextual information. This includes architectural aspects of the solutions as well as information on their inherent variability. We consider other modeling approaches (e.g. goal models, ontologies) to be relevant, however, we argue that product line variability models are more suitable for this approach because variability models have a predefined semantics for configuration purposes. These models have an inherent ability (this is what they were defined for) to document options, alternatives and constraints, which is needed in our approach.

Our research is based on the idea that end-users are able to express individual needs with natural language text descriptions [2]. We focus on end-users that have experience in using service-based systems. Our aim is providing a "smart" tool, which allows end-users to enter their needs using natural language text. Analyzing these needs the tool identifies relevant context stored in product line variability models and based on this information it presents a dynamic questionnaire to the user. We envision that the questionnaire stimulates the requirements elicitation process. In ideal cases, answering the questions will enable the end-user to automatically customize the requested service-oriented application. In the long run, individual end-user needs are also used to maintain and evolve the product line variability model. As new relevant information can be mined from the users' needs, the product line models need to be continuously maintained and evolved to ensure the correctness and completeness of the codified information.

2.1 Approach Overview

An overview of the planned conceptual solution is presented in Figure 1. It depicts the key activities and the flow of information among the different participants. A service provider usually knows about the features of a service and how it can be adapted to different contextual situations. (1) In our approach this knowledge is codified in the form of product line variability models. (2) The variability model is used as input for an end-user requirements elicitation tool. The user enters natural language text and answers the questions presented by the tool. (3) The tool attempts to configure the required product based on the answers of the user. (4) The variability model is updated each time the user comes up with new contextual information. (5) The user's answers and the underlying product line model allow the generation of a service-based prototype application.

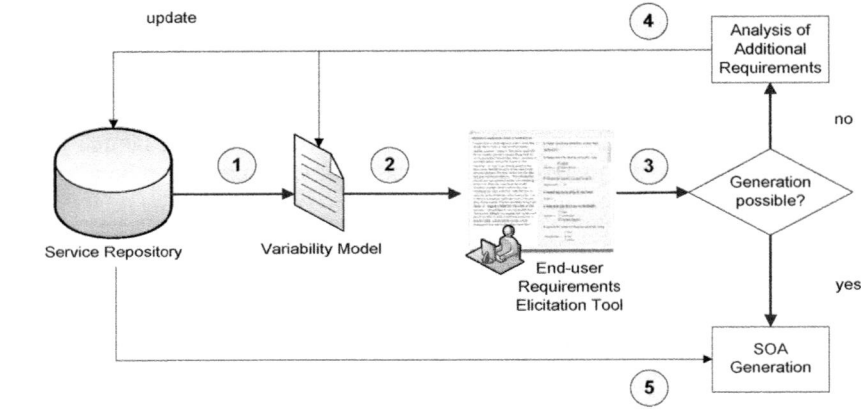

Fig. 1. Overview of different activities associated with requirements elicitation using codified context knowledge models of service-based applications

2.2 Possible Tool Support

We have started working an early tool prototype called EuReCuS (End-user Requirements Elicitation and Customization of Services), which enables end-users to enter a user story using natural language text and presents relevant questions, as the user enters her story. EuReCuS is currently utilizing the product line variability modeling capabilities of the DOPLER [3, 4] tool suite. DOPLER variability models consist of decisions, the users can take and rules that need to be considered when selecting services based on the users answers to the relevant questions.

We envision that EuReCuS will enable end-users to document their needs with the help of a seemingly simple text editor. The text editor is however sensitive to what the user is typing. It is linked to the variability model execution engine to identify relevant questions and pass the end-user's answers on these questions.

Based on the entered text the tool identifies relevant decisions within the variability model and it displays corresponding questions to the end-user. Using interactive UI elements the end-user is able to answer the upcoming questions (see Figure 2). The

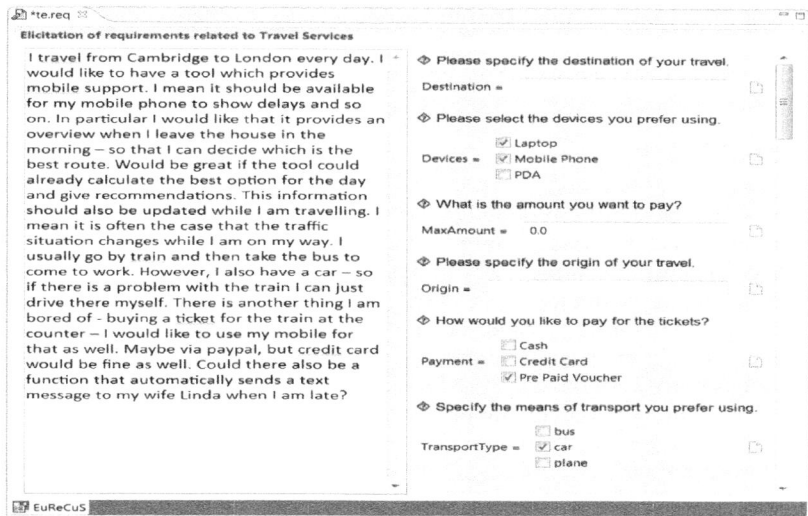

Fig. 2. Screenshot of an early EuReCuS tool prototype, depicting the text editor on the left and the set of automatically identified relevant contextual questions on the right

answers are then passed to the variability modeling execution engine. The model execution engine passes information about selected services to the service composer. The output is an automatically generated customized application.

2.3 Application Scenario

To highlight the application of our approach we prepared an example discussing how an end-user would use the developed EuReCuS tool in order to document requirements and customize a software solution. We decided to use an example which discusses everyday needs of an end-user named Tom. His requirements describe how a future software system should support his daily commuting (see Figure 2).

Tom, not being an RE expert and unfamiliar with requirements documentation, will most likely not document fully specified requirements descriptions. We expect Tom to provide a mixture of needs, rationale descriptions, and uncertainties documented in a kind of user story. In general Tom's description is supposed to include a lot of contextual information. Tom, for example, could describe needs using statements such as: *I would like to have a tool which provides mobile support and this (travel) information should also be updated while I am traveling.* Using the EuReCuS text editor Tom is not forced to describe his needs following a predefined structure. Furthermore, the approach is not limiting Tom's creativity as he is allowed to document whatever comes into his mind.

While Tom is brainstorming his vision of the future system he is presented with some multiple choice questions. For example, analyzing Tom's description and using keyword matching our tool comes up with more detailed questions referring to the type of mobile device Tom is envisioning to use (e.g. Please specify the devices you prefer using). The system will provide possible answers, such as Laptop, Mobile

Phone, and PDA which allows Tom to think about alternative options. Although he did not mention support for his Laptop in his initial description, he now might discover that he actually wants to use the envisioned system on his laptop as well.

3 Related Work

Several attempts have been made in the past to introduce feature modeling as a means to involve end-users in service customization. For example, the authors in [9] classify web services features from the users' point of view and propose to use feature diagrams for modeling flexibility of the Web Services. In [7], authors introduce feature modeling and configuring techniques in domain engineering into service-oriented computing, and correspondingly propose a business-level service model and an end-user friendly service customization mechanism. Hartman et al. [5] have introduced the concept of a "Context Variability model", which contains the primary drivers for variation, e.g. different geographic regions. However, the motivation behind this research was not to support end-users during requirements elicitation. The context variability model constrains the feature model, which allows modeling multiple product lines supporting several dimensions in the context space.

We also acknowledge related work in the area of natural language processing (NLP) for requirements engineering [8]. Currently, it is not our aim to understand the text. In these early steps we need to focus on extracting concepts contained in the user story in order to provide adequate options to the user. In [10], authors present tools and techniques to form service queries from incomplete requirements specifications And [6] presents an approach for identifying ambiguities in natural language requirements specifications using tools based on linguistic instruments.

4 Summary and Next Steps

Reuse-based system development requires changes in RE. Instead of being a front-end activity in the software engineering process and focusing on defining requirements for the development of software systems, the focus shifts towards mapping user needs to existing artifacts. This implies that knowledge about existing functionality is available and can guide requirements elicitation and system analysis. Product line variability models seem to be suitable for modeling and presenting contextual information. We foresee that making existing domain knowledge explicit might stimulate end-user's creativity and trigger new requirements.

Applying the proposed approach, in ideal cases, end-users will be able to construct tailored applications themselves. However, even if no solution can be generated automatically, our approach allows end-users to define a prototypic configuration of a service-based system. Nevertheless, we want to highlight potential risks and threats.

So far we did not conduct any experiment revealing that our basic assumption – that end-users can successfully apply the described approach – is true. As a next step we plan to use a more sophisticated tool prototype to explore the feasibility of the discussed approach. If end-users are in general are able to apply the approach we plan to focus on improving it. For example, the approach relies on natural language processing for identifying the key concepts in user stories and mapping them to modeled knowledge in variability models. This automation step could be a source of errors and has potential for further research. The use of product line variability models seems a logical choice, however we plan to investigate the use of other kinds of models (goal models, ontologies). We further plan applying our approach using real-service repositories, empowering users to customize service-oriented applications themselves. This will provide us with further feedback and will allow improving the approach and the tool.

References

1. Papazoglou, M.P., Traverso, P., Dustdar, S., Leymann, F.: Service-Oriented Computing: State-of-the-art and Research Challenges. IEEE Computer 40(11) (2007)
2. Seyff, N., Graf, F., Maiden, N.: Using Mobile RE Tools to Give End-Users Their Own Voice. In: International Conference on Requirements Engineering (RE 2010), Sydney, Australia, pp. 37–46 (2010)
3. Dhungana, D., Rabiser, R., Grünbacher, P., Lehner, K., Federspiel, C.: DOPLER: An Adaptable Tool Suite for Product Line Engineering. In: 11th International Software Product Line Conference (SPLC 2007), Kyoto, Japan, pp. 10–14 (2007)
4. Dhungana, D., Grünbacher, P., Rabiser, R.: Domain-specific adaptations of product line variability modeling. In: IFIP WG 8.1 Working Conference on Situational Method Engineering: Fundamentals and Experiences, Geneva, Switzerland (2007)
5. Hartmann, H., Trew, T.: Using Feature Diagrams with Context Variability to Model Multiple Product Lines for Software Supply Chains. In: 12th International Software Product Line Conference, Limerick, Ireland, pp. 12–21 (2008)
6. Kiyavitskaya, N., Zeni, N., Mich, L., Berry, D.: Requirements for tools for ambiguity identification and measurement in natural language requirements specifications. Journal Requirements Engineering 13(3), 207–239 (2008)
7. Robak, S., Franczyk, B.: Modeling web services variability with feature diagrams. In: Chaudhri, A.B., Jeckle, M., Rahm, E., Unland, R. (eds.) NODe-WS 2002. LNCS, vol. 2593, pp. 120–128. Springer, Heidelberg (2003)
8. Ryan, K.: The role of natural language in requirements engineering. In: Proceedings of IEEE International Symposium on Requirements Engineering, pp. 240–242. IEEE Computer Society Press, Los Alamitos (1992)
9. Wang, J., Yu, J.: A Business-Level Service Model Supporting End-User Customization. In: Service-Oriented Computing - ICSOC 2007 Workshops, Vienna, Austria, pp. 295–303 (2007)
10. Zachos, K., Maiden, N.A.M., Zhu, X., Jones, S.V.: Discovering web services to specify more complete system requirements. In: Krogstie, J., Opdahl, A.L., Sindre, G. (eds.) CAiSE 2007 and WES 2007. LNCS, vol. 4495, pp. 142–157. Springer, Heidelberg (2007)

Interview Patterns for Requirements Elicitation

Lauri Ann Scheinholtz[1,2] and Ilona Wilmont[3]

[1] Mithun Training & Consulting, Leusden, The Netherlands
[2] Laquso, Eindhoven University of Technology, Eindhoven, The Netherlands
la.scheinholtz@mithun.nl
[3] Institute for Computing and Information Sciences, Radboud University Nijmegen,
Nijmegen, The Netherlands
i.wilmont@science.ru.nl

Abstract. [**Context and motivation**] The requirements engineer as a link between software makers and software users is a firmly established role. However, people from a variety of backgrounds execute this role, making standardization, uniformity, and maturity of the role very difficult. [**Question/problem**] In this paper, we provide an initial step towards easy to understand support for the execution of requirements elicitation interviews. [**Principal ideas/results**] We present our work in progress on a framework for analyzing the types of questions used during requirements elicitation interviews, what responses they elicit and to what extent those responses are of desirable quality. [**Contribution**] Successful requirements engineering strongly depends on the right questions being asked in such a way that the user stakeholder can provide the right details in his response. Identifying these questions and guiding inexperienced requirements engineers during this challenging task promises to improve the quality of requirements elicitations.

Keywords: Requirements elicitation support, asking, types of questions, quality of responses.

1 Introduction

In this paper we analyze the process of a requirements elicitation interview with a user stakeholder. We specifically focus on what kinds of questions to ask in order to induce deep thinking, which has been shown to result in more elaborate responses and better understanding [5]. Human limitations concerning information processing and problem solving, and the tendency to make a biased selection of information, are recognized as problematic in requirements engineering [4]. The use of a requirements determination strategy enhances specification and elicitation of the appropriate requirements. Davis [4] has identified four such strategies: (1) asking, (2) deriving from an existing information system, (3) synthesis from characteristics of the utilizing system, and (4) discovering from experimentation with an evolving information system. We focus on the first strategy, since *asking* the wrong questions during a requirements interview has been identified as a fundamental mistake [9].

D. Berry and X. Franch (Eds.): REFSQ 2011, LNCS 6606, pp. 72–77, 2011.

Firstly, we discuss our method for analyzing the interviews. Then, we provide a brief description of a pilot study in which we applied our framework to an interview.

2 Methods

In order to find interview patterns that lead to successful elicitation, the *types of questions* asked are categorized according to basic communications theory [8], and related to the *response quality* they have induced, which is inspired by learning theory [5].

2.1 Categorization of Questions

We assign 4 tags to each question, which make a question type. An overview is presented in figure 1, with an explanation of tags following below.

- **Open**: Expansive, specify a topic and allows for considerable freedom.
- **Closed**: Narrow and restrictive in focus.
- **Highly**: Open or Closed to the greatest degree.
- **Moderately**: Placing a certain amount of restriction on answer possibilities.
- **Neutral**: No overt direction or pressure from the questioner.
- **Leading**: Suggest an expected or desired answer.
- **Primary**: Introducing new (sub)topics that can stand alone.
- **Probing**: Attempt to elicit a further response following a primary question. Types of probes:
  - **Silent**: The use of silence and nonverbal cues.
  - **Nudging**: The use of a 1 to 2 word prompt.
  - **Clearinghouse**: Encourage respondents to volunteer information the interviewer may not think to ask about.
  - **Informational**: Questions that get additional explanations.
  - **Restatement**: A restatement of all or part of the original question.
  - **Reflective**: Reflects answer just received to verify one's interpretation.
  - **Mirror**: Summarizes parts of the interview to ensure understanding.

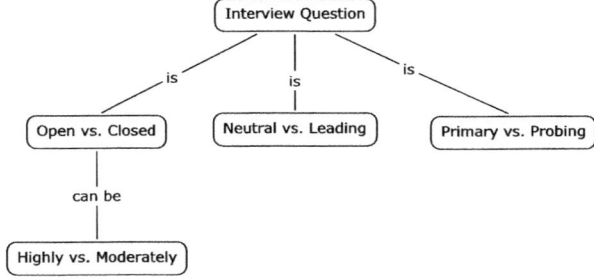

Fig. 1. Structure of the question tags

2.2 Achieving Effective Thinking

An individual's mental problem representation significantly influences the ease with which problems can be solved [2,6]. Experts reason according to principles, whereas novices tend to look mostly at visible surface characteristics of a problem [1]. Experienced requirements practitioners describe that most of their best practices are guided by intuition and 'gut feeling' (research in progress). This intuition can be termed *procedural knowledge* [7]; implicit memories that typically cannot be explicitly described, but are crucially important in order for the practitioner to function.

One way to assess this is by direct observation of users performing their daily tasks, but insights from learning theory [5] show that certain types of questions can be used to make people more consciously aware of everything they know. These questions focus particularly on constructing meaningful relations between chunks of knowledge. In collaborative settings such as a requirements elicitation session, knowledge building occurs through people reacting to each other and thereby changing each other's insights. These so called *socio-cognitive* learning processes are facilitated through cognitively oriented activities: experiences, behaviors and interactions that often induce deep cognitive, metacognitive (monitoring one's own learning) and socio-cognitive processes [5].

We distinguish between superficial thinking and deep thinking [10]. Superficial thinking is encouraged through factual questions, which are good for knowledge retelling tasks. Factual learning involves memorization, achieved through repetition, rehearsal and retelling, and basic comprehension, which happens through summarization and paraphrasing [5]. Eliciting facts is an essential part of requirements elicitation, but more is required when we truly want to gain insight into the domain. The higher level cognitive processes we want to induce for this task are analytical thinking, integration of ideas and logical reasoning. An overview of activities to achieve this type of thinking as described in [5]:

- *Elaborating on content* to add details and examples, relating new material to what one already knows. Elaborations are incorporated into existing knowledge, reorganizing mental models and thereby improving both the domain expert's and the requirements engineer's understanding of the domain.
- *Explaining ideas and concepts* to relate the why and how of issues being explained to what is already known. Again, this improves insight.
- *Asking thought-provoking questions* to encourage people to think with and about the material, which are thought to establish elaborate cognitive representations of knowledge, facilitating the connection of new ideas with prior knowledge.
- *Argumentation* through evidence based reasoning to substantiate or change views on one's claim. Besides its convincing power, argumentation can be used to explore issues and create deeper understanding of them.
- *Resolving conceptual discrepancies* between an individual's own understanding and others' views on issues, also through substantiating and explaining one's own views.
- *Modeling of cognition* by taking skilled use of questioning and explaining by others as an example to refine one's own skills.

3   Pilot Study and Observations

To test our system of analysis we have conducted a single interview with a representative from a Dutch company. One of the authors, who simultaneously works as an expert interviewer, has conducted the interview, while the other was observing. In addition, we have done an audio recording and a transcription of the interview. Preparation of the interview is up to the interviewer. In this case, the interviewer did not like preparing a structured guide so the questions are purely triggered by the respondent's answers. Analysis is primarily done after the interview has been transcribed.

When considering the notion of *quality* of the observed responses in relation to the question categories used, we analyze to what extent the interactions show superficial thinking activities, and to what extent they show deep thinking activities. We look at how the information integrates into a coherent whole, and whether there has been too much emphasis on facts and too little on insight in the domain or vice versa. Another important aspect to consider is whether there is consent over the elicited requirements and domain insights, and whether there has been active stakeholder participation. Anecdotal evidence from practitioners so far shows that a sense of ownership over the product of a requirements session greatly improves the chances of active stakeholder involvement as the project progresses. We acknowledge that at the time of writing this paper, determining the quality of questions and responses remains a subjective issue involving human interpretation of the described indicators. Therefore, the analysis results serve to reflect on the quality of the interview. However, we ultimately aim to create a framework which can assign a predefined conclusion to requirements interview flows.

In this case, the closed questions greatly outnumber the open questions, with 72 to 4 respectively. In 3 cases the interview deviates from the desired focus, and the interviewer asks two, mainly leading, questions at once. The prominent pattern here is asking closed leading questions to keep the interviewee on track. A fragment of the interview serves as an illustration.

Interviewer
Can you tell me (...) why it is you're interested in, say, templating techniques?
Interviewee
That's a good question (...) right now we have a text based approach (...) where requirements consist of a description (...) the rationale, the source and (...) well I think that's it (...) What I see is that we have difficulties in writing a good rationale (...) it's also difficult to say in a requirement what the priority is (...)
Interviewer
Well, it's a hard thing to do, especially (...) because of safety regulations and one assumes everything gets a pretty decent priority
Interviewee
Yeah, but our problem is that if we have to design it (...) And not able to create a design as expected then we have to give feedback to them and if the priority is low perhaps they can accept it, if the priority for that requirement

is high then you have another discussion I think. Today we don't have that in place because every requirement has the same priority (...) And also the source and the rationale are not often eh mentioned (...) But we believe that it's due to that they write eh.. very detailed information in it, and then it's always difficult to have a rationale for it. If you have a higher level description you probably could come up with a better rationale. (...)

Interviewer
Oh well, rationale may or may not be affected by level of detail, the rationale for any single requirement regardless of level of detail should exist, you know.. (...) Now, the question really at that point is, does anyone who's writing the requirements know the rationales, or is it just there because we've always had a requirement like this, (...)?

Interviewee
Nah, I think it's a combination (..) not everybody was very experienced in writing requirements (...) or maybe sometimes they just don't know (...) and sometimes I think it's due to the level of detail (...) for example, there is a document that says: well, after this event a timer should be reset to zero (..) and then start counting up and once the level of this is reached then something should happen. And what he really means is that he wants a delay (...) he can't find a rationale why the timer should be reset to zero after the event

The interviewer asks a *moderately open primary neutral* question to start a new topic. A reasoned argumentation for the interest in templating techniques is asked for, and the respondent does not have a straight answer. He begins reasoning by relating back to what he knows and sees in daily practice (difficulties in writing rationales and prioritizing requirements). The interviewer then assents to this by offering a reason why prioritizing requirements might be hard. The respondent does not entirely agree, and he continues by mentioning an example of where wrong prioritization causes trouble and offers a new cause: too much detail in the requirement description, which may hide the essence of it. The interviewer then expresses a slight doubt about this problem cause, probably stemming from her own experience. A few sentences later, the interviewer offers a new problem cause to be examined: whether people know what the rationales are. It is a *highly closed primary leading* question, which suggests several possibilities for the respondent to consider in his answer, but the respondent refutes them as problem causes and relates several of his experiences to the problem. Then he poses an hypothesis: "I think it's due to the level of detail" which he examines and substantiates with an example from his experience.

The cognitive processes in this example, such as examining problems, naming and testing of hypotheses and integrating ideas were abundantly present throughout the entire interview in the interviewee's responses. The main pattern we could distinguish was that the interviewer kept reviewing and reconceptualizing the information provided by the interviewee, and this triggered the interviewee to provide more information. This information came mostly in the form of either eliciting situational information from memory, or providing an hypothesis, examining it with examples from his experience, or refuting and correcting the reconceptualization the interviewer had provided using specific examples from his memory.

4   Interpretations and Future Research

Our pilot interview has shown that the framework can provide a workable way of analyzing the structure and interactions of a requirements interview. The pattern of reacting to closed questions, often by refuting the claims made in them, has been a very prominent pattern throughout the interview. When relating it to the cognitive processes we consider in our framework, this is continuous resolving of cognitive discrepancies. The respondent is offered a view, possible problem cause or solution, and it mismatches with his own views and experiences and therefore he is triggered to react and correct and change the interviewer's views.

We do feel the cognitive framework needs further refining, especially when using it to analyze the *process* of the interview. On the one hand, it is easy to distinguish between the relevant higher-level cognitive processes, or whether the interview is eliciting information from explicit memory. However, the framework focuses mainly on inducing cognitive processes desirable in collaborative problem solving or discussion situations, where people use their implicit procedural skills to accomplish a goal. In the case of an elicitation interview in which there is a clear division of roles between one person asking and the other person answering, largely from explicit memory, the framework provides irrelevant details.

Our future work will further test the framework with more data. It will be interesting to investigate the specific influence the limitations of human working memory capacity [3] have on interviews. We will adjust the focus of the cognitive framework so that we may have one part that works for assessing procedural skills, and another for analyzing mostly explicit knowledge elicitation. We feel these two aspects of human memory are equally important, and deserve equal attention when used in requirements engineering.

References

1. Bransford, J.: How people learn: Brain, mind, experience, and school. National Academies Press, Washington (2000)
2. Chi, M., Feltovich, P., Glaser, R.: Categorization and representation of physics problems by experts and novices*. Cognitive science 5(2), 121–152 (1981)
3. Davidson, J., Sternberg, R.: The psychology of problem solving. Cambridge University Press, Cambridge (2003)
4. Davis, G.: Strategies for information requirements determination. IBM Systems Journal 21(1), 4–30 (2010)
5. King, A.: Scripting collaborative learning processes: A cognitive perspective. In: Scripting Computer-Supported Collaborative Learning, pp. 13–37 (2007)
6. Newell, A., Simon, H.: Human problem solving. Prentice-Hall, Englewood Cliffs (1972)
7. Squire, L.: Memory and brain. Oxford University Press, USA (1987)
8. Stewart, C., Cash, W.: Interviewing: Principles and practices. McGraw-Hill, New York (2003)
9. Wetherbe, J.: Executive information requirements: getting it right. Mis Quarterly 15(1), 51–65 (1991)
10. Zhang, L., Sternberg, R.: The nature of intellectual styles. Lawrence Erlbaum, Mahwah (2006)

A Heuristic Approach for Supporting Product Innovation in Requirements Engineering: A Controlled Experiment

Sascha El-Sharkawy and Klaus Schmid

Universität Hildesheim, Institut für Informatik
31141 Hildesheim, Germany
{elscha,schmid}@sse.uni-hildesheim.de

Abstract. [**Context and motivation**] While requirements engineering earlier focused on gathering requirements, it has been recognized today that creativity and innovation are required as a basis for novel products. [**Question/problem**] We described earlier an approach to support creativity in requirements engineering. Here, we focus on a thorough validation of the approach. [**Principal ideas/results**] Our approach uses semantic-based technologies to derive new idea triggers. Here, we show an evaluation of this approach. We find that the approach provides better results than other existing creativity techniques like random triggers. [**Contribution**] The paper provides evidence for creativity enhancement using our approach. It also shows how a controlled experiment to analyze creativity in requirements engineering can be performed.

Keywords: Creativity support, product innovation, experimentation, model-based assistance, elicitation support.

1 Introduction

Product innovation is an important challenge for companies that want to be competitive in the market. The core problem in product innovation is *creativity*. It provides the basis for innovation and all other steps in innovation build on this. Thus, in order to improve product innovation, we must support people in being more creative. Therefore in recent years many papers in the area of requirements engineering dealt with innovation and creativity [7, 13, 17].

Despite this abundance of techniques, only very little IT-support for creativity has been developed [5]. While there are many tools that support the recording and management of ideas, like mind-mapping respectively innovation management tools, the creation of ideas itself has rarely been addressed and remained a purely people-oriented activity. To improve upon this situation was one goal of the *idSpace* project [6]. It aimed at the development of a product innovation platform that could support work teams that collaborate in a distributed manner.

As part of this project a tool to support creativity was developed. This tool takes advantage of semantically linked requirements/ideas to generate new idea triggers, which can enhance creativity. The basic approach that was developed was already discussed in a different paper [18].

D. Berry and X. Franch (Eds.): REFSQ 2011, LNCS 6606, pp. 78–93, 2011.

In this paper we describe an approach for supporting creativity through heuristics that exploit semantic relations among requirements. The main contribution is the description of an experiment to evaluate the outcome of this approach.

In Section 2 we will discuss related work. Section 3 will describe the basic representation approach that was used in the *idSpace* platform. Section 4 provides an overview of the heuristic approach to identifying new idea triggers that is used in our experiment. Subsequently, Section 5 presents our experiment that analyzed the overall effectiveness of the approach. Finally, in Section 6, we will conclude.

2   Related Work

Over time many techniques have been developed to support people in idea creation. In fact, catalogues have been developed to provide an overview of techniques [12]. We created the Creativity Technique Selector [3] as a tool to understand and organize this plethora of techniques. It currently categorizes over 180 different techniques and can filter them based on several criteria.

While requirements engineering was initially regarded as gathering somehow pre-existing requirements, it has already been recognized since the mid 90s that this is not the whole truth [14]. Over time it has been increasingly understood that requirements are invented and created [13, 15, 9, 17, 10]. Most work in this area focused on individual case studies or discussed the topic in general. In [8] Kerkow et al. provide guidance for creativity workshops based on lessons learned from several case studies.

In some cases, specific, new techniques were developed. An example of this is the EPMcreate technique [10]. This work is probably closest to our approach, although their approach does not exploit complex semantic relationships among ideas.

Berry et al. also evaluated their approach experimentally. In [16] they perform an experimental evaluation where they compare EPMcreate with a variant of their approach. They also analyzed to what extend their approach can be applied by individuals instead of groups in [11].

3   Context of the Approach

Most current creativity techniques assume that project stakeholders are present at the same place at the same time. This is a problem, especially in distributed work settings, which are increasingly common in globalized software engineering. The *idSpace* project [6] aimed at developing a web-based collaboration platform for distributed product innovation – distributed in time and in space.

The idSpace platform actively supports the creation of new ideas. This is different from most innovation support tools, which focus only on managing ideas. It also enables storage, processing and management of ideas. For supporting the creation of new ideas several capabilities for transforming the stored ideas are offered. The results are not expected to be immediately new and adequate ideas, but rather they provide triggers to humans to find better ideas than they would without them.

The approach taken in the idSpace platform is to have a common idea repository, which is realized using topic maps [19]. A meta-model was developed for storing

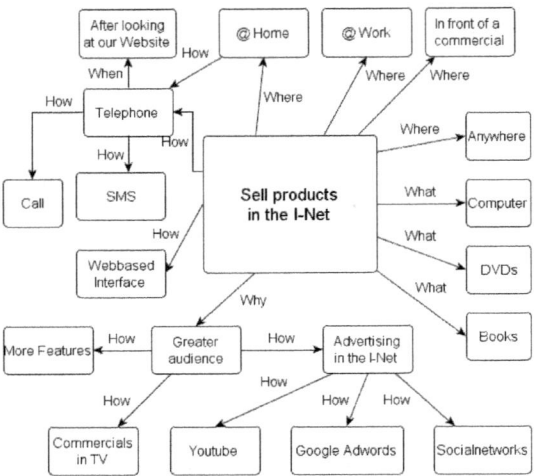

Fig. 1. Example topic map with trace of ideation, only using 5W1H

ideas and requirements [1]. The meta-model provides sophisticated means of relating ideas and describing ideation traces. However, for the purpose of this paper a simplified approach will be used. An example for a resulting idea map based on this simplified representation is shown in Figure 1. Here, boxes represent individual ideas (or requirements) while the arrows describe the relation that exists between the ideas. All relations are supposed to be based on creativity techniques. In the example above the 5W1H technique was used to create ideas for a new web shop. The 5W1H technique is based on the trigger questions Where, What, Why, When, Who and How, hence its name. These idea triggers reappear in the figure as associations.

In the work we report on here, we focused on the two creativity techniques 5W1H and SCAMPER and the associations they imply [12]. Certainly any other technique, which links several ideas with a *Statement* how they are derived, could also be used. For this our Creativity Technique Selector identifies 25 creativity techniques.

4   Heuristic Generation of Idea Triggers

In this section, we will describe the basic approach we use to support idea generation. This is only a summary to keep this description mostly self-contained, while a more detailed description is given in [4, 18].

Many creativity techniques rely in one way or the other on prompting people to perform mental operations with the expectation that this will help people to generate new, innovative ideas. However, they typically do this in an undirected fashion, e.g., a technique like SCAMPER expects that a person will take some aspect of any existing idea and will try to substitute it with something else ('S' stands for substitute). However, the technique does not provide any support on what idea to use, how to substitute, etc. Our approach is similar in the sense that it provides an idea trigger, however, it is substantially different in the sense that specific ideas to look at and links to establish between them are explicitly proposed. Thus, our approach is much more selective

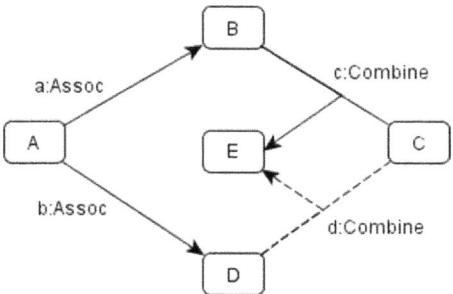

Fig. 2. Heuristic production rule r_1

and focused. This is achieved by relying on an explicit semantic representation of ideas and their associations. Based on this information our approach uses a form of graph rewriting to propose new triggers.

4.1 Overview of the Heuristics

In Section 3 we introduced our idea representation formalism. We can also interpret it as a labeled and directed graph. In this formalism we can describe our rules as graph transformations. Technically, these are single pushouts (SPO) [2]. Here, we will use a shorthand notation and represent the subgraph that needs to be recognized along with the inserted association in a single graph. This is possible due to the rather simple nature of our graph transformations. This is shown in Figure 2: everything except the dashed association corresponds to the pattern that must be recognized in the existing idea map, while the dashed association is inserted once the pattern is recognized.

We describe six rules ($r_1 - r_6$), which we developed. These were partially revised over earlier publications [4, 18]. Here, we present the latest status, which provided the basis for the experimental evaluation. The main difference from earlier publications is that we removed one of our transformation rules, because in the example that was used for the experiment we could not find an application. We also identified a new rule r_4, which was not described before. This rule was also evaluated during the experiment. So far, we created and tested the rules only for 5W1H and SCAMPER, but we assume the rules can also be adapted for other creativity techniques.

The first rule (r_1) is shown in Figure 2. It adds a new combine association to the current topic map. (Combine is one of the relations induced by SCAMPER.) The rule relies on analogical reasoning. The key idea is that B and D are in some respect similar as they are connected with A by the same association. Thus, in a form of analogical reasoning the idea D might play the same role as B in the combine relation.

The restrictions induced by this idea are formalized in terms of several constraints (Statement(x) provides the name of the association):

- Assoc is a set of triggers from arbitrary creative techniques
- Statement(c) = Statement(d) = Combine
- Statement(a) = Statement(b)

The next rule (r_2) is given in Figure 3. This rule is a form of transitivity. The idea is that while not necessarily all relations are transitive, the answers to questions like what, where, why or relations like substitute are still often transitive. Thus it might be worthwhile as a heuristic. We allow its application with any kind of association.

There are also some constraints that must be observed:

- Assoc is a set of triggers from arbitrary creative techniques
- Statement(a) = Statement(b) = Statement(c)

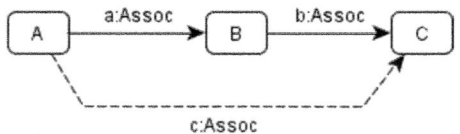

Fig. 3. Heuristic production rule r_2

The third rule (r_3) again relies on analogous reasoning. It shows actually the most basic form of analogy: A is connected with B and B is connected with C. As D is connected with A in the same way as B is, it is reasonable to assume that D is in some way like B and can thus be in the same relation with C. The rule is shown in Figure 4.

Again the constraints are chosen to express this reasoning:

- Assoc is a set of triggers from arbitrary creativity techniques
- Statement(a) = Statement(c)
- Statement(b) = Statement(d)

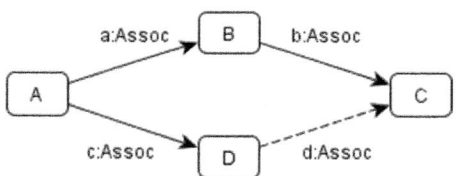

Fig. 4. Heuristic production rule r_3

Rule (r_4) is specific to the combine relation (so far). It relies on the idea that the result of a combination may often inherit important properties from its constituents. In our case these properties are expressed through associations: thus, if a certain relation exists between A and one of the constituents (e.g., B), it might be the case that the same relation is meaningful for the result as well. The rule is illustrated in Figure 5.

This leads to the following constraints:

- Assoc ⊂ 5W1H
- Statement(a) = Statement(c)
- Statement(b) = Combine

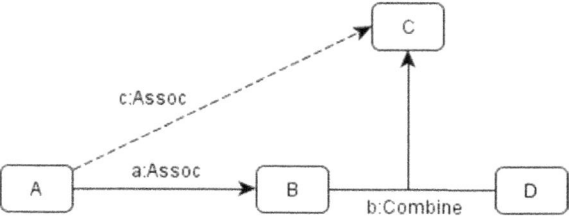

Fig. 5. Heuristic production rule r_4

The next transformation (r_5) is shown in Figure 6, which may look like transitivity, but is actually rather different. It shares, however, the basic idea that something is propagated. The rationale behind this rule is that statements exist that describe transformations of a given idea, but essentially the result remains of the same type as the original. In the techniques we looked at, these are statements like Substitute, Adapt and Modify from the technique SCAMPER. Those are combined with triggers, originating from other techniques.

This pattern is more restricted than the others. According to our analysis the rule is applicable with the following associations:

- Assoc_1 = {What, Where, Who, How} $\subset$ 5W1H
- Assoc_2 = {Substitute, Adapt, Modify} $\subset$ SCAMPER
- Statement(a) = Statement(c)

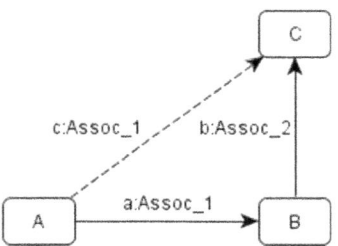

Fig. 6. Heuristic production rule r_5

Rule six (r_6) is again based on the idea that the constituents of a combine statement may have characteristics similar to the result. This is particularly true, if both constituents are in some sense similar. In this case it can be expected that the result will have the same characteristic. It can thus be regarded as a stronger form of rule r_4). This rule is shown in Figure 7.

The associated constraints are shown below:

- Assoc = {What, Where, Who, When} $\subset$ 5W1H , but could be extended with triggers from other creative techniques
- Statement(a) = Statement(b) = Statement(d)
- Statement(c) = Combine

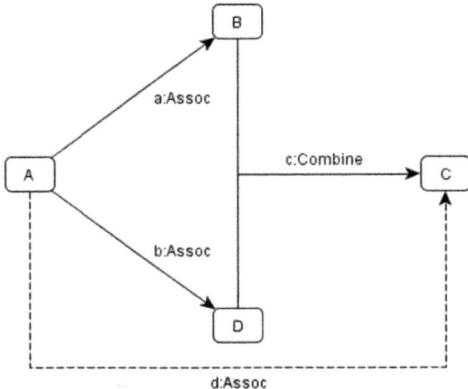

Fig. 7. Heuristic production rule r_6

The various heuristics can be subdivided into three categories:

- Analogy: some sort of reasoning is transferred from one relation to the other, though this reasoning need not be correct.
- Transitivity: this is like the standard mathematical relationship, however, correctness is not ensured.
- Propagation: some relation is propagated through another relation. Transitivity can be seen as special case of this.

4.2 Use of the Heuristics

The induced associations that are the results of the heuristics described above can be regarded as suggestions to the user. They are not ideas by themselves, but we assume that wondering about whether they are correct, special conditions under which they are right, etc. may lead to new ideas and insights.

With respect to creativity support, we can categorize the suggestions that are given from the heuristics in the following way.

- *Correct:* the suggested association is correct.
- *Helpful:* the suggested association is not necessarily correct, but it leads to a new interesting idea.
- *Innovative:* the suggested association is not necessarily correct, but it leads to a helpful idea, which the users classify as innovative.
- *Wrong:* the suggested association is not correct and does not help the user achieve creative outcomes.

Of course wrong / incorrect associations are of little interest. In our experiment we focus on the first three types, were we assume the categories to be increasingly relevant to creativity from correct to innovative.

5 Experiment

The main contribution of this paper is a experimental evaluation of the approach. The focus is to better understand whether our approach truly improves creativity and which heuristics contribute how much. We did thus set up an experiment to determine to what extend the various heuristics support a creative process. In particular, we decided to analyze whether the suggestions are regarded by the subjects as:

- correct associations,
- leading to helpful ideas,
- leading to innovative ideas.

In the remainder of this section, we describe this experiment. Section 4.1 outlines the overall setup of the experiment. Section 4.2 provides the detailed structure, while Section 4.3 describes the execution of the experiment. In Section 4.4 we analyze the results and in Section 4.5 we discuss the threats to validity of the experiment.

5.1 Experimental Setup

While the idSpace platform is available and includes an implementation of our approach, we decided that it provides just too open an environment for a thoroughly controlled experiment. We thus decided to use a questionnaire-based approach.

The independent variables in the experiment are the heuristics. The dependent variables are the support the heuristics provide for correct associations, helpful ideas and innovative ideas. However, this leads to a major problem: independent of what one presents to subjects who try to identify requirements, they may always come up with innovative requirements. We addressed this issue, by introducing a random heuristic as baseline. This baseline works by randomly selecting concepts and introducing a new (random) association among them. We call this new heuristic the baseline heuristic r_b. This is indistinguishable for the subjects from the tested heuristics, but it enables us to use the difference in effect of analyzed heuristic vs. baseline heuristic as a basis for our evaluation. As a result we did arrive at the following hypotheses to test in our experiment (for each r_i; $1 \leq i \leq 6$):

- H_{1ia}: the subjects identify more associations as correct using r_i than using r_b.
- H_{1ib}: the subjects identify the proposed associations more often as helpful using r_i than using r_b.
- H_{1ic}: the subjects identify the proposed associations more often as leading to innovative ideas using r_i than using r_b.

r_b denotes the baseline rule which randomly generates associations. H_{0ia} to H_{0ic} are identified correspondingly.

The application of the rules is not deterministic. Rather many different results can be triggered based on the existing description of the requirements. Thus we decided that each subject should get several examples for each rule. For each rule 8 different examples were generated. Further, in order to keep the overall time for the subjects limited, we grouped participants in two groups with exactly identical setup, but different samples for the heuristics. Thus grouping was not done for blocking or a similar setup, but rather it was merely done to reduce the number of tasks per subject to 4 examples for each of the 7 rules (6 rules plus random suggestions). As a consequence and contrary to typical experiment setups this implies that no comparison between the two groups were done. The experiment subjects were acquired through email lists and notices at blackboards at the university. As a result of the acquisition approach we mainly got students from the information systems study programs, but also students from other fields took part (e.g., from cultural sciences).

5.2 Experiment Structure and Material

As mentioned above, we decided to perform the major part of the experiment using questionnaires, without any tool support. The main part of the experiment consisted of one session and was planned for a maximum of two hours, in order to avoid that subjects get too tired of that they would abandon the experiment prematurely.

Our experimental material was built upon an E-Shop example. Its requirements were inspired to some degree by real functionality of amazon.com, but it had already been augmented in previous internal sessions. It was fully documented according to our approach and consisted of 63 different ideas connected with 67 associations.

The examples that were generated for the heuristics were depicted in the questionnaire as shown in Figure 8. The right side displays the suggestion and the left side shows where to find the relevant ideas in the idea map. During the experiment the subjects got an overview map covering the whole E-Shop, so they could put the proposed associations in context. Each set of eight examples was divided into two sets, consisting of four examples, and each set was allocated for one of the two groups. Thus, each group questionnaire had 28 examples.

Instead of creating only two questionnaires, one for each group, we generated for each participant an individual questionnaire, where the different examples are in a random order to avoid order and learning effects.

For each suggested association, the participants got four tasks to solve.

1. They had to answer the question, whether the suggestion is correct.
2. They should write down up to three ideas triggered by the suggestion.
3. They should evaluate how helpful the suggestion was in finding new ideas.
4. In case the suggestions trigger new ideas, the participants should score the innovative aspect of their ideas.

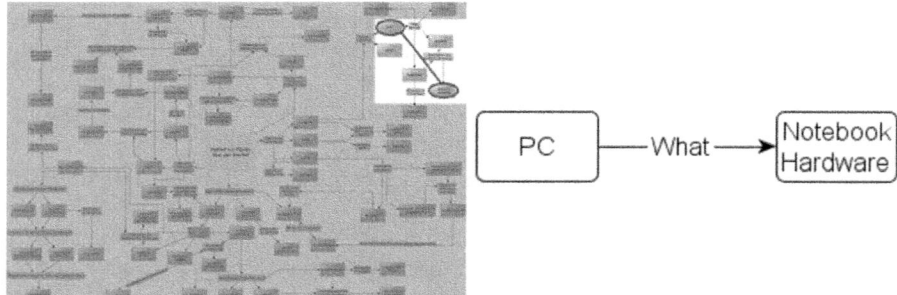

Fig. 8. One suggested association for rule r_6

To facilitate appropriate analysis afterwards, we used a four-level Likert scale with intermediate levels (thus three additional values) for the first and the third question. For the second question space was offered to answer free text. These answers were not included in the analysis. Rather this question should provide real test conditions and ensure that people really thought in terms of new ideas. For answering the last question, a semantic differential was used.

Besides this main questionnaire a pre-questionnaire was used, which aimed to identify major differences among participants regarding prior exposure to creativity techniques. It was prepared in the hope to identify any correlation between unusual results and subject characteristics. The participants should answer eight yes/no questions regarding their knowledge of and experience with:

- creativity techniques,
- brainstorming,
- 5W1H,
- SCAMPER.

The participants were also asked about their degree program and their semester.

5.3 Experiment Execution

Prior to the main experiment execution, a pre-evaluation was done with two group members who had not been involved with the overall approach and experiment setup up to this point. This led only to minor modifications of the experimental material, relating mainly to clarifications in the descriptive texts.

The main experiment execution was started with assigning the subjects randomly to the groups. However, due to some problems in group assignment it turned out that 11 people were assigned to group 1 and 9 people to group 2. Due to the specific setup of our experiment (results of both groups are simply combined), we do not assume this to be a problem for the final analysis.

In the next step a presentation was given that explained the overall procedure of the experiment, its purpose and how to deal with the questionnaires. Also the subjects were acquainted with the E-shop example. This needed about 20 minutes.

Finally, the questionnaires were distributed. They consisted of the pre-questionnaire described above and the main questionnaire containing the heuristic examples. It turned out that all participants could perform their tasks in time. Minor problems occurred as two participants did not answer a specific question. No subject dropped out during experiment execution. Speed varied significantly among participants, ranging from one to two hours.

5.4 Analysis

All data from the questionnaires was encoded into an Excel sheet. While we recorded from which groups the data came from, we combined the data sets at this point, so for the further analysis we did not differentiate among the individual examples for any heuristic any more. This was possible as both groups had done the same heuristics. The encoding was done for all answers in the following way: the Likert scale was encoded on a scale 1 to 7 (due to the intermediate values), the same for the semantic differential. For the ideas, we were not interested in the ideas themselves, but only whether someone had truly shown through ideas that the heuristics were helpful.

In a similar way, we encoded the data for the pre-questionnaire. As here we only dealt with yes/no questions except for the questions regarding to their degree program, the answers were mapped to a 0/1 scale. We analyzed this data in order to understand whether some subjects had particular knowledge and thus did perform consistently better. While there were variations in the previous exposure of people to creativity techniques, this variation was not very strong. No subject had significant knowledge or experience with creativity techniques.

We also checked the data for any outliers or other issues. For this purpose we performed some descriptive statistics to visualize the distribution of data points. We did not find any data that had to be classified as outliers. Some issues with the data were, however, found. For example people had given positive values to the category: the results were helpful, but they had not given any ideas. We are not sure, whether people had not fully understood the instructions or whether they simply wanted to save time. A substantial amount of questionnaires had these issues: 16 out of 20 participants answered at least one question incompletely. We thus decided to still include the data as it looked plausible. We also found that some subjects had noted down ideas, but had not performed the scoring for helpfulness and innovation support. In this case we pessimistically scored them using the most negative value (7).

As this may have reduced the difference among the various rules, we might have not recognized some rules that were helpful or innovative as such, even though the original data may have shown such a relation.

Before the final analysis we decided to take the fact into account that different people might be more creative than others. Thus there might be a bias towards higher or lower ratings. While we could not identify major variations, we still normalized all data by subtracting the average per person, per answer-category.

After preparing the data in this way, we had data for 7 batches of data for each of the hypotheses (one of them the baseline and the other six the data for the respective heuristics). Before performing a detailed statistical analysis, we compared the data with descriptive approaches. While some differences could be seen among heuristics, it was clear from this analysis already, that the resulting effect would be very small.

Table 1. ANOVA analysis of the heuristics vs. the random suggestions

	Correctness			Helpful			Innovative		
	F	p	rej.	F	p	rej.	F	p	rej.
r_1	14,516	$2 * 10^{-4}$	☑	2,476	0,118	☐	1,930	0,167	☐
r_2	12,802	$4,6 * 10^{-4}$	☑	1,597	0,208	☐	0,212	0,646	☐
r_3	21,532	$7,3 * 10^{-6}$	☑	7,255	$7,8 * 10^{-3}$	☑	0,824	0,365	☐
r_4	26,323	$8,4 * 10^{-7}$	☑	2,549	0,113	☐	1,972	0,162	☐
r_5	119,211	$4,9 * 10^{-21}$	☑	7,133	$8,3 * 10^{-3}$	☑	0,038	0,845	☐
r_6	40,593	$2 * 10^{-9}$	☑	10,598	$1,4 * 10^{-3}$	☑	9,352	$2,6 * 10^{-3}$	☑

We now performed a single-factor ANOVA analysis using the F-Test for all heuristic-hypothesis pairs. Table 1 shows the results of the ANOVA analysis. It was assumed as null hypothesis that the respective rule has the same distribution as the random heuristic. The column F shows the value of the F-Function the F-Test. p gives the probability of error, while *rej.* denotes whether we rejected the null hypothesis.

Thus, the results are as follows: H_{0ia} had to be refuted for all heuristics i at the α-Level 0.05. We could thus accept H_{1ia} for all heuristics. Thus, we concluded that *all* our heuristics were significantly more often *correct* than the baseline heuristic. This is by itself not too surprising as all heuristics were built to be *almost correct*.

H_{0ib} could be refuted only for three of the heuristics at the α-Level 0.05. These were r_3, r_5 and r_6. Correspondingly we could accept H_{1ib} for them. So only for heuristics r_3, r_5 and r_6, we can accept that they were significantly more *helpful* than the random baseline heuristic.

We analyzed all 6 heuristics with respect to their innovation support. Only for one of these heuristics we could refute H_{0ic} at the α-Level 0.05: heuristic r_6. This means we found one heuristic, which leads to *significantly more innovative results* than random stimuli. While we could observe the result empirically, again r_6 does not appear to be fundamentally different from the other heuristics. Neither from the perspective of the overall pattern, nor based on the characteristics shown in Table 2.

In the analysis of the results it should be noted that our statements regarding the various heuristics refer always to a comparison with random suggestions. As these random suggestions already offer idea triggers (cf. creativity technique "random stimuli"), the statement "correct" means six of the heuristics are significantly better than random stimuli. Similarly the results on helpful and innovative imply significant advances over this baseline.

Table 2. Characterization of the Heuristics

Rule	Type	arity of induced assoc.	# techniques involved	# nodes	# assocs
r_1	Analogy	ternary	1-2	5	3 (+1)
r_2	Transitivity	binary	1	3	2 (+1)
r_3	Analogy	binary	1-2	4	3 (+1)
r_4	Propagation	binary	2	4	2 (+1)
r_5	Propagation	binary	2	3	2 (+1)
r_6	Propagation	binary	1-2	4	3 (+1)

We summarized some characteristics of these rules in the hope of learning why the heuristics differed in terms of results. The characterization of the rules was chosen based on the hypothesis that more complex rules may lead to more innovative results. In order to describe complexity we identified several candidate characteristics. Table 2 shows these characteristics. The column *arity of induced association* describes whether the rule induces a binary or ternary association. The involved number of different creativity techniques is given in the column *#techniques involved*. Thus, in some rules exactly 1 or 2 different techniques involved, while the constraints of r_1, r_3 and r_6 allow both the application with 1 or with 2 different techniques. The columns *#nodes* and *#assocs* describe the number of nodes and associations, respectively. In the last column one always finds *(+1)* as one association is added by each rule.

However, as one can see, the various rules are rather similar according to all these criteria. In particular, these characteristics cannot explain why r_3, r_5, r_6 led to more positive results than the others.

5.5 Threats to Validity

While the results of our study are rather positive, it is important to analyze the threats to validity. We will follow here mainly the outline given in [20]:

Internal Validity: As this is a (student) experiment, we focused on achieving high internal validity. The first observation is of course the number of replications. While two groups were formed, this was done in a way so that the data from the two groups could be combined (group formation was only done to reduce work-time per subject). As a result we have per heuristic and hypothesis 80 different data points. While this is not extremely high and comes only from 20 different subjects, it is already a significant data set. Our approach to address learning and ordering effects was two-fold: for each question, subjects had only four examples. This should achieve a reduction of learning and fatigue effects. Further, the examples for a specific heuristic were distributed randomly over the questionnaire. This randomization was even performed differently for each individual subject. Thus, while probably learning and ordering effects exist with this kind of task, we think that extensive measures were taken to address them.

During the execution of the experiment no issues were raised. Thus, we assume the questionnaires mostly worked fine. However, when evaluating the results, we realized that in several cases subjects marked the heuristics as helpful or innovative, but did not provide examples for induced ideas. We are not sure in these cases what the reason was for this, but assume it was mostly due to the desire by the subjects to save time, but it may also point to a different problem: subjects may have characterized results as helpful or innovative, although they did not lead to them to new ideas.

We had no drop-outs during the experiment. The subjects were somewhat heterogeneous (e.g., information science vs. cultural science). However, the vast majority had an information science background. We found no significant differences among the subjects in terms of results.

External Validity: It is clear that this approach cannot be used as a independent creativity technique. It is expected to be part of a larger cycle of innovation support, which is supported by the idSpace platform. The presentation in the idSpace platform is slightly different, leading to a threat to validity. However, the portlet that represents the approach in the final platform basically presents the same results (in a very similar format) as we had in the experiment. Also, interacting with paper and pencil versus with a computer program may have a significant impact on results. Thus, the external validity may depend strongly on the specific realization of the approach.

Most subjects who participated in the experiment were bachelor students, thus the results can probably not be compared directly with professionals. The experimental situation is significantly different from a normal work situation. This may have a further effect. Further the example that we choose (E-Shop) was chosen to improve external validity as we expect that all subjects have experience with such an example.

Construct Validity: in order to ensure high construct validity, we differentiated between correct, helpful and innovative associations. This allows a fine-grained analysis of the contribution that the associations make for creativity. We also analyzed the results relative to random associations. As this is also a creativity technique this ensures that really improvement of creativity is measured.

The subjects had to make the proposals and to evaluate them regarding the innovative contribution. We choose this approach as it is typical for practice in an ideation session. Thus, we do not regard it as a major threat to construct validity. We even regard this as more appropriate for rating creativity than evaluation by an external person, as this may introduce issues due to differences in standards between creative person and evaluator. Thus, this may lead to situations where many results are mistaken with good results.

The experimental setup required that an ideation map with already gathered ideas be given to the subjects at the beginning of the experiment. Of course this influences the results. However, this threat exists in all experiment setups that use prepared material. The map was also constructed before a decision regarding the experiment was made. Thus, we do not assume that it introduced a significant bias.

Conclusion Validity: The α-Level of 0.05 is a very tough level to make, especially in such cases that are very difficult to quantify and analyze as the situation we have here. Nevertheless for three, respective one, heuristic we could make the conclusion that they are significantly more helpful (resp. innovative) for new ideas than the baseline. As all other factors were well controlled, we can assume that this conclusion has very significant validity.

6 Conclusion

In this paper, we described the evaluation of an approach for deriving creative triggers from a knowledge map of requirements. We provided a brief description of the construction of the knowledge map; this was already described in detail in [18]. Our approach has also been implemented in the idSpace platform [4].

In this paper, we described some modifications of the heuristics of our approach over previous publications. However, our main contribution, is a description of a student experiment that analyzes the effectiveness of our creativity technique in a strongly controlled setting. At this point most efforts on the validation of approaches to creative requirements engineering relied on case studies. Our analysis contributes to the still small body of knowledge of strongly validated studies.

In particular, we could show the contribution of our approach even under strict restrictions (e.g., α-Level of 0.05) and even though we used as baseline another creativity technique. Thus, we did show effectively that not only our approach does work, it is also more effective than an approach relying on random triggers.

The work that led to this effort is particularly geared towards innovation platforms for distributed (in time and space) working. Thus, we assume that a significant part of communication will happen through an online platform that serves requirements interchange. Our results are probably most appropriate in such a setting. Application of our approach in a group meeting is probably not straightforward.

We analyzed in our experiment not only a single technique, but simultaneously evaluated six different heuristics that can be used with our technique. The success did differ among those heuristics: some made it, others did not. This is basically what we expected and what led us to analyze several heuristics simultaneously. However, it directly leads to the next challenge: what characterizes heuristics that lead with a particularly high probability to innovative requirements? At this point there are no clear criteria based on our analysis that can be used to predict success.

In total, our study showed that while innovation can certainly not be enforced, it can obviously be assisted by our approach and the goal is to get better and more predictable at this.

Acknowledgements

We would like to thank Per Pascal Grube, who was involved in the preparation and execution of the experiment.

This work was carried out as part of the idSpace project on *Tooling and training for collaborative product innovation* http://idspace-project.org. This project was partially supported by the European Community under the Information and Communication Technologies (ICT) theme of the 7th Framework Program for R&D (FP7-IST-2007-1-41, project number 216799). This document does not represent the opinion of the European Community, and the European Community is not responsible for any use that might be made of its content.

References

[1] Aalborg University, University of Hildesheim, and University Piraeus Research Center. idspace deliverable: D2.3 – semantic meta-model integration and transformations v2 (2009), http://dspace.ou.nl/handle/1820/2157 (Online December 2010)

[2] Corradini, A., Montanari, U., Rossi, F., Ehrig, H., Heckel, R., Loewe, M.: Algebraic Approaches to Graph Transformation, Part I: Basic Concepts and Double Pushout Approach. Technical report, Università di Pisa (1996)

[3] Creativity technique selector website, http://repository.sse.uni-hildesheim.de/CreativityTechniqueSelector (Online December 2010)

[4] El-Sharkawy, S., Grube, P., Schmid, K.: Using semantically linked content to support creativity in product innovation. In: Proceedings of The First International Conference on Creative Content Technologies (CONTENT 2009), pp. 638–642 (2009)

[5] Grube, P., Schmid, K.: idspace deliverable: D2.1 state of the art in tools for creativity (2008), http://dspace.ou.nl/handle/1820/1658 (Online; December 2010)

[6] idspace project website, http://www.idspace-project.org (Online December 2010)

[7] Jones, S., Lynch, P., Maiden, N., Lindstaedt, S.: Use and influence of creative ideas and requirements for a work-integrated learning systems. In: 16th International Requirements Engineering Conference, RE 2008, pp. 289–294 (September 2008)

[8] Kerkow, D., Adam, S., Riegel, N., Uenalan, O.: A creative method for business information systems. In: 1st Workshop on Creativity in Requirements Engineering (CREARE) at (REFSQ 2010), pp. 8–21. ICB-Research Report 40 (2010)

[9] Maiden, N., Manning, S., Robertson, S., Greenwood, J.: Integrating creativity workshops into structured requirements processes. In: Fifth Conference on Designing Interactive Systems (DIS 2004), pp. 113–122 (2004)

[10] Mich, L., Anesi, C., Berry, D.: Requirements engineering and creativity: An innovative approach based on a model of the pragmatics of communication. In: Tenth International Workshop on Requirements Engineering: Foundation for Software Quality (REFSQ), pp. 129–143. Technical Report, Essen (2004)

[11] Mich, L., Berry, D., Alzetta, A.: Individual and end-user application of the EPMcreate creativity enhancement technique to website requirements elicitation. In: 1st Workshop on Creativity in Requirements Engineering (CREARE) at (REFSQ 2010), pp. 22–31. ICB-Research Report 40 (2010)

[12] Mycoted website, http://www.mycoted.com (Online December 2010)

[13] Nguyen, L., Shanks, G.: A framework for understanding creativity in requirements engineering. Information and Software Technology 51, 655–662 (2009)

[14] Potts, C.: Invented requirements and imagined customers: requirements engineering for off-the-shelf software. In: Second IEEE International Symposium on Requirements Engineering, pp. 128–130 (1995)

[15] Robertson, J.: Eureka! why analysts should invent requirements. IEEE Software 19(4), 20–22 (2002)

[16] Sakhnini, V., Berry, D.M., Mich, L.: Validation of the effectiveness of an optimized EPMcreate as an aid for creative requirements elicitation. In: Wieringa, R., Persson, A. (eds.) REFSQ 2010. LNCS, vol. 6182, pp. 91–105. Springer, Heidelberg (2010)

[17] Schmid, K.: A study on creativity in requirements engineering. Softwaretechnik-Trends 26(1), 20–21 (2006)

[18] Schmid, K.: Reasoning on requirements knowledge to support creativity. In: 2nd Intern. Workshop on Managing Requirements Knowledge (MaRK 2009), pp. 7–11 (2009)

[19] Topicmaps.org website, http://www.topicmaps.org (Online December 2010)

[20] Wohlin, C., Runeson, P., Höst, M., Ohlsson, M.C., Regnell, B., Wesslén, A.: Experimentation in Software Engineering – An Introduction. Kluwer, Dordrecht (2000)

Satisfying User Needs at the Right Time and in the Right Place: A Research Preview

Nauman A. Qureshi[1], Norbert Seyff[2], and Anna Perini[1]

[1] Fondazione Bruno Kessler - IRST, Software Engineering Research Group
Via Sommarive, 18, 38050 Trento, Italy
{qureshi,perini}@fbk.eu
[2] University of Zurich
Binzmuehlestrasse 14, 8050, Zurich, Switzerland
seyff@ifi.uzh.ch

Abstract. **[Context and motivation]** Most requirements engineering (RE) approaches involve analysts in gathering end-user needs. However, we promote the idea that future service-based applications should support end-users in expressing their needs themselves, while the system should be able to respond to these requests by combining existing services in a seamless way. **[Question/problem]** Research tackling this idea is limited. In this research preview paper we sketch a plan to investigate the following research questions: How can end-users be facilitated by a system to express new needs (e.g. goals, preferences)? How can the continuous analysis of end-user needs result in an appropriate solution? **[Principal ideas/results]** In our recent research, we have started to explore the idea of involving end-users in RE. Furthermore, we have proposed an architecture that allows performing RE at run-time. The purpose of the planned research is to combine and extend our recent work and to come up with a tool-based solution, which involves end-users in realizing self-adaptive services. Our research objectives include to continuously capture, communicate and analyze end-user needs and feedback in order to provide a tailored solution. **[Contribution]** In this paper we give a preview on the planned work. After reporting on our recent work we present our research idea and the research objectives in more detail.

Keywords: Requirements Engineering, End-User Involvement, Self Adaptive Systems.

1 Introduction

End-users are among the key stakeholders who are invited to participate in requirements elicitation activities, which are typically mediated by analysts [1]. The aim of such approaches is to discover requirements that can satisfy the needs of the majority of users, so individual user needs are not considered per-se, but rather generalized into categories [2]. However, novel software paradigms such as services-oriented computing suggest that identifying individual end-user needs is essential to provide a customized and tailored software system [3].

The evolution of web services into the Internet of Services allows integrating existing services into Service-Based Applications (SBA) that can dynamically provide the

D. Berry and X. Franch (Eds.): REFSQ 2011, LNCS 6606, pp. 94–99, 2011.

required functionality. In this context[1], self-adaptivity is pointed out as a key feature. Self-adaptive systems can manage dynamic events occurring at run-time, such as unavailability of services, hardware and platform changes as well as the change of a user's preferences and needs. Engineering such applications significantly challenges the role of Requirements Engineering (RE). Usually, RE activities are carried out at the outset of the whole development process, but in the context of self-adaptive SBA, they are also needed at run-time thus enabling a seamless SBA evolution. This also includes that SBA should be able to capture, analyze and satisfy end-user needs while they emerge.

The aim of our research is to support "On-line" requirements acquisition by involving the end-user and the system itself. To fulfill this aim, requirements capturing and analysis capabilities need to be provided, thus enabling end-users to communicate (new) needs, which are then turned into new (or changed) requirements. These requirements have to be satisfied through a combination of available services or left as new requirements to be addressed off-line within a software evolution process. In this paper, we illustrate our planned research aiming at investigating the above described idea. We will combine and extend our recent work to come up with a tool-based approach that involves end-users in the realization of their needs using self-adaptive SBA.

The paper is organized as follows. In Section II we revisit our recent work on end-user driven requirements elicitation (iRequire approach [4]) and Continuous Adaptive RE (CARE framework [5,6]). In Section III we discuss our planned research towards "On-line" RE. We illustrate our proposal with a motivating application example. Section IV gives a conclusion and provides an overview on first steps.

2   Background and Recent Research

The rise of mobile technology and the increasing use of mobile applications by end-users challenge the role of RE in system development, but also provide new opportunities for our field. Our recent work on iRequire [7] and CARE [5,6] complement each other and provide significant potential for collaborative research and highlight new research challenges for the field of RE. Before highlighting the potential of the planned collaborative research the next paragraphs give an overview on our recent work.

2.1   End-User Driven Requirements Elicitation with iRequire

The goal of the conducted research on iRequire is to develop and evaluate a tool-supported requirements discovery method for end-users [7]. The iRequire approach enables end-users to capture individual needs in situ without the help of an analyst. In addition to requirements discovery, the method supports the on-site identification of contextual information. Installed on the end-user's smartphone the iRequire tool supports blogging needs anytime and anywhere. Following four simple steps, the end-user is able to document upcoming needs in a structured way. In particular, the iRequire tool provides the following key features: *Taking a picture of the environment:* iRequire uses a mobile device built-in camera to allow end-users to capture pictures of their environment or objects which are related to the documented needs. An example could be an

---

[1] http://www.s-cube-network.eu/; www.secse-project.eu/

end-user who takes a picture of a bus stop countdown display and comes up with the need i.e. "I'd like to have the same information on my mobile". *Documenting end-user needs:* The key functionality provided by iRequire is to enable end-users to blog their needs and ideas in situ. This can be done using text-based requirements descriptions. Additionally end-users can audio record their needs. *Describing the relevant task and providing a rationale:* This feature supports end-users in describing which tasks or activities will be supported by a documented need. Furthermore, end-users are able to report why a need is important to them. *Summary on documented need:* This feature allows the end-user to review the captured information. iRequire displays a summary on the documented need before storing the captured information in its database. The current iRequire prototype also provides initial capabilities for automated context sensing. When blogging a need iRequire automatically detects the end-user's position and stores this information together with the requirement description in a local database.

2.2   Continuous Adaptive RE (CARE) Framework

CARE [5] suggests that user needs (along with contextual information) can be analyzed by software systems. Instead of a human analyst, it is the system, which compares upcoming needs with existing requirements specifications and which transcribes them into adequate service requests. These service requests do not only reflect end-user needs and can be used to discover and select appropriate services-based solutions, they also hold relevant information for future system monitoring. Please note that we take into account that user's goals, preferences and context information will be monitored by the system. In the case of a change, the system evaluates the given conditions/events and adapts itself to the most feasible solution (service). The overall aim of CARE is to continuously capture and operationalize user's changing requirements. The main activities of the CARE framework, along with the Companion application that instantiates it [5,6] are: *Service Request Acquisition:* This activity aims at acquiring user needs in a structured way (represented in XML) to capture the users changing requirements as service requests. Service requests (RRA) can either be gathered from the user or the system itself identifies requests based on monitoring. *Service Lookup:* This activity foresees an automated service lookup based on operationalized user requests. A service monitoring agent provides the information about the availability of a new or competing relevant service to satisfy the user needs. *Service Selection:* It ensures the invocation and composition of the available services. This activity is supported by the feedback control agents to evaluate the service request and the monitored information about the services to be invoked. *Update Requirements Specification:* This activity is managed by a reasoner agent, which refines the requirements specification based on service requests and service descriptions. The reasoner agent performs the update operation using a shared ontology and the existing requirements specification.

3   On-line Requirements Engineering

The main goal of the planned research is to develop a tool-supported On-line RE method which enables end-users to communicate their needs in situ, expecting to receive appropriate solutions at the right time and in the right place. The planned work will be based on, but go beyond, the scope of our recent work on iRequire and CARE. It will be structured along the following research objectives (RO) and intended activities to realize them:

RO 1: *Support end-users in communicating needs & feedback.* This research objective focuses on exploring novel tool-supported approaches which enable end-users to communicate ideas, wishes, needs and feedback about the satisfaction on the given solution.

Our recent research on iRequire provides first insights on how to support end-users in documenting needs in situ. We plan to integrate iRequire and CARE, for example by using the iRequire tool as a part of CARE's service request acquisition activity. iRequire further could act as front end which would allow communicating system changes to end-users based on CARE's monitoring capabilities. We also plan to extend iRequire by improving its automated context sensing features. However, we envisage that the planned research also calls for novel approaches which will support end-users in giving feedback on generated solutions. Such feedback can provide an objective measure to evaluate the usefulness of the analysis and the solution provided [8].

RO 2: *Capture relevant user-centric information.* This objective highlights the importance of user-centric information including user's goals, preferences, resources, assets, personal information as well as the current location as an input to perform On-line RE activities.

We plan to capture user-centric information in a so called *"user's personal space"*. This on-line knowledge repository can be accessed by a variety of devices (e.g. smartphones) anytime and anywhere. Our aim is to integrate this repository with the CARE and iRequire data models. We plan to exploit appropriate knowledge representation techniques to represent the "user's personal space" and reason on partial knowledge, uncertainty and temporal relations. We foresee that the information stored in the "user's personal space" will be helpful to refine new or changed user requests and will provide support in ranking possible alternative solutions.

RO 3: *Continuous on-line analysis of new needs and solution provisioning.* This objective focuses on the continuous analysis of new and emerging needs by providing a solution to them.

Our recent research on CARE is directed to provide a continuous RE approach. It acquires and refines user's needs at run-time and provides a solution (services) to them. We plan to enhance this by investigating reasoning mechanisms to reason for run-time refinement of requirements. This is necessary for taking the adaptation decision for solutions provisioning. We aim to leverage existing AI planning approaches to provide automated reasoning over the "user's personal space" e.g. preference-based reasoning. This improves the quality of the solution and increases end-user goal satisfaction [9].

3.1   Application Example

In this section we exploit a possible application example. We envisage *iCompanion* as a self-adaptive service based application, which enables an end-user to express and communicate needs in situ. Further it instantly performs a continuous on-line analysis of user needs and provides service-based solutions. It is aware of the user's personal space and by monitoring the user's context (location, device and environment) it supports

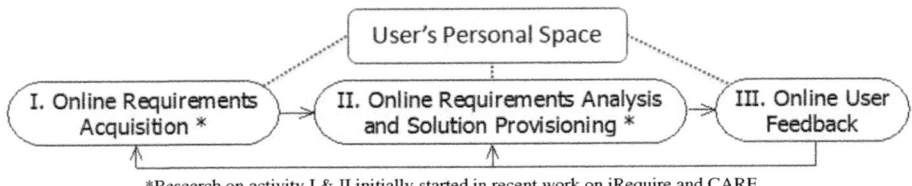

*Research on activity I & II initially started in recent work on iRequire and CARE.

Fig. 1. On-line RE Activities Realized by *iCompanion*

the user accomplishing their goals. Fig.1 presents activities performed by the intended iCompanion. These activities (labeled as I-III)[2] are needed to support On-line RE. Further Fig.1 shows the user's personal space, a repository, which is fed and exploited by iCompanion while performing these activities. We now elaborate the example to highlight the benefits of our planned research.

We envision that iCompanion is available on an end-user's smartphone. For instance while the user is in a shopping mall and about to buy several products. As the supermarket has re-arranged the location of products the user needs help in finding what she is looking for. She communicates this need using iCompanion (activity I shown in Fig.1). After analyzing her need, iCompanion identifies an appropriate solution (activity II in Fig.1) by automatically detecting the user's current location (via monitoring). iCompanion then provides an interactive map of the supermarket. Using this map the user is able to follow the optimal route to get the requested products. However, the supermarket does not provide all the requested products any more (e.g. low fat products). The user communicates her request to "*find low fat products*" with a rationale to "*eat healthier*". This rationale becomes a new goal, which is stored in the user's personal space (activity I & II shown in Fig.1). While exploiting her personal space as input (e.g. information about her goals) the iCompanion performs an on-line analysis (activity II shown in Fig.1) and identifies a service which fulfills the user's needs. The detected service is not only able to search for products in near supermarkets, it also allows to look for bargains and further it is able to detect the distance to the supermarket where the product is available. Using this recommended service the user is shown a direct path to the supermarket where she can buy the requested product. In due course iCompanion requests feedback (activity III shown in Fig.1) on the provided solution. Subsequently, this feedback is stored as part of the user's personal space and could be used to improve the quality of the solutions provided by iCompanion.

4   Discussion and Conclusion

We are aware of the fact that the proposed research still is challenged by several issues. Particularly we would like to highlight that the automated composition of services based on end-user needs strongly depends on the quality of transcribing end-user needs into service requests and the availability of adequate services. As discussed in [10] we consider four different types of adaptation. If the automated propagation of a solution is not possible we still consider involving human analysts. However, this is not the focus of

---

[2] Activities can be executed sequentially or in an interleaved manner.

the planned research. We do expect several benefits from combining our recent work on iRequire and CARE. As highlighted in Section 3, iRequire already instantiates CARE's service request acquisition activity. The continuous analysis of requirements, which is supported by the CARE framework provides benefits for iRequire. Monitoring of the user's personal space allows the analysis of new needs expressed by the user or by the system. Subsequently to reason for adapting to the most feasible solution on the fly.

To provide continuous analysis and solution provisioning based on available services efficient reasoning is required. For this, we need to monitor the available user-centric information stored in the user's personal space. Another important facet worth to consider in our research is the role of domain assumptions. Such assumptions might change over time and could provoke the system to adapt. Such adaptations might require re-planning and are not fully covered by our planned research. Nevertheless, the quality of the generated solution is critical, as it has to satisfy a users needs. Apart from satisfying functional needs we consider that quality attributes (e.g. privacy, performance) significantly influence the users satisfaction. For this, end-user involvement in providing feedback on the quality of the solution is central to our proposed approach. We consider our planned work on "On-line" RE to be the first step towards a new RE paradigm which strengthens the role of end-users in system development and allows the tailoring of software to individual end-user needs.

References

1. Grünbacher, P., Seyff, N.: Requirements negotiation. In: Aurum, A., Wohlin, C. (eds.) Engineering and Managing Software Requirements, pp. 143–162. Springer, Heidelberg (2005)
2. Viller, S., Sommerville, I.: Social analysis in the requirements engineering process: from ethnography to method. In: IEEE Int. Symposium on Requirements Eng., pp. 6–13 (1999)
3. Sutcliffe, A., Fickas, S., Sohlberg, M.: Personal and contextual requirements engineering. In: 13th IEEE Int. Requirements Eng. Conf., pp. 19–28 (2005)
4. Seyff, N., Graf, F., Maiden, N.: End-user requirements blogging with irequire. In: 32nd ACM/IEEE Int. Conf. on Software Engineering, pp. 285–288 (2010)
5. Qureshi, N.A., Perini, A.: Requirements engineering for adaptive service based applications. In: 18th IEEE Int. Requirements Eng. Conf., pp. 108–111 (2010)
6. Qureshi, N.A., Perini, A.: Continuous adaptive requirements engineering: An architecture for self-adaptive service-based applications. In: First Int. Workshop on Requirements@Run.Time (RE@RunTime), pp. 17–24 (2010)
7. Seyff, N., Graf, F., Maiden, N.: Using mobile re tools to give end-users their own voice. In: 18th IEEE Int. Requirements Eng. Conf., pp. 37–46 (2010)
8. Schneider, K., Meyer, S., Peters, M., Schliephacke, F., Mörschbach, J., Aguirre, L.: Feedback in context: Supporting the evolution of IT-ecosystems. In: Ali Babar, M., Vierimaa, M., Oivo, M. (eds.) PROFES 2010. LNCS, vol. 6156, pp. 191–205. Springer, Heidelberg (2010)
9. Robinson, W.N.: Seeking quality through user-goal monitoring. IEEE Software 26, 58–65 (2009)
10. Qureshi, N., Perini, A., Ernst, N., Mylopoulos, J.: Towards a continuous requirements engineering framework for self-adaptive systems. In: First Int. Workshop on Requirements@Run.Time (RE@RunTime), pp. 9–16 (2010)

Flexible Sketch-Based Requirements Modeling

Dustin Wüest and Martin Glinz

Department of Informatics, University of Zurich, Switzerland
{wueest,glinz}@ifi.uzh.ch

Abstract. **[Context and motivation]** Requirements engineers and stakeholders like to create informal, sketchy models in order to communicate ideas and to make them persistent. They prefer pen and paper over current software modeling tools, because the former allow for any kind of sketches and do not break the creative flow. **[Question/problem]** To facilitate requirements management, engineers then need to manually transform the sketches into more formal models of requirements. This is a tedious, time-consuming task. Furthermore, there is a risk that the original intentions of the sketched models and informal annotations get lost in the transition. **[Principal ideas/results]** We present the idea for a seamless, tool-supported transition from informal, sketchy drafts to more formal models such as UML diagrams. Our approach uses an existing sketch recognizer together with a dynamic library of modeling symbols. This library can be augmented and modified by the user anytime during the sketching/modeling process. Thus, an engineer can start sketching without any restrictions, and can add both syntax and semantics later. Or the engineer can define a domain-specific modeling language with any degree of formality and adapt it on the fly. **[Contribution]** In this paper we describe how our approach combines the advantages of modeling with the freedom and ease of sketching in a way other modeling tools cannot provide.

Keywords: Requirements sketching, adaptable formalization, requirements modeling.

1 Introduction

When modeling requirements during requirements elicitation, stakeholders and requirements engineers would benefit from being able to freely draw sketches first and convert these into models later. This is due to the fact that sketching fosters creativity [7,3] and can also be applied by stakeholders who do not master a modeling language with a formal syntax. However, the power and ease of sketching comes at the expense of a *media break*, i.e., of later having to re-create the sketched models from scratch in a modeling tool in order to be able to manage requirements properly. This re-creation process is time consuming, error-prone, and can lead to a loss of information [5].

Sketch recognition tools have been created to relieve the task of converting sketches into models (e.g. [4,10]). However, such tools rely on predefined notations, so that the user needs to know the underlying modeling language and is restricted to its vocabulary. Hence, in terms of expressivity and creativity, sketch recognition tools do not help. Moreover, they introduce the problem of sketch recognition errors.

D. Berry and X. Franch (Eds.): REFSQ 2011, LNCS 6606, pp. 100–105, 2011.

In this paper, we give a preview of a new approach that (i) allows users to sketch any informal models, (ii) provides means for assigning syntax and semantics to sketched elements on the fly, and (iii) supports the transformation of sketches into classic semi-formal models (e.g., a class diagram or a statechart) by a semi-automated method, thus avoiding media breaks. The goal of our approach is to unite the flexibility of unconstrained sketching with the power of formal modeling.

The rest of the paper is structured as follows. In the next Section we give an overview of our planned research. Section 3 discusses related work. In Section 4 we conclude the paper.

2   Flexible Sketch-Based Requirements Modeling

2.1   Main Goal

The goal of the planned research is to provide a sketch-based modeling approach. We envision that our approach allows requirements engineers and stakeholders to sketch any informal models. Users should not be restricted in what they may draw, nor should they need to decide for a specific notation beforehand. Further, our approach should support the semi-automated transition of sketches into classic models. Our key research activities include: (i) identify the needs of requirements engineers with respect to sketch-based modeling, (ii) provide method and tool support, and (iii) evaluate the approach and demonstrate its practical benefits.

We plan to realize tool support by incorporating an existing sketch recognition framework that compares drawn shapes with the symbols included in a library. In contrast to other approaches, our symbol library does not hold a predefined modeling language, but is dynamic: users can augment and modify it at any time during the modeling process (see Fig. 1). Syntax and semantics can be added to the sketches on demand, and modeling may be performed on various levels of formality.

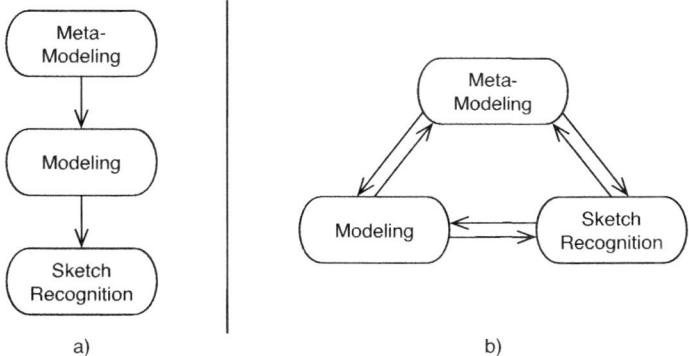

Fig. 1. (a) Existing sketch recognition approaches restrict users to do tasks in a given order. (b) Our envisaged approach allows to change flexibly between tasks.

2.2   Scenarios for Flexible Sketch-Based Requirements Modeling

We illustrate the usefulness of our approach with two typical elicitation scenarios. Both describe a meeting of a requirements engineer with stakeholders in an early phase of elicitation.

Scenario 1. A requirements engineer and two stakeholders stand in front of an electronic whiteboard. The interface of our envisaged tool is projected onto the whiteboard. The stakeholders start to sketch requirements. They do not use a specific notation since they are not familiar with modeling languages. Towards the end of the meeting, there are annotated rectangles, circles, and arrows on the board. In a discussion with the stakeholders, the requirements engineer clarifies the meanings of the symbols. After the meeting, the engineer selects one of the drawn symbols and assigns a type to it. The tool adds the symbol to the symbol library. Similar symbols are then identified automatically. Next, the engineer selects one of the arrows and defines it as a Connector that determines the order of two connected symbols. The engineer also defines the type of the connection as being a temporal relationship. The other arrows are recognized automatically. The engineer has now a minimalistic modeling language and a formalized version of the sketched model in that language. The engineer further defines new symbols that represent the drawn symbols in a formalized version of the sketch, and can now switch between the sketch version and the formal version.

Scenario 2. Some days before the meeting, the stakeholder sends a documentation of a domain-specific language (DSL) including two notations to the requirements engineer, who is also knowledgeable in metamodeling. The stakeholder intends to use the same language in the meeting. With the help of the documentation, the engineer creates the DSL description within our software tool. This work results in two symbol libraries, one for each notation. When the engineer and the stakeholder meet, most of the symbols drawn by the stakeholder are immediately recognized by the software tool. Some symbols are not identified because they are distorted. The engineer selects them and assigns the correct type manually. The stakeholder also introduces a new symbol not included in the DSL description. The engineer adds the symbol to the description by assigning a type to it. In total, the stakeholder draws two diagrams using the notations that are part of the DSL. Both diagrams include the same rectangular symbol, but it has a different meaning in each of the diagrams. To enable correct symbol recognition, the engineer tags the elements of the first diagram (e.g. by encircling them) and assigns the proper symbol library to the tagged elements. Then the engineer does the same for the second diagram.

2.3   The Elements of Our Approach

In the following paragraph we discuss the required features and components of a software tool that supports the activities described in the scenarios.

Modeling Interface. A tool following our approach has to support both informal and formal requirements modeling activities. On one hand, it must allow unconstrained sketching on an empty canvas. On the other hand, the tool must provide a way to edit (e.g. scale, move, copy) objects and to formalize the sketches. Both modes must be integrated in a unified, unobtrusive, simple interface.

Symbol Libraries and Multiple Contexts. A symbol library includes symbols that can be recognized when a user is drawing them. Symbol libraries must be modifiable at any time. Further, we envision separate libraries for different modeling languages, and therefore a tool must be able to manage a list of symbol libraries. People like to use and mix different visual conventions [5], thus the tool must support the use of different notations at the same time. When a user starts to draw symbols that are part of multiple symbol libraries (which can happen very quickly for overloaded, simple shapes such as rectangles or circles), it is impossible for the tool to detect the correct language automatically. Even if the user adheres to one particular language such as UML, some shapes have different meanings in different diagram types. Thus a user must have the option to tag parts of the sketch and define the context by choosing the correct library for the recognition from a list. Explicitly assigning contexts also helps when symbols are used inconsistently.

Sketch Recognition Framework. A recognition framework processes sketches on two levels. Low level recognition combines groups of individual pen strokes to distinct symbols. High level recognition compares drawn symbols with those in the symbol library. For our tool, the recognition framework must be able to handle a dynamic symbol library. Sketch recognition algorithms can be divided into two categories: while an *offline* algorithm starts the recognition process only after the user has finished sketching, an *online* algorithm starts processing right away when the user begins to draw, and takes temporal properties of drawn strokes into account. These temporal properties provide additional hints for the sketch recognition engine. As our approach is interactive, we will need an online algorithm. We plan to modify an existing online sketch recognition algorithm such that it fits our needs.

Modeling Language Definition. The tool must provide an interface that helps users in defining a modeling language. Users must be able to easily add new symbols to the symbol library. They also need convenient means for adding syntax and semantics to symbols. No scripting or programming should be required during the metamodeling task. Creating a lightweight, sketch-based interface that also allows to add all kinds of syntax and semantics is a challenging task. This is probably the most critical part of the tool. Therefore, our work will not only be based on research in the fields of requirements engineering (RE) and sketch recognition, but also relies on findings from work in the human-computer-interaction domain. The interactivity and the flexibility of a tool add a great deal to its usability. The graphical user interface for the language definition needs to be seamlessly integrated into the sketch environment.

2.4   Benefits and Limitations

Our tool will allow requirements engineers to formalize sketches into models without having to recreate them, and therefore eliminate media breaks. It gives them the flexibility to co-evolve diagrams and meanings of the drawn elements, and also allows them to define a DSL first, start sketch-based modeling using this DSL and then augment or modify the DSL in the modeling process.

The co-evolution usage style is more flexible than any existing tool-supported approach, but is probably limited to simple, lightweight modeling languages. Otherwise, this style requires too much metamodeling overhead and can only be used properly by metamodeling experts. Working with a lightweight modeling language [6] matches our intention of supporting early requirements engineering. At this stage, when stakeholders and requirements engineers sketch their intentions and creative ideas, using a lightweight language is crucial, because adherence to a sophisticated modeling language would impede the creative flow [7,3].

The DSL style has similarities to using a meta-edit tool (the modeling language definition has to be entered first), but gives more freedom to users as it allows adding or modifying symbol definitions during the modeling process. This style is particularly useful when metamodeling experts predefine a symbol library for a standard modeling language such as UML, which then can be extended by requirements engineers with domain-specific elements.

2.5   Current Research Status

A literature review has shown that while there is a lot of ongoing research in sketch recognition, sketch-based tools do not focus on the RE domain and also have deficiencies in terms of flexibility and ease of sketch-based modeling. From discussions with requirements engineering experts about this topic, we conclude that our approach will provide value to requirements engineers. We currently have completed a preliminary concept of our approach. Right now we are comparing different sketch recognition concepts and look at theories about graphical user interfaces. Future steps include the creation of a tool prototype, its evaluation with a case study, and its improvement.

3   Related Work

Related research in this area includes software tools that incorporate a natural drawing interface and a sketch recognition engine, e.g. SUMLOW [4], and Tahuti [10]. These tools use predefined libraries and thus only support certain languages.

Some meta-tools allow users to define their own languages, e.g. Marama [9] and MetaEdit+ [11]. The meta-tool then builds the actual modeling tool. If users want to change the language, they have to go back to the meta-tool, modify the definitions, and tell the meta-tool to rebuild the modeling tool.

Domain-independent sketch recognition toolkits like SketchREAD [1] and InkKit [12] can handle additional domain languages. These notations must either be scripted/ programmed or imported via a library plug-in. Thus, these tools are better suited for developers rather than requirements engineers.

Gross [8] and Avola et al. [2] present sketch recognition frameworks that work with dynamic libraries of user defined shapes. While Avola et al. focus on the technical details of sketch recognition, Gross additionally enables users to define some spatial constraints between shapes. Apart from this, none of the two approaches support user defined syntax and semantics. We will reuse a sketch recognition framework like the one presented in [2] for our work.

4   Conclusions

State-of-the-art sketch-based interfaces either lack formalization functionality or restrict users to use specific modeling languages. Although some of the discussed tools can be used for requirements engineering, they are not built for this purpose. We envisage a tool that is tailored to the needs of requirements engineers and allows unconstrained sketching with a subsequent, semi-automated formalization of the sketches. With this approach we overcome media break problems. As we are at the beginning of our research, next steps include building and evaluating a prototype tool in order to assess the usefulness of such a tool and our approach.

References

1. Alvarado, C., Davis, R.: SketchREAD: a Multi-Domain Sketch Recognition Engine. In: 17th Annual ACM Symposium on User Interface Software and Technology, pp. 23–32. ACM, New York (2004)
2. Avola, D., Del Buono, A., Gianforme, G., Paolozzi, S., Wang, R.: SketchML: a Representation Language for Novel Sketch Recognition Approach. In: 2nd International Conference on Pervasive Technologies Related to Assistive Environments, pp. 1–8. ACM, New York (2009)
3. Black, A.: Visible Planning on Paper and on Screen: the Impact of Working Medium on Decision-Making by Novice Graphic Designers. Behavior and Information Technology 9, 283–296 (1990)
4. Chen, Q., Grundy, J., Hosking, J.: SUMLOW: Early Design-Stage Sketching of UML Diagrams on an E-Whiteboard. Softw. Pract. Exper. 38(9), 961–994 (2008)
5. Cherubini, M., Venolia, G., DeLine, R., Ko, A.J.: Let's Go to the Whiteboard: How and Why Software Developers Use Drawings. In: 2007 SIGCHI Conference on Human Factors in Computing Systems, pp. 557–566. ACM, New York (2007)
6. Glinz, M.: Very Lightweight Requirements Modeling. In: 18th IEEE International Requirements Engineering Conference, pp. 385–386. IEEE Computer Society, Washington (2010)
7. Goel, V.: Sketches of Thought: a Study of the Role of Sketching in Design Problem-Solving and its Implications for the Computational Theory of the Mind. Ph.D. thesis, University of California at Berkeley, Berkeley (1991)
8. Gross, M.D.: Stretch-A-Sketch: a Dynamic Diagrammer. In: 1994 IEEE Symposium on Visual Languages, IEEE Computer Society, Washington (1994)
9. Grundy, J., Hosking, J.: Supporting Generic Sketching-Based Input of Diagrams in a Domain-Specific Visual Language Meta-Tool. In: 29th International Conference on Software Engineering, pp. 282–291. IEEE Computer Society, Washington (2007)
10. Hammond, T., Davis, R.: Tahuti: a Geometrical Sketch Recognition System for UML Class Diagrams. In: 2002 AAAI Spring Symposium on Sketch Understanding, pp. 59–68. AAAI Press, Menlo Park (2002)
11. Kelly, S., Lyytinen, K., Rossi, M.: MetaEdit+: a Fully Configurable Multi-User and Multi-Tool CASE and CAME Environment. In: Constantopoulos, P., Vassiliou, Y., Mylopoulos, J. (eds.) CAiSE 1996. LNCS, vol. 1080, pp. 1–21. Springer, Heidelberg (1996)
12. Plimmer, B., Freeman, I.: A Toolkit Approach to Sketched Diagram Recognition. In: 21st British HCI Group Annual Conference on People and Computers, pp. 205–213. British Computer Society, Swinton (2007)

Use Cases versus Task Descriptions

Soren Lauesen and Mohammad A. Kuhail

IT University of Copenhagen, Denmark
slauesen@itu.dk, moak@itu.dk

Abstract. **[Context and motivation]** Use cases are widely used as a substantial part of requirements, also when little programming is expected (COTS-based systems). **[Question/problem]** Are use cases effective as requirements? To answer this question, we invited professionals and researchers to specify requirements for the same project: *Acquire a new system to support a hotline.* **[Principal ideas/results]** Among the 15 replies, eight used traditional use cases that specified a dialog between users and system. Seven used a related technique, task description, which specified the customer's needs without specifying a dialog. **[Contribution]** It turned out that the traditional use cases covered the customer's needs poorly in areas where improvement was important but difficult. Use cases also restricted the solution space severely. Tasks didn't have these problems and allowed an easy comparison of solutions.

Keywords: use case; task description; requirements; verification; COTS.

1 Background

Traditional requirements consist of a list of system-shall-do statements, but don't describe the context of use. IEEE-830, for instance, uses this approach [6]. The lack of context makes it hard for users to validate such requirements, and developers often misunderstand the needs (Kulak & Guiney [9]). Jacobson introduced use cases in the late 1980s [7]. They describe the dialog (interaction) between a system and a user as a sequence of steps. Use cases seemed to provide what traditional requirements lacked, and they became widely used as a substantial part of requirements. Soon other authors improved on the basic idea and wrote textbooks for practitioners, e.g. Cockburn [3], Kulak & Guiney [9], Armour & Miller [2], Constantine & Lockwood [4].

Use cases have developed into many directions. Some authors stress that use cases should be easy to read for stakeholders and that they should not be decomposed into tiny use cases [3], [8]. The CREWS project claimed that use cases should be detailed and program-like with *If* and *While*, and have rules, exceptions and preconditions (reported in [1] and questioned in [5]). In contrast, Lilly [15] and Cockburn [3] advise against program-like elements. Other authors claim that use cases must have dialog details to help developers [17], [19].

In this paper we will only discuss how use cases handle the user-system interaction. This is the most common use in literature as well as in practice.

Virtually nobody discusses whether use cases in practice are suited as verifiable requirements. Use cases seem to be intended for system parts to be built from scratch,

D. Berry and X. Franch (Eds.): REFSQ 2011, LNCS 6606, pp. 106–120, 2011.

but this situation is rare today. What if the use case dialog differs from the dialog in one of the potential systems? Should we discard the system for this reason?

As a consultant, Lauesen had observed how use cases were used as a main part of requirements in large software acquisitions, even though the customer expected a COTS-based system with little add-on functionality. Usually the use cases were not used later in the project. However, in one large project the customer insisted on them being followed closely. As a result, the system became so cumbersome to use that the project was terminated [18].

Task Description is a related technique that claims to cover also the case where the system is not built from scratch. One difference is that tasks don't describe a dialog between user and system, but what user and system have to do together. The supplier defines the solution and the dialog - not the customer. The task technique was developed in 1998 (Lauesen [10], [11]) and has matured since [12], [13].

To get a solid comparison of the two approaches, we looked at a specific real-life project, invited professionals and researchers to specify the requirements with their preferred technique, and compared the replies.

2   The Hotline Case Study

The case study is an existing hotline (help desk). Hotline staff were not happy with their existing support system and wanted to improve the one they had or acquire a new one, probably COTS-based.

Lauesen interviewed the stakeholders, observed the existing support system in use, and wrote the findings in a three-page analysis report. Here is a brief summary: The hotline receives help requests from IT users. A request is first handled by a 1st level supporter, who in 80% of the cases can remedy the problem and close the case. He passes the remaining requests on to 2nd line supporters. A supporter has many choices, e.g. remedy the problem himself, ask for more information, add a note to the request, transfer it to a specialist, order components from another company, park the request, and combinations of these. The hotline is rather informal and supporters frequently change roles or attend to other duties.

We invited professionals to write requirement specifications based on the analysis report. The invitation emphasized that we looked for many kinds of "use cases" and didn't care about non-functional requirements. It started this way:

We - the IT professionals - often write some kind of use cases. Our "use cases" may be quite different, e.g. UML-style, tasks, scenarios, or user stories. Which kind is best?

Participants could ask questions for clarification, but few did. The full analysis report is available in [14]. It started this way:

A company with around 1000 IT users has its own hotline (help desk). They are unhappy with their present open-source system for hotline support, and want to acquire a better one. They don't know whether to modify the system they have or buy a new one.

An analyst has interviewed the stakeholders and observed what actually goes on. You find his report below. Based on this, your task is to specify some of the requirements to the new system: use cases (or the like) and if necessary the data requirements.

We announced the case study in June-July 2009 to members of the Requirements Engineering Online Discussion Forum <re-online@it.uts.edu.au>, to members of the Danish Requirements Experience Group, and to personal contacts. The British Computer Society announced it in their July 2009 Requirements Newsletter. We got several comments saying: *this is a great idea, but I don't have the time to participate.* Lauesen wrote special requests to Alistair Cockburn and IBM's Rational group in Denmark, but got no reply.

We received 15 replies. Eight replies were based on use-cases and seven on tasks. Some replies contained separate data requirements, e.g. E/R models, and some contained use cases on a higher level, e.g. business flows. When identifying verifiable requirements, we looked at these parts too. The full replies are available in [14]. Here is a profile of the experts behind the replies:

Replies based on use cases. Decreasing requirement completeness:

Expert A. A research group in Heidelberg, Germany. The team has industry experience and has taught their own version of use cases for 7 years.
Expert B. Consultant in California, US. Has 15 years professional requirements experience. Rational-certified for 11 years.
Expert C. A research group at Fraunhofer, Germany.
Expert D. Researcher at the IT-University of Copenhagen. Learned use cases as part of his education in UK, but has no professional experience with them.
Expert E. Consultant in Sweden with ten years experience. Specialist in requirements management. Have classes in that discipline.
Expert F. A software house in Delhi. Write use cases regularly for their clients. Were invited to write a reply on a contract basis, and were paid for 30 hours.
Expert G. Consultant in Sweden with four years experience in requirements.
Expert H. Consultant in Denmark with many years experience. Teaches requirement courses for the Danish IT association.

Replies based on task descriptions. Decreasing requirement completeness:

Expert I. Consultant in Sweden with many years experience. Uses tasks as well as use cases, depending on the project. Selected tasks for this project because they were most suitable and faster to write.
Expert J. Help desk manager. Has 15 years experience with programming, etc.
Expert K. A recently graduated student who has used tasks for 1.5 years. Little program experience.
Expert L. Researcher at the IT-University of Copenhagen. Has 25 years industry experience and has later used tasks for 10 years as a consultant and teacher.
Expert M. GUI designer with one year of professional requirements experience.
Expert N. Leading software developer with 12 years experience. Learned about tasks at a course and wrote the reply as part of a four-hour written exam.
Expert O. A research group in Bonn. Germany. The team has several years of industry experience, but little experience with the task principle.

3   Evaluation Method and Validity

We evaluated the replies according to many factors, but here we deal only with these:
A.   Completeness: Are all customer needs reflected in the requirements?

B. Correctness: Does each requirement reflect a customer need? Some requirements are incorrect because they are too *restrictive* so that good solutions might be rejected. Other requirements are incorrect because they are *wrong*; they specify something the customer explicitly does not want.
C. Understandability: Can stakeholders understand and use the requirements?

Validity threats. For space reasons we don't discuss all the validity threats here, but only the most important ones:

* Lauesen has invented one of the techniques to be evaluated. His evaluation of the replies might be biased. We have reduced this threat by getting consensus from several experts, as explained in the procedure below.
* The experts didn't have the same opportunities for talking to the client, as they would have in real life. True, but it seemed to have little effect. During the consensus procedure, there was no disagreement about which requirements were justified by the analysis report and which were not.
* Lauesen studied the domain and wrote the analysis report. This gave him an advantage. True, but it had no influence on the other six task-based replies. Further, when ranking the task-based replies on completeness (Figure 5), Lauesen (Expert L) was only number 4. (His excuse for the low ranking is that he spent only one hour writing the solution, plus 5 hours pretty-typing it without improving it in other ways.)

Procedure

1. The two authors have different backgrounds and independently produced two very different replies, Kuhail's based on use cases (Expert D) and Lauesen's on tasks (Expert L). We evaluated all replies independently. Each of us spent around 1 to 3 hours on each reply.
2. We compared and discussed until we had consensus. As an example, one of us might have found a missing requirement in reply X, but the other could point to where the requirement had been stated in the reply. We had around 5 points to discuss for each reply.
3. For each reply, we sent our joint evaluation to the experts asking for comments and for permission to publish their reply and our comments. We also asked for comments to our own solutions. Some authors pointed out a few mistakes in our evaluation, for instance that we had mentioned missing requirements in their reply that were not justified by the analysis report; or that our own solutions missed more requirements than we had noticed ourselves. We easily agreed on these points. Other authors said that our evaluation basically was correct, and that they were surprised to see the task approach, and considered using it in the future.
4. Finally we asked two supporters (stakeholders) to evaluate the four representative replies presented below. It was of course a blind evaluation. They had no idea about the authors.

We asked the supporters these questions in writing:

a. *How easy is it to understand the requirements?*
b. *Which requirements are covered* [met] *by the system you have today?*
c. *Which requirements specify something you miss today?*[want-to-have]

d. Do you miss something in addition to what is specified in the requirements?
e. Are some requirements wrong?
*f. Could you use the requirements for evaluating the COTS system you intend to
    purchase?*

The supporter got an introduction to the case and the style used in the first reply. He/she was asked to read it alone and answer the questions above. He/she spent between 30 and 50 minutes on each reply. Next we met, looked at the reply and asked questions for clarification. We handled the other replies in the same way.

Karin, senior supporter: The first supporter was Karin Tjoa Nielsen. Karin had been the main source of information when Lauesen wrote the analysis report. She is not a programmer but has a very good understanding of users' problems and the hotline procedures. She read the replies in this sequence: Expert H (tiny use cases), Expert L (Lauesen tasks), Expert A (program-like use cases), Expert K (tasks).

Morten, supporter with programming background: The second supporter was Morten Sværke Andersen. Morten is a web-programmer, but had worked in the hotline until two years ago. He had never seen use cases, but had worked with user stories. He read the replies in this sequence: Expert L (Lauesen tasks), Expert H (tiny use cases), Expert A (program-like use cases), Expert K (tasks).

4 Sample Replies and Stakeholder Assessment

We will illustrate the replies with the four examples summarized in Fig. 1. We chose them because they are short, well-written examples of tiny use cases, program-like use cases, and task descriptions.

Tiny use cases: Expert H's reply consists of seven use cases. Fig. 2 shows one of them in detail (*Transfer request*). It describes the dialog when a supporter wants to

Expert H (tiny use cases)	Expert A (program-like use cases)	Expert L (Lauesen) (tasks - no dialog)	Expert K (tasks - no dialog)
UC1. Record new request	UC1. Trigger and control hotline problem solution	T1: Report a problem	T1: IT users (report problem + follow up)
UC2. Follow up on request	UC2. Accept request	T2: Follow up on a problem	
UC3. Add request data	UC3. Clarify request	T3: Handle a request in first line	T2.1: First line
UC4. Transfer request	UC4. Handle request	T4: Handle a request in second line	T2.2: Second line
UC5. Update request	UC5. Set support level	T5: Change role	T2.3: Both lines (change state)
UC6. Retrieve statistics	UC6. Get statistics	T6: Study performance	
UC7. Generate reminder (system-to-system use case)	UC7. Warn about orphaned requests (system-to-system use case)	T7: Handle message from an external supplier	
		T8. Update basic data	
Length: 5500 chars. **Time**: 2.5 hours.	**Length**: 9900 chars. **Time**: Unknown.	**Length**: 4600 chars. **Time**: 6 hours.	**Length**: 2900 chars. **Time**: 3 hours.

Fig. 1. Overview of four replies

transfer a help request to another supporter. The steps alternate between *The system does* and *The user does*. Deviations from this sequence are recorded as variants below the main flow, e.g. the variant that the user wants to filter the requests to see only his own.

Expert H's use cases have a simple flow with few deviations from the main flow. They are examples of *tiny use cases*, where each use case describes a simple action carried out by the user.

The reply is easy to read. However, it gives an inconvenient dialog if the system is implemented as described. As an example, several use cases start with the same steps (UC 1, 2 and 3). If implemented this way, the supporter will have to select and open the request twice in order to add a note to the request and then transfer it (a common combination in a hotline.)

Supporter assessment: The supporters were confused about the supplementary fields with goal, actor, etc. and ignored them as unimportant. Apart from this, they found the reply easy to read, but concluded that it contained only few and trivial requirements. As an example, Morten considered the entire use case in Fig. 2 one trivial requirement. *It is more of a build-specification*, he said. They noticed several missing or wrong requirements.

USE CASE #04	Transfer request
Goal	Transfer a request to a specific hotline employee
Level	User goal (sea level)
Precondition	User is logged in and has the right to transfer requests
Postcondition	N/A
Primary, Secondary actors	Hotline
Trigger	Primary actor

NORMAL FLOW	
Step	**Action**
1	The system shows a list of all open requests
2	The user selects a support request
3	The system shows request data for the selected request
4	The system shows a list of hotline employees
5	The user chooses a hotline employee from the list
6	The system changes Owner to the selected employee and changes state to "2nd level"
7	The system updates the request

VARIANTS	
Step	Action
2a **1** **2**	**User wants to filter his own requests** The system shows a list of all open requests with the user as Owner The use case goes to step 2

Fig. 2. Expert H: Dialog steps in one column. Tiny use cases.

Program-like use cases: Expert A's reply also consists of seven use cases. Fig. 3 shows one of them in detail (*Handle request*). It describes the dialog when a supporter takes on a help request and either corrects the problem or transfers the request to

Name	Handle request	
Actor	Supporter (first/second line)	
Supporting Actors	IT user	
Goal	Solve a problem.	
Precondition	[Workspace: request]	
Description	**Actor**	**System**
	A1) VAR1) the actor takes on an open request from his/her line. [Exception: No open requests] VAR2) the actor receives a request forwarded to him/her.	S1) If VAR1) The system records the actor as owner of the request. [System function: take on request]
	A2) [optional *] The actor adds information [Include UC Clarify request]	
	A3) [optional X] The actor forwards the request. VAR1) forward to second line VAR2) forward to specific expert (no matter what line) [include UC Handle request]	S3) The system forwards the request [System function: forward request] If VAR1) The system changes the owner to "not set" and the status to "second line" If VAR2: The system sets the expert as the owner and notifies him/her about the forwarded request. If he/she is logged in at the moment, the system sends an alert in a way designed to attract his/her attention (e.g. a pop-up window). Else it sends the alert as soon as the expert logs in.
	A4) [optional *] The actor looks up information of the request.	S4) The system provides information about the request. [System function: show request details]
	A5) [optional X] The actor solves the problem and closes the request.	S5) The system closes the request. The system sends the user a notification. [System function: close request]
Exceptions	[There are no open requests]: The system contains no open requests.	
Rules	None	
Quality Requirements	None	
Data, Functions	System functions: take on request, show request details, add information to description field . . .	
Post conditions	The request is closed in the system.	
Included UCs	Clarify request; Handle request	

Fig. 3. Expert A: Dialog steps in two columns. Programs-like use cases.

someone else. The steps are shown as two columns, one for the user actions (A1, A2, etc.) and one for the system actions (S1, S2, etc.). Variants are shown right after the related step. There are many variants, if-statements, included use cases, rules and exceptions. Special notation is used to show whether a step is optional, and whether it terminates the use case if done. The description is a kind of program that specifies the possible sequences.

The optional steps may be carried out in any order, which gives the user much freedom to choose the sequence.

Some of A's use cases involve several users and describe a kind of dialog between them. As an example, use case *Clarify Request* describes that a supporter can require more information from the IT user, what the user does, and how a (new) supporter handles it.

Expert A's use cases are very different from H's. As an example, H's entire use case 4 (Transfer request) is just step A3 in A's *Handle request*. While an H use case shows a tiny part of the dialog, an A use case covers a more coherent period.

Supporter assessment: Karin (the senior stakeholder) couldn't understand the program-like details and ignored them. She found the rest okay to read and used it as a checklist. She identified many lines as requirements that were *met* or *want-to-have*. She also noticed some missing or wrong requirements. Morten (the programmer) found the reply very hard to read and spent a lot of time checking the program-like parts. *If I had been asked to read this first, I wouldn't have done it.* He found many parts wrong or dubious. He concluded that the use cases were useless for checking against a new system, since it might well work in some other way.

Task descriptions (Lauesen): Expert L's reply consists of eight task descriptions. Fig. 4 shows one of them in detail (Handle *a request in second line*). It describes what a second-line supporter can do about a request from the moment he looks at it and until he cannot do more about it right now (a *closed task*). He has many options, e.g. contact the user for more information, move to the problem location, order something from an external supplier - or combinations of these.

At first glance, task descriptions look like use cases, but there are several significant differences:

1. The task steps in the left-hand column specify what user and computer do together without specifying who does what. Early on you don't know exactly who does what, and in this way you avoid inventing a dialog. Variants of the task step are shown right after the step, e.g. *1a* about being notified by email.
2. You can specify problems in the way things are done today, e.g. *1p* about spotting the important requests. You don't have to specify a solution.
3. The requirements are that the system must support the tasks and remedy the problems as far as possible. You can compare systems by assessing how well they do this.
4. In the right-hand column you may initially write examples of solutions, later notes on how a potential system supports the step. The left-hand side is relatively stable, but the right-hand side is not. Sometimes the system can carry out the entire step alone, for instance if it automatically records the IT user's name and email based on the phone number he calls from.

5. The steps may be carried out in almost any order. Most of them are optional and often repeatable. The user decides what to do. The steps are numbered for reference purposes only. (Cockburn and others recommend this too, but it is hard to realize with use cases, because dialogs are a step-by-step sequence.)

Problem requirements. In the example there are four problems in the way things are done today. Some of them, for instance 7p, are very important but not easy to solve.

When a step has an example solution, the solution is not a requirement. Other solutions are possible. Steps without a solution may have an obvious one that the analyst didn't care to write (e.g. step 6) - or he cannot imagine a solution (e.g. 7p). Both are okay.

Lauesen's task list is quite different from expert H's use case list. As an example, H's use case 3, 4 and 5 are steps in Lauesen's *Handle a Request in Second Line*. The relationship to A's use cases is more complex. An A use case may go across several

C4. Handle a request in second line

Start: The supporter gets an email about a request or looks for pending requests.
End: The supporter cannot do more about the request right now.

Subtasks and variants:		Example solutions:
1	Look at open second-line requests from time to time, or when finished doing something else.	
1p	**Problem:** In busy periods it is hard to spot the important and urgent requests.	Can restrict the list to relevant requests. Can sort according to reminder time, priority, etc.
1a	Receive email notification about a new request	
2	Maybe contact the user or receiver to obtain more information.	p, q: Problems today
3	Maybe solve the problem by moving to the problem location.	a, b: Variants of the subtask
4	Maybe work for some time on the problem. Inform others that they don't have to look at it.	Put the request in state *taken*.
5	Maybe order something from an external supplier and park the request.	The system warns if no reminder time has been set.
6	In case of a reminder, contact the supplier and set a new reminder time.	User and computer together
6p	**Problem:** The user doesn't know about the delay.	The system sends a mail when the reminder time is changed.
7	Maybe close the case.	The system warns if the cause hasn't been set.
7p	**Problem:** To gather statistics, a cause should be specified, but this is difficult and cumbersome today.	Maybe: The user decides
7q	**Problem:** The user isn't informed when the request is closed.	The system sends a mail when the request is closed. The supporter has the possibility to write an explanation in the mail.
8	Maybe leave the request in the "in-basket" or transfer it to someone else.	

Fig. 4. Expert L (Lauesens): Tasks- no dialog. Problems as requirements.

users and a large time span. In contrast a task should cover what one user does without essential interruptions from Start (trigger) to End (done for now). This is the *task closure* principle.

Supporter assessment: The senior supporter was excited about this reply: *This is so clear and reflects our situation so well. It is much easier to read than the first one I got. I hope I don't step on someone's toes by saying this.* Although she correctly understood the left-hand side, she tended to consider the example solution a promise for how to do it. Morten read this reply as the first one. He was excited about the start and end clauses because they reflected the real work. He was puzzled about the distinction between first and second line, because the hotline didn't operate in that way when he worked there. Initially he hadn't marked the problems as requirements, but later included them. Both supporters marked most of the steps as requirements that were *met* or *want-to-have*. They didn't notice any missing or wrong requirements.

We have seen also in other cases that the two-column principle and the problem requirements are not fully intuitive. However, once reminded of the principle, readers understand the requirements correctly. (The reply started with a six-line explanation of the principles, but the supporters didn't notice it.)

The senior supporter decided to evaluate the system they intended to buy by means of the task descriptions (she still didn't know whom the author was). She did this on her own a few days later, and concluded that most requirements were met - also those that earlier were *want-to-have*. She could also explain the way the new system solved the *want-to-have* problems.

Task description: Expert K's reply consists of four tasks, very similar to Lauesen's, but K hasn't covered statistics and maintenance of basic data. For space reasons we don't show a detailed task. In general all the task replies are rather similar. We chose K's reply because the author had no supporter experience, had experience with tasks in real cases, and followed the principle of task closure.

Supporter assessment: The senior supporter read this reply a few months after reading the first three replies. She found also this reply easy to read. She had marked eight of the requirements with a smiley and explained that these requirements showed that the author had found the sore spots in a hotline. (Seven of these requirements were problem requirements.) She had marked all the requirements as *met* in the new system, but explained that they currently worked on improving the solution to one of the problems (quick recording of problems solved on the spot). She had noticed that requirements for statistics were missing.

Morten also read this a few months later. He was asked to compare the reply against the old system, since he didn't know the new one. He found the tasks easy to read and noticed six requirements that were not met in the old system (five of them problem requirements). He didn't notice that requirements for statistics were missing.

He also made comments that showed that the task principles had to be reinforced. He surprisingly suggested that the step *estimate solution time* should be deleted - otherwise supporters would be annoyed at having to make an estimate. He forgot that all task steps are optional, and you don't have to carry out an optional step. In a few places he complained about missing or bad *solutions*. He forgot that the solution side is just examples. The supplier should give the real solution.

5 Completeness - Dealing with Existing Problems

Requirements are complete when they cover all the customer's needs. Completeness of the ordinary requirements varied within both groups of replies due to participant's experience, time spent, etc. However, the two groups handled the present problems very differently. If requirements don't cover these problems, the customer may end up getting a new system without noticing that the problems will remain.

The analysis report mentions nine problems in the existing hotline, e.g.: *In busy periods, around 100 requests may be open (unresolved). Then it is hard for the individual supporter to survey the problems he is working on and see which problems are most urgent.*

In principle requirements can deal with such a problem in three ways:

1. Specify a solution to the problem.
2. Ignore the problem.
3. Specify the problem and require a solution (a *problem requirement*).

Problem requirements are unusual in traditional requirements, but are used extensively in tasks. The use case replies deal with problems by either specifying a solution or ignoring the problem.

All the use case replies ignored the problem with the busy periods. Expert A confirmed our suspicion that it was because they couldn't see a solution.

Expert A explained: *We do not think that this can be solved by the system. The system gives all the important information (e.g. date placed) for the user to decide.*

With tasks you can just record the problem, for instance as in Fig. 4, 1p. Lauesen's experience from many kinds of projects is that recording the problem helps finding a solution later, for instance the one outlined in Fig. 4, 1p. Even if the analyst cannot imagine a solution, a supplier may have one. As an example, we considered problem 7p (specifying the cause of requests) hard to solve until we saw a product with a short experience-based list of the most common causes. They covered around 90% of the help requests. The customer could gradually add more causes.

The analysis report mentions nine problems. For each reply we checked which problems it covered, either as a problem requirement or as a solution. Fig. 5 shows the results. The problem above is recorded as problem A. None of the use case replies deal with it. Problems that have an easy solution, for instance problem I, are covered by most replies.

Tasks cover these nine problems significantly better than use-cases do:

- Number of problems covered by a use case reply: 3.8 ± 1.2
- Number of problems covered by a task reply: 6.5 ± 1.9

The difference is significant on the 1% level for ANOVA ($p=0.6\%$) as well as for a t-test with unequal variances ($p=0.5\%$).

The standard deviations are due to differences in expertise, time spent, simple mistakes, etc. Not surprisingly, the deviation for task replies is larger because some task participants had little task experience (N and O).

Maiden & Ncube [16] observed that when comparing COTS products, all products meet the trivial requirements. Selection must be based on the more unusual requirements. In the hotline case, the problem requirements are the ones that will make a difference to the customer, while the ordinary requirements will be met by most systems.

Use-case based:	A: Hard to spot important requests	B: Difficult to specify a cause. May change later	C: User: When can I expect a reply?	D: Forgets to transfer requests when leaving	E: Cumbersome to record on-the-spot solutions	F: User: When is it done?	G: Nobody left on 1st line	H: Reminder: Warn about overdue requests	I: Today it is hard to record additional comments	Total
Expert A				1	1	1	1	0.5	1	5.5
Expert B		0.5	1		1	1		0.5	1	5
Expert C				0.5		1	1	0.5	1	4
Expert D				1			1	1	1	4
Expert E					1		1	1	1	4
Expert F						0.5	1	1	1	3.5
Expert G			0.5					0.5	1	2
Expert H						0.5		0.5	1	2
Total UC	0	0.5	1.5	2.5	3	4	5	5.5	8	
Task-based:										
Expert I	1	1	1	1	1	1	1	0.5	1	8.5
Expert J	1	1	1	1	1	1	1		1	8
Expert K	1	0.5	1	1	1	1	1	1		7.5
Expert L	1	1	1	1	1	1		1		7
Expert M	1	1	0.5		0.5	1	1		1	6
Expert N	1	1			0.5	1			1	4.5
Expert O					0.5	1	1		1	3.5
Total tasks	6	5.5	4.5	4	5.5	7	5	2.5	5	

Fig. 5. Problem coverage: 1 =fully covered, 0.5 = partly covered

6 Too Restrictive Requirements

In the hotline case the purpose is not to develop a new system, but to expand the existing one or acquire a new one (probably COTS-based). With the task technique stakeholders check how well the system supports each task step and each problem. In order to compare systems, they check each of them in the same way.

We couldn't see how the use cases handled this situation. The use cases specify a dialog in more or less detail, and it seems meaningless to compare this dialog with a different dialog used by an existing system. The requirements arbitrarily restrict the solution space. So we asked participants how their use cases could be used for comparison with an existing system. Here are some of the replies:

Expert F: *We will* make *use of something that we call a decision matrix. We have prepared a sample for your reference where we are comparing the present Hotline system with the system that we propose...*

Their matrix shows nine features to compare, e.g. *Reminder management* and *Automatic request state management*. They have no direct relation to the use cases. F explained that their use cases specified a new system to be developed from scratch.

Expert H: *Use Cases are an optimal source for defining Test Cases. So running these Test Cases against different proposals and the existing system, it will be clear which systems fulfill most of the functional requirements. The tests can be run "on paper" since many solutions have not been developed yet.*

This seems a good idea. The only problem is at what detail you define these test cases. Assume that you use the use cases directly as test scripts. You would then test *Transfer request* (Fig. 2) by trying to select a request from the list, checking that the system shows request details and a list of hotline employees. But what about a system where you don't need to see the details, but transfer the request directly from the list? You would conclude that the system doesn't meet the requirements (actually it might be more convenient). One of the supporters (Morten) actually tried to verify Expert A's program-like use cases in this way, but became so confused that he gave up.

Hopefully, the testers have domain insight so that they can abstract from the details of the use case and make the right conclusion. If so, most of this use case is superfluous. You could omit everything except the heading *Transfer request* and simply test that the system can transfer a request, and make a note about how easy it is to do so. The other supporter (Karin) actually verified all use cases in this way.

Expert A: *Our requirements only describe the to-be system. They cannot be used to compare the other systems with the current (open source) system. However, they could be used to see whether the supplier's system (if not available, the description of the system) meets our requirements.*

Expert A (another team member): *I think the purpose of your [Lauesen's] specification is quite different from ours. We want to provide a specification that describes the solution to the problems on a high level. For the purpose of choosing between solutions your specification is much better, but this was not so prominent in the experiment description that we considered it the major context.*

The other use-case replies follow the same lines. They describe a future solution in detail.

Why did all the use case authors describe a future solution and later realize that it wasn't useful as requirements in this case? The analysis report said that the customer wanted to modify the existing system or buy a new one - not build a new one. We believe that use case principles and current practice are the causes:

1. Use case principles force you to design a dialog at a very early stage. In this way you design key parts of the solution rather than specifying the needs.
2. Use cases are so widely used that nobody questions their usefulness.
3. Few analysts know alternative requirements that are verifiable, not solutions, and reflect the context of use.

7   Wrong Requirements

The supporters and we noted several wrong requirements in the use cases. As an example, Expert C mentions these two business rules:

R1. Only problems with high priority may be requested via phone or in person.
R2. For statistical purpose it is not allowed to create a request for more than one problem.

None of these rules are justified in the analysis report, and it would be harmful to enforce them. Should hotline reject a user request if it contains more than one problem? The hotline would surely get a bad reputation.

We believe that use case theory and templates cause these mistakes. Many textbooks on use cases emphasize rules, preconditions, etc. and their templates provide fields for it. Most replies used such a template, and as a result, the authors were tempted to invent some rules, etc. Often these rules were unnecessary or even wrong.

In order to avoid this temptation, tasks do not have fields for preconditions or rules. When such a rule is necessary to deal with a customer need, it can be specified as a task step, e.g. *check that the request has a high priority,* as a constraint in the data model, or in other sections of the requirements [13].

8 Conclusion

In this study we compare real-life use cases against the related technique, task description. We deal only with use cases that specify the interaction between a human user and the system. We do not claim that the findings can be generalized to other kinds of use cases, for instance system-to-system use cases.

The study shows that with use cases the customer's present problems disappear unless the analyst can see a solution to the problem. The consequence is that when the customer looks for a new system, he will not take into account how well the new system deals with the problems. Even if the analyst has specified a solution, a better solution may not get the merit it deserves because the corresponding problem isn't visible in the use cases.

Task descriptions avoid this by allowing the analyst to state a problem as one of the "steps", with the implicit requirement that a solution is wanted (a *problem requirement*). Example solutions may be stated, but they are just examples - not requirements. In practice, stakeholders need some guidance to understand this principle.

The study also shows that use cases in practice produce too restrictive requirements for two reasons: (1) They force the analyst to design a dialog at a very early stage, in this way designing a solution rather than specifying the needs. Often the dialog would be very inconvenient if implemented as described. (2) Many use case templates provide fields for rules, preconditions, etc. and these fields encourage analysts to invent rules, etc. Often they don't reflect a customer need and may even be harmful.

Task descriptions don't specify a dialog but only what user and system need to do together. The supplier defines the solution and the dialog, and stakeholders can compare it against the task steps to be supported. Tasks don't tempt the analyst with fields for rules, etc. When rules are needed, the analyst must specify them as separate task steps or in other sections of the requirements.

References

1. Achour, C.B., Rolland, C., Maiden, N.A.M., Souveyet, C.: Guiding Use Case Authoring: Results of an Empirical Study. In: Proceedings of the 4th IEEE International Symposium (1999)

2. Armour, F., Miller, G.: Advanced Use Case Modeling. Addison-Wesley, Reading (2001)
3. Cockburn, A.: Writing Effective Use Cases. Addison-Wesley, Reading (2000)
4. Constantine, L.L., Lockwood, L.A.D.: Software for Use: A practical guide to the Models and Methods of Usage-Centered Design. Addison-Wesley, New York (1999)
5. Cox, K., Phalp, K.: Replicating the CREWS Use Case Authoring Guidelines. Empirical Software Engineering Journal 5(3), 245–268 (2000)
6. IEEE Recommended Practice for Software Requirements Specification, ANSI/IEEE Std. 830 (1998)
7. Jacobson, I., Christerson, M., Johnsson, P., Övergaard, G.: Object-Oriented Software Engineering - a use case driven approach. Addison-Wesley, Reading (1992)
8. Jacobson, I.: Use Cases: Yesterday, Today, and Tomorrow. IBM Technical Library (2003)
9. Kulak, D., Guiney, E.: Use Cases: Requirements in Context. Addison-Wesley, Reading (2000)
10. Lauesen, S.: Software requirements - styles and techniques. Addison-Wesley, Reading (2002)
11. Lauesen, S.: Task Descriptions as Functional Requirements. IEEE Software, 58–65 (March/April 2003)
12. Lauesen, S.: User interface design - a software engineering perspective. Addison-Wesley, Reading (2005)
13. Lauesen, S.: Guide to Requirements SL-07 -Template with Examples (2007) ISBN: 978-87-992344-0-0, http://www.itu.dk/people/slauesen/SorenReqs.html#SL-07
14. Lauesen, S., Kuhail, M.A.: The use case experiment and the replies (2009), http://www.itu.dk/people/slauesen/
15. Lilly, S.: Use Case Pitfalls: Top 10 Problems from Real Projects Using Use Cases. IEEE Computer Society, Washington, DC, US (1999)
16. Maiden, N.A., Ncube, C.: Acquiring COTS software selection requirements. IEEE Software, 46–56 (March/April 1998)
17. Rosenberg, D., Scott, K.: Top Ten Use Case Mistakes, Software Development (2001), http://www.drdobbs.com/184414701
18. Sigurðardóttir, Hrönn Kold: Project manager for the Electronic Health Record system at the Capital Hospital Association (H:S): Draft of PhD thesis (2010)
19. Wirfs-Brock, R.: Designing Scenarios: Making the Case for a Use Case Framework, Smalltalk Report (November/December 1993), http://www.wirfs-brock.com/PDFs/Designing%20Scenarios.pdf

E-Service Requirements from a Consumer-Process Perspective

Martin Henkel and Erik Perjons

Department of Computer and Systems Sciences, Stockholm University
Forum 100, SE-16440, Kista, Sweden
{martinh,perjons}@dsv.su.se

Abstract. **[Context and motivation]** When designing e-services it is important that they fit smoothly into the service consumers' business processes. If the e-services do not fit there is a risk that they will not be used by the consumers; the investment and effort to use the e-services might be too high. **[Question/problem]** In this paper, we aim at describing an approach for analysing requirements on e-services from the service consumers' perspective. **[Principal ideas/result]** The approach supports the identification and analysis of problems that e-services can cause in consumers' business processes. The presented approach is also supporting identification of tentative solutions such as changes in the e-services, business processes, IT systems or legal regulations. **[Contribution]** The approach contributes to the area of e-service requirements analysis by taking a consumer and process centric perspective. The approach is grounded in and illustrated by a case at the Swedish Tax Agency.

Keywords: process analysis, e-service requirements, e-service design.

1 Introduction

Generally, e-services can be used in a wide range of situations. For example, e-services can be used for information exchange; for ordering of products; or for more elaborative business collaborations. Central to service usage can arguably be the interaction between the service provider and the service consumer (sometimes called the "service user"). In order for the service consumer to use an e-service, the service needs to be valuable for the consumer [1]. However, the consumer value of the service can be hampered if the consumer needs a large investment or effort in order to use the service. In a commercial setting this can mean that the consumer may not use the service for requesting information or for ordering of products. Likewise, for an e-service provided by the government, such as online tax declaration/tax return, this can mean that the consumer will not use the e-service. Instead, the consumer will send in the tax declaration using paper forms and traditional channels, which will increase the administrative costs for the tax agency.

The adjustment effort, or investment, that is needed for a consumer to use an e-service can be particularly unfortunate for the use of governmental e-services. The reason behind this is that some governmental e-services at a first glance give little immediate consumer value. For example, companies that are submitting tax

D. Berry and X. Franch (Eds.): REFSQ 2011, LNCS 6606, pp. 121–135, 2011.

declarations do not get any immediate value in return. (Of course, companies do get something in return, in the form of public roads etc [2].) Thus, the effort of using this kind of governmental e-services needs to be low in order for consumers to start using them. This is especially true if there are alternative ways of achieving the same result. For example, many companies have developed a business process for manually managing tax declarations using paper forms and traditional channels. Using the e-service instead may cause changes in the company's business processes as well as supporting IT systems, which, in turn, may require extra investments and/or efforts. These changes in the process can be at best annoying for the company, or in the worst case require substantial investments to be dealt with.

The problem addressed in this paper is that e-services can cause problems in consumer processes. That is, requirement elicitation activities for designing e-services need to broaden their scope and also consider the e-services' impact on the consumers' business processes.

The goal of the paper is to present an approach for identifying and analysing problems related to the e-services impact on the consumers' business processes. The approach also supports identification of tentative solutions. These solutions consist of a combination of changes on the service provider's and/or the service consumers' sides. More precisely, the suggested solutions consist of improvements in the consumers' business processes enabled by changes in the provider's e-services; the provider's business and legal regulations; or the consumers' IT systems.

The approach is grounded in and illustrated by a case study performed at the Swedish Tax Agency. The work is a part of a research project, named SAMMET [3]. One of the problems investigated in the project was that an e-service developed by the Swedish Tax Agency was not used as much as expected. The e-service was aiming at supporting companies to send in tax declarations to the Swedish Tax Agency electronically. However, a large group of companies were continuing to use paper forms and traditional channels instead of using the e-service. In order to analyse the limited use of the e-service, we investigated the e-service design as well as the IT and business context on both the service provider's and service consumers' sides. We then designed and applied the approach presented in this paper.

The approach is theoretically grounded in a four-aspect process framework [4] [5]. The process framework enables a structured approach to the process analysis and to structure the outcome of the approach. To aid the identification of possible solutions we furthermore apply a set of solution areas, based on that changes can be made to both IT and business on the consumers' and provider' sides of an e-service.

The remainder of this paper is structured as follows. In the next section, we describe research related to the approach. In Section 3, we give a short overview of the approach. In section 4-6, we describe the approach in detail. We also illustrate the approach using the Swedish Tax Agency case. Section 7 concludes the paper.

2   Related Research

Identifying, designing and implementing e-services introduce new challenges for business and IT architects. Compared to traditional information systems, service based systems are typically distributed among organisations. This means when designing and analysing e-services there is a need to consider a wider scope of requirements stemming from both the service provider and the service consumers. These issues have been addressed in the new subarea of requirements engineering that investigate service analysis and design. In this section, we describe how the approach presented in this paper relates to other research on e-services.

The relation between e-services and processes is discussed frequently in the literature. Particularly, the use of e-services is seen as a vehicle for process improvements. This view is predominant in the realm of Service Oriented Architectures, SOA. Several authors argue that e-services, and SOA, will be a base for building new, improved business processes [6][7]. In this paper, we take a different view: the view that a service can adversely affect the process it is used in. As a result, the findings can be used for e-service improvements as well as business process improvements.

There exist several methods on how to gather requirements for, and design e-services. Closest to the approach presented here are methods [8] [9] [10] that employ process models to design e-services. However these methods focus on the use of processes to create new e-services. In comparison to these methods, we use processes as a mean to analyse existing e-service designs, and to provide solutions for a better fit of the e-services in the service consumers' processes. Furthermore, the mentioned process based approaches focus on the activities and their relation in the processes for analysis, while we here apply a more elaborate four-aspect process framework. This enables us to perform a more detailed process analysis.

The view that information systems need to be analysed and evaluated in their context is argued for by several authors. For example, Scriven [11] argues that effects of a program should be evaluated by the effects as perceived by its users, as this way of evaluating is likely to catch unintended side-effects. This is in contrast to evaluate a service against its set up goals or intended effects. To rather examine the *unintended effects* is in line with the approach presented in this paper, since we try to discover problems or unintended effects that the use of a service has on a process.

The importance of studying e-services in their context is also pointed out by Goldkuhl [12]. Goldkuhl points out that e-services can have positive as well as negative effects for both service consumers and providers. In this paper, we focus on negative effects on the consumer side. Furthermore, Goldkuhl presents a generic method of how a software system in general should be designed to fit a certain organizational context [12]. However, the generic method does not include any concrete guidelines for how the analysis should be carried out. The approach presented in this paper is a first step towards aiding business and e-service analysts and designers with concrete guidelines how to perform this kind of analysis.

There also exist methods that makes use of goal models, such as i*, to design e-services [13][14][15]. We do not apply goal models in our analysis, this would be a possible extension to capture alignment problems between e-services and high-level organizational goals. However, one benefit with the approach is that the approach still could be used if no goals are identified at the consumers' side. Another benefit is that the approach is concrete and highly focused on the day-to-day activities in the consumers' processes.

It is interesting to note that technically oriented service design principles, such as loose coupling [7] and service composability [6], are expressing the desire to design e-services that are affecting its usage context as little as possible. The reason behind these technical design principles is to create services that are usable in different technical settings. These kinds of principles are seldom found in more user interface and user-interaction oriented literature. The driver behind the approach presented in this paper is similar to the technical design principles - to create services that do not impose restrictions in their context of use.

3   Overview of the Approach

The goal of the approach presented in this paper is to identify and analyse problems that e-services cause in consumers' business processes. More precisely, we will focus on negative unintended effects on the processes, that is, the limitations that the e-services impose on the consumer processes.

The approach consists of three steps: *consumer process identification, consumer process analysis* and *solution summary*. To perform each step we provide one instrument in each of the steps. For example, the consumer process identification is supported by the use of a set of guiding questions. The three step approach is presented in Figure 1. Inputs to the steps are shown as arrows to the left side of boxes and output is represented as arrows from the right side of the boxes. The instruments used are represented as arrows associated with the bottom side of the boxes.

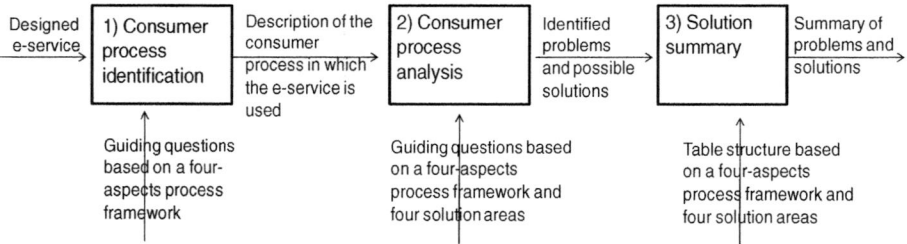

Fig. 1. Overview of the approach

Each of the three steps and used instruments are described in detail in Section 4, 5 and 6. These sections also show how the approach was applied in a case at the Swedish Tax Agency. The steps in the approach are briefly summarised below:

Step 1 - Consumer process identification. The aim of this step is the description of a consumer process in the form of its activities, the order of activities, the structure and content of information used and produced in the activities, as well as needed roles for service interaction. The step includes both the direct interaction required to use the e-service, and the wider context of the service use, i.e. the activities that precede and follows the service interaction. To guide the process identification, we provide an instrument in form of *a set of guiding questions* based on a *four-aspect process framework*.

Step 2 - Consumer process analysis. During this step the consumer process is examined to find problems caused by the e-service, as well as tentative solutions to these problems. To guide this step we propose an instrument in the form of another set of *guiding questions*. These questions are based on a combination of the aforementioned four aspect-process framework, and *four solution areas*. The four solution areas are: changes in the service consumers' business processes, changes in the e-service, changes in the provider's business rules (including legal regulations), and changes in the consumers' IT systems.

Step 3 - Solution summary. The problems and solutions found in the previous process analysis step are summarised according to the process aspects as well as the solution areas. To guide this summary, we provide an instrument in form of a simple table structure, describing problems and for each problem possible solutions. The table structure also shows how a solution in the form of a consumer process change must be supported by a change in at least one of the solutions areas: the service provider's business rules, the service provider's e-service or the service consumers' IT systems.

All three steps above could be performed by a process/e-service analyst in collaboration with the consumers of the e-service. In the case study presented in this paper, we used the guiding questions of step 1 and 2 in interviews with service consumers. However, the questions could also be used to guide workshops with several consumers present. The instrument in step 3 can be performed by a business analyst, in combinations with other approaches to estimate the cost of performing the changes, and to prioritize the changes.

4   Process Identification

In order to identify and describe the consumer process we need to examine not only the activities of the process that are directly interacting with the service, but also the activities that precede and follow the *service interaction*. We denote the activities that precede and follow the service interaction activities as the *service context*. Thus, in this step of the approach we will identify both activities within the service interaction and in the service context.

  A process is not only about the activities and their relations. To analyse service-based business process in depth, we also need to identify the process' use of information and role responsibilities. To cover all aspects of a process during the identification step, we rely on an existing four-aspect process framework [4][5]. According to this framework, a process can be described in four aspects:

- *Functional* - Describes the set of activities that are within the process
- *Behavioral* - Describes how the activities are interlinked, i.e. their order of execution and how the activities are synchronized in time.
- *Informational* - Describes the needed information that is used and produced by the activities within the process.
- *Organizational* - Describes who is responsible for executing the activities. This is commonly described by using roles.

The four aspects are interrelated. Thus, to describe a process in detail all four aspects need to be used. The four aspects should therefore not be seen as orthogonal. Instead, process analysts can use an aspect as a mean to intentionally focus on some characteristic of the process in detail, while putting other characteristics in the background.

To cover all the above process aspects, and to cover both the service interaction and its context, we propose an instrument which consists of a set of simple guiding questions, see Table 1. The guiding questions are based on the four-aspect process framework described above. As shown in Table 1, we propose to have separate questions for the service interaction and the service context. This is to avoid a too narrow focus in the process analysis.

Table 1. Process identification questions, based on process aspects

Process aspect	Within service interaction	In the service context
Functional	Which activities are needed within a service interaction in order to use a specific e-service?	Which activities are needed for preparation and handling of the result of a service interaction for the e-service?
Behavioural	Which order of activities is needed within a service interaction in order to execute a specific e-service? What requirements are put on the timing and performance on these activities?	Which order of internal activities is needed in order to prepare for the service interaction? How are the activities that handle the result of the interaction coordinated?
Informational	Which structure and content have the information that is sent to external parties during the service interaction?	Which structure and content of the internal information are needed for preparation, and handling of the result, of the use of the e-service?
Organizational	Which organizational role(s), or individual(s) are needed to participate in the service interaction in order to execute a specific e-service?	Which organizational role(s), or individual(s) are needed for the preparation before service interaction, and for handling of the result of a service interaction?

In order to identify and describe the consumers' tax declaration processes in the case study at the Swedish Tax Agency, we performed eleven semi-structured interviews with consumers of the tax agency's e-service. Out of the eleven interviews, six where performed with personnel at companies that worked as ombudsmen for tax declarations. These companies managed tax declarations of VAT and salaries for other companies. Thus, they had worked with the tax agency's e-service in different organisational settings. The other five interviews where performed with accountants working with the e-service at the company by which they are employed. Out of the eleven companies three had over 250 employees. During the interviews the guiding questions ensured that we identified information about the tax declaration processes with enough width and detail to get a good ground for further analysis.

The interviews led to a generalized graphical process model of the consumer's tax declaration process, and also textual descriptions. Figure 2 shows the resulting process diagram drawn by using the Business Process Model Notation (BPMN). The process is a simplification of both the service interaction and the service context that is performed at the companies. To simplify the process we only show the VAT process in Figure 2, and not the handling of the tax on salaries. Furthermore, we assume that all companies hand in declarations monthly. In reality smaller companies are allowed to do tax declarations quarterly or yearly. We have also removed some of the activities that some individual companies perform internally.

In the Tax Agency case there where substantial similarities in how the service consumers performed the tax declaration process, we therefore drew one generic process model. Other options would be to draw one process model per consumer, or one per consumer segment. The later, having a process model per consumer segment, can be beneficial when having a wide range of different consumers.

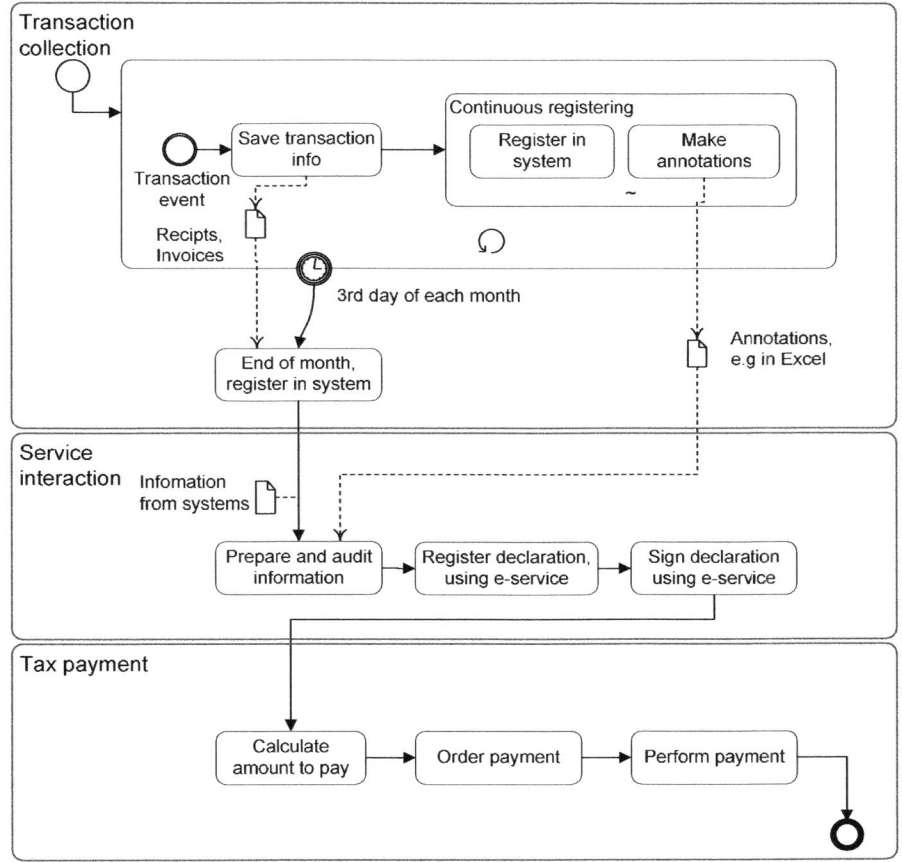

Fig. 2. The e-service consumer process

The tax declaration process (see Figure 2) starts with a *transaction collection phase* where the companies save receipts and invoices. Some of the companies perform continuous registration of the transactions in their systems. For special transactions, such as those that involve several countries, a special annotation is made, e.g. in an excel sheet or word document. All transactions need to be entered in the system on the 3rd day of each month at the latest. This phase is part of the service context.

During the *service interaction phase* the information that has been collected is prepared and audited for the declaration, this includes considering the special annotations done previously. The information is then manually registered in the tax declaration e-service, and signed using a digital certificate.

During the *tax payment phase* the correct amount tax is paid by the companies by issuing a payment order. This phase is part of the service context.

Even though it is simplified, the textual process description above, and the model shown in figure 2, constitutes the result of the first step of the approach. The next step of the approach is to identify problems in the process.

5 Process Analysis

The four process aspects described earlier (functional, behavioural, informational and organisational) are excellent as a means to describe a process, but we cannot rely on it alone to identify problems in the process. The reason is that the four aspects only suggest certain areas of a business process to focus on when describing and analysing a business process. To identify the problems, the consumer process also needs to be related to optimal solutions that the current process diverts from. In a sense, a problem exists when there is a gap between a desired state of affairs and the actual. However, if no optimal solution is available, further means are needed, such as means for identifying the lack of resources in existing processes or finding alternative solutions to the existing one. Therefore, we propose *four solution areas* for solving problems in the consumer process.

The solution areas that we propose are based on the idea that solutions can exist in the form of business changes or IT changes. Furthermore, these business and/or IT changes can be implemented at the consumer's or provider's sides. This combination gives four solution areas, as shown in figure 3.

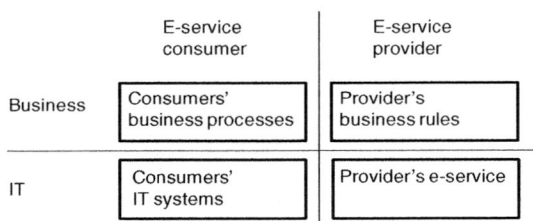

Fig. 3. The four pre-defined solution areas

The four solution areas are described below:

- *Provider's e-service*, i.e. the e-service designed and offered by the provider of the service (and used by the consumer).
- *Provider's business rules*, i.e. the business rules that govern the design and use of the e-service at the provider's side of the interaction. For example, when it comes to governmental e-services, this can be legal or organisational regulations.

- *Consumers' business process*, i.e. the internal business process in which the e-service is used by the consumer of the service.
- *Consumers' internal IT system*, which supports the internal business process in which the e-service is used.

By combining the four aspects framework with the four solution areas, *problems* can be found as well as tentative *solutions*. Each problem will be associated with a certain process aspects, while solutions are related to solution areas. The solutions consist of a combination of changes on the service provider's and/or the service consumer's sides. More precisely, the suggested solutions consist of improvements in the consumer's business process *enabled by* changes in the provider's e-services; the provider's business rules; or the consumer's IT systems. For example, there might be activities in the consumers' business process that can be removed (problems in the functional aspect of the process) by an improved design of the providers business rules (a solution area).

To guide this step we propose an *instrument* in form of a set of guiding questions, based on this combination of the four aspect-process framework and the four *solution areas*. The guiding questions are presented in the next sub-sections, describing how the process can be analysed aspect by aspect.

5.1 Analysing the Functional Process Aspect

The functional aspect of a process concerns the activities carried out in a process, in our approach, the service consumer process. The activities can be a part of the service interaction, that is, they can be depending on interaction with the e-service. The activities can also be in the service context, that is, they can be performed before or after the service interaction.

E-Services that do not fit well with the consumer process will require additional activities compared to e-services that are designed with the consumer process in mind, or will include manual activities that could be automated. During the process analysis of the functional aspect we can thus examine if there are any unnecessary extra activities needed to use the service, and if there are unnecessary manual activities which could be automated. To guide the analysis of the functional aspect we can use two simple questions, based on the reasoning above:

- QF1 - Are there any extra activities in the process that can be avoided using an alternative design of the provider's e-service, provider's business rules, or consumers' internal IT systems?
- QF2 - Are there any manual activities in the process that can be automated using an alternative design of the provider's e-service, provider's business rules, or consumers' internal IT systems?

In the Tax Agency case (see Figure 2), we can firstly conclude (by using question QF2) that the submission of the tax declaration requires the companies (i.e. service consumers) to manually enter the figures into the Swedish Tax Agency's (i.e. service provider's) e-service (the Register declaration activity in Figure 2). This activity could have been automated if there was a possibility to interconnect the consumers' internal IT support with the Swedish Tax Agency's system. Thus, we conclude that there is an alternative design that concerns the consumers' internal IT systems, and the provider's e-service design.

We can also conclude (by applying question QF1) that there are activities that are used for overcoming limitations in the service consumers' IT systems, namely the "Make annotations". These annotation activities are performed because the current IT support does not fully support the Swedish VAT regulations. In this case, these annotation activities would not be necessary if the e-service and IT systems where designed to follow the same standard procedures and rules, and have open interfaces. This problem can be related to two solution areas, an alternative internal IT system design or an alternative design of the Swedish Tax Agency's business rules. Even if it is unlikely that the Swedish VAT rules will be changed to conform to system implementations at the service consumers' side, posing the questions reveals that there are discrepancies between the IT systems that the service consumers' use and the business rules at the service provider's side imposed via the service.

5.2   Analysing the Behavioural Process Aspect

The behavioural aspect of a process concerns the control flow, i.e. in which order the activities are arranged in relation to each other. The control flow is expressed using a set of basic control flow constructs: sequence, synchronizations and conditional branching.

Ideally the service would not affect a process' behavioural aspect. This means that the service should introduce as few sequences, synchronizations and conditional branches as possible. When analyzing how the service causes problems in a process we can thus look for process flow constructs that are unnecessary with alternative solutions. To aid in analyzing the process we have three basic questions, based on the three types of flow constructs:

- QB1 - Are there any unnecessary constraints put on the sequencing of activities in the process that can be avoided using an alternative design of the provider's e-service, provider's business rules, or consumers' internal IT systems?

- QB2 - Are there any extra complexity in the process due to conditional branching that could be avoided by an alternative design of the provider's e-service, provider's business rules, or consumers' internal IT systems?

- QB3 - Are there any unnecessary constraints put on the process hindered because of the need to perform synchronization of parallel flows that can be avoided using an alternative design of the provider's e-service, provider's business rules, or consumers' internal IT systems?

Looking at the Tax Agency case (see Figure 2), we can see that the behavioural aspect is quite simple - there are few uses of branching and parallel flows. The most complex part of the process is actually before the interaction with the service occurs, i.e. when the information to put into the tax declaration is collected in the "Save transaction" and "Register in system". We can conclude (with the aid of question QB1) that all "Save transaction" and "Register in system" activities must be performed before the service is used. This can be considered as a requirement put on the behavioural aspect of the process. Another design of the provider's e-service and business rules that allows continuous reporting of transactions would get rid of this dependency between activities.

Even if it is not shown in the example process, the use of the e-service also put requirements on the process synchronization. When a company declares in and outgoing VAT it also needs to declare the paid salaries for the same month. This means that two sub-processes, the salary process (not shown) and the VAT process (shown in Figure 2), need to converge/synchronize in a single activity, the "Register declaration" activity. This dependency can be found by using question QB3. The reason behind the need to declare both VAT and salaries at the same time can be traced back to the use of paper forms - it was considered simpler to just use a single paper form for both declarations. A simple solution can be found in the e-service solution area – just separate the handling of VAT and tax put on salaries.

5.3 Analysing the Informational Process Aspect

The informational aspect of a process concerns the information structures needed for performing its activities. The information structures include the information sent and received from the service under study, as well as information that are internal to the process, i.e. the information sent and received in the service context. Services that do not fit well with the process will require the information to be restructured, for example by requiring that the information is sent in several "documents" rather than one. To discover the services impact on the informational aspect we provide the following guiding question:

- QI1 - Are there any unnecessary re-packaging of information that can be avoided by using an alternative design of the provider's e-service, provider's business rules, or consumers' internal IT systems?

In the Tax Agency case (see Figure 2) we have already seen that the functional aspect of the process is affected because supporting IT systems are not following the same standard procedures and rules as the e-service designed by the Swedish Tax Agency. This mismatch also affects the informational aspect. Even thought detailed document flow is not provided in the sample process, we can see (using QI1) that the extra information provided during the "Make annotations" is required to be merged into the main declaration information in the activity, i.e. "Prepare and audit information". In essence this means that an information requirement is affecting not only the informational aspect, but also the functional, because there is a need to have extra activities to produce the requested information. As stated in Section 5.1, the alternative solution to this problem is potentially to change the provider's business rules or the consumers' IT systems.

5.4 Analysing the Organisational Process Aspect

The organisational aspect of a business process concerns who is responsible for executing the activities. In some process modelling notations, such as BPMN and UML Activity diagrams, swim lanes/partitions are used in the diagram to group together activities that a role is responsible for or should be performed by. Roles can be representing an entire organisation (i.e. "Manufacturer", "Service consumer"), or roles within an organisation (i.e. "Accountant", "CIO").

When analysing if an e-service causes problems in the process organisational aspect, we need to examine which roles are needed to perform the service interaction, and the activities that are executed before and after the interaction. To discover limitations to the use of roles and individuals we propose to use the following questions:

- QO1 - Are there any unnecessary use of specific roles that can be avoided by using an alternative design of the provider's e-service, provider's business rules, or consumers' internal IT systems?
- QO2 - Are there any unnecessary limitation of the number of actors/individuals that can take different roles and that can be avoided by using an alternative design of the provider's e-service, provider's business rules, or consumers' internal IT systems?

The organisational aspect (in the form of swim lanes/partitions) is not shown in the process of the Tax Agency case (Figure 2) to avoid cluttering. The use of the declaration e-service does not impose any restrictions on who performs each activity - except when it comes to the signing of the declaration. This can only be done by someone who is authorized signatory of the company (typically the owners and CEO) or an appointed ombudsman for declarations. Thus, posing the QO1 question points us towards some restrictions in the service design. The solution, if needed, is to be found in the areas of changed provider's business rules. The rules could be changed so there is a possibility for more roles to sign the declaration than is allowed today according to rules at the Swedish Tax Agency.

It is interesting to note that the restrictions of requiring a traditional authorised signatory is somewhat amended by the possibility to appoint a specific individual as ombudsman. However, the use of ombudsman to perform the signature is quite limited - since there can only be a single individual appointed for each company (this limitation is exposed by asking the questions QO2). The Swedish Tax Agency is currently investigating the possibility of changing the regulations so that a company can have several ombudsmen that are allowed to sign the declarations. This change is clearly in the provider's business rules solution area.

6 Solution Summary

The result from the previous step is a number of problems that an e-service causes in a consumer's business process as well as potential solutions. Each problem is associated with a certain process aspects, and the solutions are related to solution areas as well. However, each problem can have several solutions, and each solution require a mix of changes in different solution areas. This will give a rather complex picture of problems and possible solutions. Thus, the identified problems and solutions need to be presented so that the managers and e-service designers can get an overview, and, thereby, make rational decisions which solution to choose to solve a certain problem. Therefore, in this step, we introduce an instrument in form of a simple table structure.

Table 2. Overview of the problems and solutions

Aspect	Problem	Consumer Process Improvement	Provider Rules	Provider E-Service	Consumer IT systems
Functional	Manual entry of declarations	Remove activity, let the system interact with e-service		New service API needed	×
Functional	Unnecessary annotations activities	Remove activities, let the IT system handle this	Change tax rules to fit systems	×	
Functional	Unnecessary annotations activities	Remove activities, let the IT system handle this			Change systems to fit rules
Behavioral	Transactions handled on a monthly basis	Remove the monthly collection of transactions	Allow continuous reporting	×	×
Behavioral	Merged handling of VAT and salaries	De-couple the VAT and salary declarations		Separate VAT and salary entry	
Informa-tional	*(same as functional and behavioral in the case)*				
Organisational	Limited set of roles allowed to sign	Let the signing activity be performed by more roles	Expand the roles allowed to sign	×	
Organisational	Only one individual can act as ombudsman	Let any individual in a role sign	Allows several ombudsmen to sign	×	

The table structure is as follows (see Table 2, in which we applied the table structure on the Tax Agency case): The two leftmost columns describe the process aspects and the identified problems. The following four columns show the solution areas. Each row represents a problem, and if a problem got several solutions it is simply repeated in several rows (see for example row 2 and 3). For every problem there is a consumer process solution that addresses the problem. However the consumer process change must be supported by a change in at least one of the solutions areas: the service provider's business rules, the service provider's e-service or the service consumers' IT systems.

A change in a solution area, which aims to enable a change in the consumers' business processes, can also cause changes in other solution areas. To indicate this in the table, we simply put a cross in the areas that can be caused. For example, a problem identified from the Tax Agency case is that transactions can only be handled on a monthly basis (see row four in Table 2). The problem can be solved by changing the consumers' processes so that they can manage such continuous reporting. This requires that the service provider's business rule change so that continuously reporting can be allowed at the Swedish Tax Agency. However, such a change of the provider's business rule can, in turn, cause changes in both the design of the e-service and the consumers' business processes and IT systems. Note that six out of seven proposed changes primarily affect the e-service provider. The changes in the consumer process are positive effects of these changes, i.e. they represent improvements from the consumer's perspective.

In the described Tax Agency case, the informational problems described in Section 5.3 overlap with the behavioural and functional problems described in Section 5.1. We therefore exclude the informational problems from the table.

The table can also be used as a basis for further detailing of the solutions. For example, there might be different cost associated to performing each solution.

7 Conclusion

In this paper, we have presented an approach for identifying and analysing problems related to the e-service impact on the consumers' business processes, as well as identifying tentative solutions. The approach is based on four well-known process aspects. Since the process aspects are well-known, the novelty of the approach lies elsewhere. Firstly, we consider a larger process scope than just the service interaction, that is, we advocate the analysis of its service context as well. Secondly, we use the four aspect framework to drive the analysis, but we provide a set of guiding questions, based on the framework, for simplifying the analysis. Furthermore, the usage of the questions ensures that no aspect of the process is overlooked. Thirdly, to aid both the problem and the solution identification we introduce a set of solution areas. The solution areas and process aspect are combined to get an overview of the identified problems and solutions. Again, in order to simplify this step, we provide a set of guiding questions to use. Finally, we present a table structure to visualise the complexity of problems and possible solutions and how a solution require of a mix of changes in different solution areas.

The presented approach leaves rooms for future research. The process perspective misses to describe things not related to activities and their inputs and outputs [16]. Thus, there is a need to combine the approach with other approaches to cover other effects of service use that cannot be described in the form of a process. Using goal models and value models could be candidates in this area [14]. Another limitation of the approach is that it cannot directly be applied to organisations that do not work according to a business process structure. For example, some work requires a more flexible ad-hoc working structure. Further work thus entails modifying the approach to cope with these circumstances. Finally, we would like to validate the approach in several case studies. Despite these areas for improvements we consider the approach to be a valuable part of any e-service designers' toolkit.

Acknowledgements

The SAMMET project is partially funded by the Swedish agency for innovation systems (VINNOVA). The authors would like to thank the persons that participated in the interviews, as well as the personnel at the Swedish Tax Agency.

References

1. Edvardsson, B., Gustafsson, A., Johnson, M.D., Sandén, B.: New service development and innovation in the new economy. Studentlitteratur, Lund (2000)
2. Hruby, P., Kiehn, J., Scheller, C.: Model-Driven Design Using Business Patterns. Springer, Heidelberg (2006) ISBN 978-3540301547
3. SAMMET, SAMMET Project site (2010), http://www.dsv.su.se/sammet (accessed 2010-12-05)
4. Jablonski, S.: Workflow-Management-Systeme: Modellierung und Architektur. Thomson Publishing (1995)
5. Rausch-Scott, S.: TriGSflow - Workflow Management Based on Object-oriented Database Systems and Extended Transaction Mechanisms, PhD Thesis, University of Linz (1997)
6. Erl, T.: SOA Principles of Service Design. Prentice Hall, Englewood Cliffs (2007) ISBN 978-0132344821
7. Josuttis, M.: SOA in Practice: The Art of Distributed System Design. O'Reilly Media, Sebastopol (2007) ISBN 978-0596529550
8. Arsanjani, A., et al.: SOMA: A Method for Developing Service-Oriented Solutions. IBM Systsms Journal 47(3), 377–396 (2008)
9. Piccinelli, G., Emmerich, W., Zirpins, C., Schütt, K.: Web Service Interfaces for Inter-Organisational Business Processes – An Infrastructure for Automated Reconciliation. In: Proceedings of the 6th International Enterprise Distributed Object Computing Conference (EDOC 2002), Lausanne, Switzerland, September 17-20, pp. 285–292. IEEE Computer Society Press, Los Alamitos (2002)
10. Papazoglou, M.P., Yang, J.: Design Methodology for Web Services and Business Processes. In: Buchmann, A., Casati, F., Fiege, L., Hsu, M.-C., Shan, M.-C. (eds.) TES 2002. LNCS, vol. 2444, pp. 54–64. Springer, Heidelberg (2002)
11. Scriven, M.: Evaluation Thesaurus. SAGE Publications, Thousand Oaks (1991) ISBN 9780803943643
12. Goldkuhl, G.: Socio-instrumental service modelling: An inquiry on e-services for tax declarations. In: Persson, A., Stirna, J. (eds.) PoEM 2009. LNBIP, vol. 39, pp. 207–221. Springer, Heidelberg (2009)
13. Gordijn, J., Yu, E., Raadt van der, B.: e-Service Design Using i* and e3 value Modeling. IEEE Software 23(3), 26–33 (2006)
14. Henkel, M., Johannesson, P., Perjons, E., Zdravkovic, J.: Value and Goal Driven Design of E-Services. In: The IEEE International Conference on e-Business Engineering (ICEBE 2007), Hong Kong, China, October 24-26 (2007)
15. Bleistein, S., Cox, K., Verner, J., Phalp, K.: Requirements engineering for e-business advantage. Requirements Engineering 11(1), 4–16 (2006)
16. Goldkuhl, G., Röstlinger, A.: The significance of work practice diagnosis: Socio-pragmatic ontology and epistemology of change analysis. In: Goldkuhl, G., Lind, M., Ågerfalk, P.J. (eds.) Proceedings of Action in Language, Organizations and Information Systems, pp. 27–50 (2003)

Is It Beneficial to Match Reusable Services Earlier?

Sebastian Adam, Oezguer Uenalan, and Norman Riegel

Fraunhofer IESE, Fraunhofer Platz 1, 67663 Kaiserslautern
{sebastian.adam,oezguer.uenalan,
norman.riegel}@iese.fraunhofer.de

Abstract. **[Context and motivation]** Achieving a tight fit between requirements and reusable assets is not the usual case in practice, even if especially
SOA makes such promises. The very early consideration of existing services
and their alignment with requirements have therefore been recommended by
several references, as otherwise the fit will rather depend on luck. **[Question /
problem]** However, empirical evidence about the benefits of such "match
early" approaches is rare, at least with regard to SOA. **[Principle ideas /
results]** This paper therefore describes two empirical studies done to investigate
possible benefits. **[Contribution]** The results of a controlled experiment performed in this regard have not confirmed any claimed benefits from a statistical
point of view. However, the application of "match early" in an industrial case
study indicates benefits especially with regard to effectiveness.

Keywords: requirements engineering, SOA, reuse, empirical study.

1 Introduction

The paradigm of SOA [1] promises high flexibility for enterprises and their application landscapes. In particular, services are expected to be reused and recombined in
new and innovative ways without the need to make all their potential usage scenarios
explicit in advance. However, a tight fit between software services and business requirements is not the usual case in practice, and many parts of a service landscape still
have to be renewed, leading to the situation that the desired benefits of reuse in SOA
cannot be fully exploited[1].

Among others, we identified the common use of traditional requirements engineering (RE) methods in service-based application development as a reason for this loose
fit [3]. Following this traditional RE perspective, the capabilities of a given reuse
infrastructure are not considered during requirements analysis at all, leaving it up to
the developers to map requirements to existing assets [9]. The risk of this approach,
which is still being proposed even by leading vendors [16], is that requirements usually do not fit a reuse infrastructure at first glance, resulting in either time-consuming
renegotiations, or the renouncement of a high degree of reuse, respectively costly
adaptations. Hence, even if services are systematically planned for reuse (as shown in
[4], for instance), the benefits of reuse will not automatically arise.

---

[1] On average, only around 13.5% development costs are saved through reuse in SOA projects [5].

D. Berry and X. Franch (Eds.): REFSQ 2011, LNCS 6606, pp. 136–150, 2011.
© Springer-Verlag Berlin Heidelberg 2011

Unfortunately, state-of-the-art reuse approaches from the product line area (e.g., [6]), which address this problem by explicitly linking requirements with reusable assets, are not widely applied in SOA, as the underlying assumption of a stable domain and a fixed set of products is often not fulfilled in this context.

Thus, when high flexibility is required, reconciling requirements with the capabilities and constraints of a reuse infrastructure is still a challenging and often unsystematic task today [7][18]. Several references such as [3][8][9][10] therefore highlight the need to consider, align, and negotiate requirements and reuse capabilities at a very early stage already, as otherwise their fit will rather depend on luck. We call such as approaches "match-early" approaches. In addition, requirements completeness is also expected to be positively influenced when reusable assets are used as inspiration during the elicitation phase already [14].

However, empirical evidence about the benefits of such "match early" approaches is rare, at least with regard to SOA. It is therefore interesting to see whether approaches that try to align requirements and software services during early RE activities already are more beneficial than those matching late and then initiating rework if necessary. In this paper, we therefore describe and present the results of both a controlled experiment and a case study for elaborating which impacts an early match has on service-oriented development[2]. For that purpose, we have compared our own "match early" approach (see [13] for an extensive method description) with a typical "match late" approach in order to assess its feasibility, effectiveness (i.e., completeness and fitness), and efficiency. Of course, discovering, browsing, understanding, and selecting services, as well as mapping them to problems and requirements are long-lasting and complex activities, which cannot be simplified in a controlled experiment. Our research contribution is therefore just the investigation whether the point in time at which these activities take place makes a difference.

The remainder of this paper is structured as follows: In the next section, we introduce the two approaches to be evaluated. The controlled experiment and its results are then described in section 3, while section 4 adds some further experience gathered in a real world-case study. The paper closes with a discussion and a conclusion in sections 5 and 6.

2   Background

Basically, "selection" and "mapping" approaches can be distinguished in reuse-based requirements engineering. "Selection" approaches allow customers to select predefined requirements or features that are closest to their actual needs. "Mapping" approaches, in contrast, aim at aligning real customer requirements with existing features in order to select a best-fitting product and to identify necessary adaptations. These mapping approaches can be further classified into "match early" and "match late" approaches. Below, the two mapping approaches are described in more detail.

---

[2] The research described in this paper was carried out in the SoKNOS project (grant no. 01ISO7009) and the ADiWa project (grant no. 01IA08006F), both projects funded by the German Federal Ministry of Education and Research.

2.1 "Match early" Approach

"Match early" approaches are based on the assumption that requirements in reuse-based development must be less specific and less complete than in traditional development, as too stringent requirements may exclude promising reusable assets, or imply costly modifications [17]. Following a "match early" approach as described in [13] or [15], only high-level customer requirements in terms of business processes or workflows should therefore be elicited and specified in a first step (see left part of Figure 1). Based on these initial requirements, suitable software services, which could potentially support the fulfillment of the high-level requirements, are then identified, preselected, and linked to the corresponding requirements. In close discussions with the customer, it is then determined whether and how the service capabilities can actually be used to fulfill the high-level requirements. To support this decision, the high-level requirements are refined (e.g., into system use cases or more fine-grained workflows) and matched to the service capabilities while considering possible constraints. Hence, trade-off decisions can be made immediately when conflicts occur. Thus, a tight fit of requirements and software services can be achieved in a constructive rather than an analytical way, leading to less rework cycles.

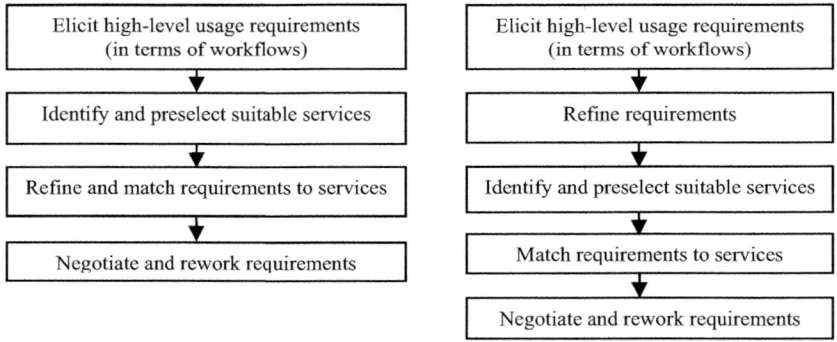

Fig. 1. Match early (left) and match late (right)

2.2 "Match late" Approach

Following a "match late" approach (see right part of Figure 1), the almost complete elicitation and specification of customer requirements is the first step. The idea behind this approach is that also detailed requirements of customers should be completely understood, as otherwise there is a risk that customers must adapt themselves to a system and not vice versa [19]. Based on such an almost complete set of requirements, suitable software services are then identified, preselected, and linked. Using different fitness measures (e.g., as proposed by [20]), conflicts between requirements and reuse capabilities can be identified. Furthermore, resolution actions including their effort and risk are determined [15]. The requirements are then negotiated with the customer and trade-off decisions are made. Thus, a tight fit of requirements and software services requires a certain number of rework cycles.

2.3 Analytic Comparison

The difference between "match early" and "match late" is essentially how much requirements engineering is done before services are identified and aligned. At first glance, it seems that "match early" is much more efficient, because rework or wasted effort is expected to be minimized. On the other hand, however, the consideration of services during elicitation and refinement takes additional time, which might exceed the time needed for negotiating conflicting requirements in case of need.

Also with regard to the effectiveness (i.e., completeness and fit), it remains unclear which approach is able to achieve higher values. Even if the potential for influence and support is basically higher in "match early", both approaches consider existing services in the end, and foster their alignment explicitly. Thus, as it is hard to compare both approaches in an analytic way, an empirical investigation seems to be justified.

3 Controlled Experiment

3.1 Experiment Organization

In this section, we present the experimental setup, including goal, participants, used material, hypotheses, etc.

3.1.1 Goal and Research Questions

Again, as discovering, browsing, understanding, and selecting services, as well as mapping them to problems and requirements are complex activities, the sole research question was the determination whether the point in time at which a mapping between software services and requirements takes place makes a difference. According to GQM [12], the derived goal of our evaluation was to analyze a *"match early" and a "match late" approach* for the purpose of *comparison* with respect to *effectiveness and efficiency* from the viewpoint of *a requirements engineer with domain knowledge* in the context of a *controlled experiment*. In particular, we would like to know:

- Can the **fit** between requirements and service capabilities be increased when existing services are considered early in the definition of requirements?
- Do requirements have **higher completeness** when existing services are considered early as inspiration?
- Do stakeholders **feel more satisfied** when they know the capabilities and constraints of a service infrastructure before they start stating their requirements?
- Can the **efficiency** of a requirements process be improved when service capabilities and constraints are considered earlier?

3.1.2 Participants (Subjects)

The participants in the experiment were 18 computer science master students (6 female, 12 male) from the Technical University of Kaiserslautern, Germany, enrolled in the Requirements Engineering lecture, as well as 12 Fraunhofer employees (2 female, 10 male) with industrial experience (>4 years on average) in RE for information systems. The participants were 28 years old on average, and all were trained in the skills, but not in the material needed for the experimental tasks. Furthermore, both parties participated voluntarily in the experiment. They were not informed about our hypotheses or study goal beforehand.

3.1.3 Experiment Design

The experiment was designed as a blocked subject-object study, where each of the participants was randomly assigned. In order to check whether both groups were quite homogenous, we analyzed the results of our pre-questionnaire (see Table 1).

Table 1. Assignment of participants to treatments

	Group 1	Group 2
Treatment	Match early	Match late
# Subjects	15	15
Average age	27	29
# Subjects with high RE experience	5	7
# Subjects with good use case performance	4	7

3.1.4 Procedure

After performing a pilot test to check the applicability of the test material, we first performed the experiment with the 12 experts, whom we assigned randomly, but with equal numbers of participants, to both groups. Before letting each participant perform the experiment, we did the pre-interview including the performance tests in order to get data about his / her experience (see Table 1 again). After giving a short introduction, each participant then got the materials according to the group he / she was assigned to. For the "match late" approach, we had prepared two material packages: one for writing the use cases without any consideration of existing services, and one package for matching the use cases with the services afterwards according to the concept of "match late". Thus, the second package was handed out after a participant had finished the instructions of the first package. After the participant had finished completely, we let him / her fill out the post-questionnaire in order to get subjective impressions. In a second round, we then performed the experiment with the student group, from which each participant was again assigned randomly to one of the two groups, comprising of an equal numbers of participants. The experiment was then held as a joint session during the weekly lecture's exercise slot (restricted to 90 min).

3.1.5 Material

The following materials[3] were prepared and provided during the experiment:

Pre-questionnaire. In order to get statistical information about each participant (sex, age, course of study, experience with RE, etc.) and to check his / her performance in explaining business process diagrams and writing use cases, a pre-questionnaire was provided. Besides closed multiple-choice questions, two tasks were included to measure the performance. The first task aimed at measuring how well each participant was able to understand the business process diagram used in the experiment (see below). Hence, the task was to paraphrase this graphical model. The second task aimed at measuring how well and how fast each participant was able to write use cases according to a tabular structure. Thus, we asked each participant to write the well-known use case "withdraw money from an ATM".

---

[3] http://www2.iese.fraunhofer.de/download/experimentPackage.zip

Scenario descriptions. The context in which the participants should imagine themselves during the experiment was an organization that aimed at introducing a service-based application to manage the business trips of its employees. Each participant was asked to play the role of an employee who is familiar with the business travel domain and with requirements engineering. Hence, the task to be performed in the experiment was to write use cases for a business travel application based on a business process diagram. However, to reflect the idea of the different match approaches, we prepared two variants of the scenario description. Hence, the "match early" group got a scenario in which each participant was explicitly asked to consider a set of reusable services right from the beginning. In contrast, the "match late" group at first only got a scenario in which each participant was asked to refine the business activities into use cases without any consideration of services. However, after this task was completed, a continuation of the scenario was provided in which each participant was asked to match a given set of services to the written use cases.

Business process diagram. The business process diagram, which was provided to both groups together with the (first) scenario, described the control flow and data flow of a business travel process ranging from the creation of a business trip application to the reimbursement of expenses. The business process diagram was drawn using the notation of EPC [11], which was taught to all participants before.

Data collection sheet. The data collection sheet was provided in order to allow each participant to track his / her start and end times during the experiment. The point in time at which tracking should be done was described in the experiment instructions.

Experiment instructions. We prepared precise, checklist-like experiment instructions for each participant. Similar to the scenario description, the experiment instructions were also split for the "match late" group.

Use case writing guideline. In order to assure that the use cases were written well, a short use case writing guideline was provided.

Use case templates. For each business activity to be refined in the form of a use case (only four business activities should be refined), we prepared one use case template. However, only the flow description was left empty; all other attributes such as goal, actor, etc. were already filled out by us.

Conceptual service descriptions. The (human-understandable) conceptual service description (CSD) was a package of ten pages, where each page described a cohesive set of functions assumed to be provided by an underlying service infrastructure. The level of abstraction was chosen on the level of Use Case steps (including parameters), i.e., system functions that could be explicitly invoked by users when doing a task (e.g., get list of all available hotels in a certain city (city, timeframe)). The CSD were prepared by a domain expert, and included all functions that are typically needed to support the administration of a complete business travel process. Thus, the descriptions simulated a service registry.

Post-questionnaire. Finally, a post-questionnaire was provided in which the participants were asked to assess certain properties of the used match method and the CSD based on a Likert scale. Furthermore, they were asked how satisfied they were with the use cases they wrote during the experiment.

3.1.6 Variables and Hypotheses

The independent variable (treatment) controlled in our experiment was the used match approach ("match early" vs. "match late") as described in section 2. In order to identify and define hypotheses and dependent variables (metrics), we refined our study goal as follows according to the GQM approach:

Table 2. Variables and hypothesis

Variable	Question	Metric	Hypothesis
Completeness	Which match approach leads to a higher degree of completeness?	Percentage of specified use case steps that are marked as being essential in a domain expert's sample solution for achieving the goal of the use case	Use cases written following the "match early" approach are more complete than use cases written following the "match late" approach $H1_0: \mu 1_{ME} \leq \mu 1_{ML}$ $H1_1: \mu 1_{ME} > \mu 1_{ML}$
Fit	Which match approach leads to a higher fit between customer requirements and service capabilities?	Percentage of specified system steps in use cases that can be realized through service functions provided in set of services	Use cases written following the "match early" approach better fit a given reuse infrastructure than use cases written following the "match late" approach $H2_0: \mu 2_{ME} \leq \mu 2_{ML}$ $H2_1: \mu 2_{ME} > \mu 2_{ML}$
Satisfaction	Which match approach leads to use cases that better reflect the customers' actual expectations?	Subjective assessment of requirements on ordinal scale using different question items (1=bad, 2=rather bad, 3=rather good, 4=good)	Participants are more satisfied with use cases written by following the "match early" approach than with use cases written by following the "match late" approach. $H3_0: \mu 3_{ME} \leq \mu 3_{ML}$ $H3_1: \mu 3_{ME} > \mu 3_{ML}$
Completion Speed	Which match approach leads to a higher degree of completeness within a certain period of time?	Percentage of specified use case steps necessary to achieve the goal of a business activity / time needed for performing the experiment (in minutes) * 60	After one hour, the use cases specified so far are more complete when following the "match early" approach than when following the "match late" approach. $H4_0: \mu 4_{ME} \leq \mu 4_{ML}$ $H4_1: \mu 4_{ME} > \mu 4_{ML}$
Alignment Speed	Which match approach leads to a higher fit within a certain period of time?	Percentage of specified system steps in use cases that can be realized through service functions described in the set of services / time needed for performing the experiment (in minutes) * 60.	After one hour, the use cases specified by following the "match early" approach so far have a better fit with the service capabilities than the requirements specified by following the "match late" approach. $H5_0: \mu 5_{ME} \leq \mu 5_{ML}$ $H5_1: \mu 5_{ME} > \mu 5_{ML}$

All metrics were immediately derived from our research questions. As we were interested in the completeness of the requirements and as the experiment produced just use cases as working results, the completeness of a use case with regard to a sample solution was apparently a meaningful metric, for instance. Accordingly, the time needed to achieve a certain degree of completeness was also a meaningful metric to measure the efficiency of the compared approaches. The same held true for the fit. With regard to satisfaction, we are aware that there are much better instruments to measure satisfaction, but such details were beyond the main scope of our study.

3.2 Experiment Analysis

In this section, we present all information that is necessary to analyze and understand the results of our experiment. However, as the interpretation of these results is also influenced by the experiences made in our case study, the interpretation will only be described in section 5.

3.2.1 Analysis Procedure

In order to perform the analysis, we reviewed all final use cases and measured the metrics after the "Negotiate and rework requirements" step. For determining completeness, we compared each participant's use cases with the domain expert's standard solution, and for the fit, we compared each use cases with the functionality provided in the CSD. Based on these measures as well as the required effort of each participant, which was tracked in addition, the completion speed and alignment speed were finally calculated. For satisfaction, we took the average of the values for the given ratings. All measured and calculated values were then used for descriptive statistics as shown in Table 3. Furthermore, we performed Mann-Whitney U tests (α=0.05) for checking our hypotheses using the SPSS tool (see Table 4). We used this test due to the small sample size and the non-normal distribution of some variables. In addition, the post-questionnaires were analyzed.

3.2.2 Results

Table 3 shows that the means of almost all measured, dependent variables are higher, respectively better in the group that used the "match early" approach. In the following, we investigate the results of the statistical tests for each hypothesis.

Table 3. Results of descriptive statistics[4]

			Match early		Match late	
			AVG	STD	AVG	STD
Completeness		All participants	62%	16%	59%	15%
		Experts	69%	16%	69%	11%
		Students	57%	15%	51%	14%
Fit		All participants	92%	8%	86%	9%
		Experts	95%	6%	89%	5%
		Students	90%	9%	85%	11%
Satisfaction		All participants	3.28	0.48	3.24	0.56
		Experts	3.68	0.40	3.52	0.32
		Students	3.00	0.36	3.04	0.64
Completion speed		All participants	63%	24%	56%	16%
		Experts	75%	25%	61%	17%
		Students	56%	22%	52%	15%
Alignment speed		All participants	94%	23%	83%	15%
		Experts	104%	28%	79%	20%
		Students	87%	18%	85%	11%

---

[4] $N_{Experts}$ = 12, $N_{Students}$=18, AVG = mean, STD = standard deviation.

H1. Completeness: As shown in Table 3, the difference between the means of "match early" (62%) and "match late" (59%) is quite low with regard to completeness. For the experts, there was no difference in the means at all. As a consequence, the execution of a significance test showed that our null hypothesis cannot be rejected.

H2. Fit: The difference between the means of "match early" (92%) and "match late" (86%) with regard to fit is also not significant based on the experiment data. However, it is interesting to see that the difference in fit between both groups is more significant for the experts than for the students. This seems to be caused by the fact that the results of the experts are more comparable and close to reality than that of the students.

H3. Satisfaction: Regarding satisfaction, there is almost no difference between "match early" (3.28) and "match late" (3.24) from a descriptive perspective. An equivalence test [2] even showed that satisfaction is equal in both groups. The null hypothesis could therefore not be rejected based on the experiment's data.

H4. Completion Speed: The difference between the means of "match early" (63%) and "match late" (56%) with regard to completion speed is also quite low. As a consequence, our significance test could not reject the null hypothesis. However, it is interesting to see that the savings achieved by the experts are higher than those achieved by the students.

H5. Alignment Speed: The difference between the means of "match early" (94%) and "match late" (83%) with regard to alignment speed is also not significant. However, the savings in average achieved by the experts and those achieved by the students are quite different (25% vs. 2%).

Table 4. Mann-Whitney U results

		p	Decision
Completness	All participants	0.646	Retain $H1_0$
	Experts	0.810	Retain $H1_0$
	Students	0.421	Retain $H1_0$
Fit	All participants	0.124	Retain $H2_0$
	Experts	0.075	Retain $H2_0$
	Students	0.344	Retain $H2_0$
Satisfaction	All participants	0.791	Retain $H3_0$
	Experts	0.382	Retain $H3_0$
	Students	0.360	Retain $H3_0$
Completion speed	All participants	0.430	Retain $H4_0$
	Experts	0.521	Retain $H4_0$
	Students	0.860	Retain $H4_0$
Alignment speed	All participants	0.158	Retain $H5_0$
	Experts	0.107	Retain $H5_0$
	Students	0.757	Retain $H5_0$

3.2.3 Threats to Validity

Wherever possible, threats to validity were constructively avoided when we setup the experiment. The complexity of the material, for instance, was largely realistic for industrial practice, and also the experiment environment was made realistic by providing a concrete scenario. Due to the assignment of each participant to one group only, there were no learning effects. Nobody had done a similar experiment before. The time for the experiment was rather low; hence, concentration problems cannot be assumed. Also, the applicability of the statistical methods was investigated carefully. Finally, the involvement of 12 experienced people allows trusting the results more than if only inexperienced students had performed the experiment. Nevertheless, we identified some potential threats to validity that might influence the results above.

Conclusion Validity: A first possible threat to conclusion validity is the reliability of measures. On the one hand, when analyzing the experimental results, the three authors of this paper shared the work of reviewing the written use cases. Due to different writing styles of the participants (even though precise use case guidelines were provided!), there is a risk that each reviewer measured the completeness, especially that of the rather bad use cases, slightly differently. For the future, we therefore have to improve the inter-rater reliability. On the other hand, the participants tracked the required time on their own. Hence, there is a risk that the time has not been exactly tracked and that small deviations might exist.

Internal Validity: One possible threat to internal validity might be the assignment of the participants. Even though both the involved experts and the involved students were internally quite homogenous as far as their education and prior knowledge was concerned, and even though they were assigned randomly to groups, the pre-questionnaires showed that there were better and more experienced people in the "match late" group than in the "match early" group (see Table 1). Hence, there is a risk that some maybe significant differences between "match early" and "match late" could not be confirmed on $\alpha=0.05$.

External Validity: The aforementioned problem might also influence external validity, because the evaluated methods do not only aim at supporting requirements engineers, but also domain experts (i.e., stakeholders) in deciding how business processes could be realized with a given service infrastructure. Finally, some students in the "match late" group did not seem to be willing to invest much rework when they detected missing requirements or misfits. A major issue regarding external validity is however the fact that the experiment only investigated whether the point in time plays a role. Of course, there are many other aspects such a browsing or negotiation support that are relevant to map requirements to existing software services. However, as already mentioned, these aspects were beyond the scope of our study.

4 Feasibility and Effectiveness in Industry

While no significant difference could be shown in the controlled experiment, it is interesting to see which effectiveness and efficiency a "match early" approach can achieve in real world projects. In a public safety project, we therefore performed three separate interviews to elicit requirements for individual incident management systems based on an existing service platform. Two interviews were performed with staff members of the German police, the other interview with staff members of a German fire station. The platform functionality included around 170 functions and was encapsulated in 17 CSD.

4.1 Goal and Research Questions

According to GQM, our case study goal was to analyze *the "match early" approach* for the purpose of *evaluation* with regard to *effectiveness* from the viewpoint of a *requirements engineer* in the context of *a real industrial project*. The questions we would like to answer in the case study were:

Q_{CS1}. Does the "match early" method lead to complete requirements from a customer's point of view?

Q_{CS2}. Does the "match early" method lead to a tight fit of requirements and service capabilities?

Furthermore, we were interested to see whether "match early" worked anyway in practice.

4.2 Case Study Performance

Each interview was performed by two interviewers. One person took the role of the moderator; the second one was responsible for creating the artifacts that were produced during the workshop (e.g., process descriptions). The interviews were performed as closed interviews and conducted along the following steps: After having identified a challenging incident scenario, a typical flow of such a scenario was sketched using a business process notation. We then presented the CSD to the stakeholders, and briefly explained the capabilities of each service one by one. The stakeholders were asked to choose from the specified services, those that seemed to be useful in the given scenario. Then, we went through the whole scenario and cooperatively annotated the business activities with our conceptual services. Then, use cases were written for each activity within the scenario with due consideration of the functionality of the annotated services.

A thread to validity was that each interview was performed by us (experienced requirements engineers). We were furthermore the ones who created the CSD and who developed the "match early" method described in [13]. Thus, the functionality of the platform as well as the methodological details were well known by us. Hence, there is a risk that interviewers who might not know the whole functionality or the method might not have produced the same good results.

4.3 Observations

In all interviews done during this case study, we gathered the following experience regarding our research questions:

Q_{CS1}. When using the already existing functionality in the form of the CSD, we could foster the consideration of functions that would otherwise have been forgotten. In particular, we experienced that the stakeholders did not have many additions when they were asked to give feedback to the written use cases. On average, only one activity per interview had been forgotten and was added. Minor corrections were incorporated in 26% of the activities. Thus, the use cases were sufficiently complete developed already during the interviews (95% completeness).

Q_{CS2}. Due to the consideration of the CSD during the interviews, we could reuse existing functionality wherever possible. The need to define already existing functions anew was therefore not given. In general, we could fully support 55 or 63 business activities with the existing services (87% fit). Hence, not much functionality was required that did not already exist on the platform.

In general, the focused and closed interviews worked very well, so the applicability in industry-size settings was shown.

5 Interpretation and Discussion

Below, the results of the controlled experiment and the case study as well as their potential implications are discussed according to the four questions we aimed to answer.

*Can the **fit** between requirements and service capabilities be increased when existing services are considered early in the definition of requirements?*

The fact that the fit was higher than 85% in both groups let us assume that a fit mainly depends on the extent to which a service infrastructure is able to satisfy the needs of a stakeholder and less on the time when it is matched. The more a set of services addresses the requirements of a certain domain, the higher the probability that these services can actually be reused. Therefore, thorough "design for reuse" is indispensable when an organization aims at successfully developing systems in a service-based way.

With regard to the "design with reuse" phase that was addressed by our study, we cannot clearly state whether it makes a difference if reuse is forced during the initial elicitation already, or during a subsequent negotiation. Even though a descriptive comparison of the means of "match early" and "match late" reveals that "match early" has a slight advantage regarding fit especially for experts, the difference was not significant based on our experimental data. We therefore recommend replicating the experiment with more experts to get significant data in this regard.

In our industrial case study using "match early", however, we experienced that in each case where a fit was basically possible, a fit was also achieved. Even if there would have been more conflicting stakes, we see no impact on our conclusions, because the required negotiation would benefit from the awareness of the available capabilities, as we experienced that it is feasible to match services and customer requirements early. Thus, the identification of deltas can be done immediately, which saves corresponding rework effort. However, we cannot make clear statements about whether "match early" is actually more beneficial in every case. We therefore claim that the exact point in time seems to be of minor importance with regard to a tight fit.

*Do requirements have **higher completeness** when existing services are considered early as inspiration?*

In our experiment, we got the impression that the overall degree of completeness rather depends on the knowledge a stakeholder has about his / her domain than on the point in time of matching. This impression is confirmed by the group-independent difference in completeness achieved by the experts, who had much domain knowledge, and that of the students, who were less experienced with the business travel domain. Furthermore, the analysis of the ATM use case task in the pre-questionnaire, which was processed very well by all participants without any service descriptions, also showed that the degree of completeness rather depends on personal domain knowledge than on usage of services as a mnemonic. Nevertheless, 100% of the experiment participants in the "match early" group and 80% of the participants in the "match late" group stated in the post-questionnaire that the services supported them at least partially in not forgetting important issues. However, with regard to our second hypothesis, our experimental data do not allow a conclusion as to whether early or late consideration of services has a higher impact on completeness.

Interestingly, the difference in the degree of completeness achieved by the students and experts differs depending on the chosen approach. While there is a significant difference ($p=0.024<0.05$) between the completeness achieved by experts and students using "match late", a significant difference between both using the "match early" approach cannot be confirmed. Therefore, it is expected that the benefit of using services early is mainly helpful for minimizing the gap between the results of experienced and inexperienced people. We therefore hypothesize that the early consideration of existing services also allows guiding or even influencing stakeholders to a certain degree.

*Do stakeholders feel **more satisfied** when they know the capabilities and constraints of a reuse infrastructure before they start stating their requirements?*

Similar to fit, satisfaction with a service-based application also mainly depends on the extent to which the underlying services address the requirements and needs of a stakeholder. In our experiment, we could even show that both methods delivered equal results with regard to satisfaction.

*Can the **efficiency** of a requirements process be improved when reuse capabilities and constraints are considered earlier?*

With regard to efficiency, we do not have any evidence that the effort for reworking requirements in case of need is significantly higher than making it right straight from the beginning. However, as shown in Table 3, experts seem to benefit more from a "match early" approach regarding efficiency than novices. The reason for this difference could be that experts are able to use the knowledge about existing services more appropriately to optimize the requirements process. Another explanation could be that the experts in the "match late" group were willing to actually perform rework when they detected that something was missing or did not fit, while this was not always the case for the students.

Also in the case study, we experienced that the "match early" approach was an efficient means for performing elicitation workshops. We expect this observation to be the main advantage of "match early", as requirements elicitation is typically not integrated with reuse infrastructure matching in today's practice (unfortunately, this setting could not be constructed in a controlled experiment). Rather, following a "match late" approach requirements are pre-processed and aligned with a reuse infrastructure in back office afterwards. If a misfit between requirements and services is detected, new elicitation workshops have to be scheduled, leading to additional effort and a delay in terms of time-to-market.

6 Conclusion

The early alignment of existing services with requirements has been recommended by several references. However, empirical studies investigating whether the point in time actually makes a difference are rare. This paper therefore described two empirical studies to investigate this issue. However, the results of these studies did not confirm any significant differences from a statistical point of view, even though "match early" seems to have slight benefits especially for experts. We therefore claim that only in contexts in which people stating requirements and people mapping requirements to service infrastructures are distributed spatially and temporally, "match early" could have actual benefits. For bringing this claim on a solid basis, we recommend performing additional field studies with experts in real-world settings.

References

1. Krafzig, D., Blanke, K., Slama, D.: Enterprise SOA: Service-Oriented Architecture Best Practices. Prentice Hall PTR, Englewood Cliffs (2004)
2. Schumacher, M., Schulgen, G.: Methodik klinischer Studien. Springer, Heidelberg (2002)
3. Adam, S., Doerr, J.: The Role of Service Abstraction and Service Variability and its Impact on Requirements Engineering for Service-oriented Systems. In: Proceedings of the 32nd IEEE International Computer Software and Applications Conference. IEEE, Los Alamitos (2008)
4. Lee, J., Muthig, D., Naab, M.: Identifying and Specifying Reusable Services of Service Centric Systems through Product Line Technology. In: SOAPL Workshop @ SPLC (2007)
5. Poulin, J., Himler, A.: The ROI of SOA – Based on Transitional Component Reuse, LogicLibrary (2006), http://www.logiclibrary.com/pdf/wp/ROI_of_SOA.pdf
6. Bühne, S., Halmans, G., Lauenroth, K., Pohl, K.: Scenario-Based Application Requirements Engineering. In: Software Product Lines. Springer, Heidelberg (2006)
7. Guelfi, N., Perrouin, G.: A flexible requirements analysis approach for software product lines. In: Sawyer, P., Heymans, P. (eds.) REFSQ 2007. LNCS, vol. 4542, pp. 78–92. Springer, Heidelberg (2007)
8. Lam, W., Jones, S., Britton, C.: Technology Transfer for Reuse: A Management Model and Process Improvement Framework. In: Proceedings of the IEEE International Requirements Engineering Conference. IEEE, Los Alamitos (1998)
9. Baum, L., Becker, M., Geyer, L., Molter, G.: Mapping Requirements to Reusable Components using Design Spaces. In: Proceedings of International Requirements Engineering Conference. IEEE, Los Alamitos (2000)
10. Halmans, G., Pohl, K.: Communicating the variability of a software-product family to customers. In: Software and System Modeling 2003. Springer, Heidelberg (2003)
11. Keller, G., Nüttgens, M., Scheer, A.-W.: Semantische Prozeßmodellierung auf der Grundlage "Ereignisgesteuerter Prozeßketten (EPK)", Universität des Saarlandes (1992)
12. Basili, V.R., Caldiera, G., Rombach, H.D.: Goal Question Metric Paradigm. In: Encyclopedia of Software Engineering, vol. 1, pp. 528–532. John Wiley & Sons, Chichester (1994)
13. Adam, S., Ünalan, Ö., Riegel, N., Kerkow, D.: IT capability-based business process design through service-oriented requirements engineering. In: Halpin, T., Krogstie, J., Nurcan, S., Proper, E., Schmidt, R., Soffer, P., Ukor, R. (eds.) BPMDS 2009 and EMMSAD 2009. LNBIP, vol. 29, pp. 113–125. Springer, Heidelberg (2009)

14. Zachos, K., Maiden, N., Zhu, X., Jones, S.: Discovering web services to specify more complete system requirements. In: Krogstie, J., Opdahl, A.L., Sindre, G. (eds.) CAiSE 2007 and WES 2007. LNCS, vol. 4495, pp. 142–157. Springer, Heidelberg (2007)

15. Mohamed, A., Ruhe, G., Eberlein, A.: MiHOS: an approach to support handling the mismatches between system requirements and COTS products. In: Requirements Engineering, vol. 12. Springer, Heidelberg (2007)

16. Klückmann, J.: White Paper. In: 10 Schritten zur Business-driven SOA. IDS Scheer AG (2007)

17. Lauesen, S.: COTS tender and integration requirements. In: Requirements Engineering, vol. 11. Springer, Heidelberg (2006)

18. O'Leary, P., Rabiser, R., Richardson, I., Thiel, S.: Important Issues and Key Activities in Product Derivation. In: Experiences from Two Independent Research Projects, Software Product Line Conference. SEI (2009)

19. Djebbi, O., Salinesi, C.: RED-PL, a method for deriving product requirements from a product line requirements model. In: Krogstie, J., Opdahl, A.L., Sindre, G. (eds.) CAiSE 2007 and WES 2007. LNCS, vol. 4495, pp. 279–293. Springer, Heidelberg (2007)

20. Alves, C.: COTS-based requirements engineering. In: Cechich, A., Piattini, M., Vallecillo, A. (eds.) Component-Based Software Quality. LNCS, vol. 2693, pp. 21–39. Springer, Heidelberg (2003)

Requirements Engineering for Embedded Systems:
An Investigation of Industry Needs

Ernst Sikora[1], Bastian Tenbergen[2], and Klaus Pohl[2]

[1] Automotive Safety Technologies GmbH, 85080 Gaimersheim, Germany
ernst.sikora@autosafety.de
[2] paluno – The Ruhr Institute for Software Technology,
University of Duisburg-Essen, 45127 Essen, Germany
{bastian.tenbergen,klaus.pohl}@paluno.uni-due.de

Abstract. **[Context and Motivation]** Requirements engineering (RE) research is expected to provide methods that address the specific challenges of industrial systems engineering. **[Question/problem]** For this purpose, researchers need a detailed understanding of the needs and expectations that the industry has regarding RE methods. **[Principal ideas/results]** To identify the key industry needs, we have conducted an in-depth study with representatives from large, internationally operating companies in the domain of embedded systems in Germany. **[Contribution]** This paper reports on the identified industry needs related to the topics natural language vs. requirements models, support for high system complexity, quality assurance of requirements, and intertwining of RE and design.

Keywords: Embedded Systems; Industry Survey; Requirements Models; System Complexity.

1 Introduction

The embedded systems industry expresses a strong demand for new and improved development methods to address major challenges such as barely manageable system complexity and the strict quality demands related to high-assurance systems. Requirements engineering (RE) research is expected to provide RE methods that satisfy the essential needs and constraints of RE practice in this domain. RE researchers and method developers hence need a thorough understanding of the industry needs and constraints. However, there is no recent, systematic attempt to reveal the essential needs and constraints in the embedded systems domain that RE approaches should address. To close this gap, we have conducted a study with the following research question: *What are current industry needs concerning methodological support for requirements engineering in the embedded systems domain?*

We have investigated this research question by means of an in-depth study with seven large internationally operating companies in Germany from five different branches of the embedded systems domain see Section 3.1. While a number of industry surveys have already been conducted and reported in the past, some topics that are of critical importance for RE methods have been investigated with insufficient depth or even been completely neglected. Our study therefore focused on the following topics:

D. Berry and X. Franch (Eds.): REFSQ 2011, LNCS 6606, pp. 151–165, 2011.

- *Topic 1*: Use of natural language vs. requirements models
- *Topic 2*: Support for high system complexity
- *Topic 3*: Quality assurance for requirements
- *Topic 4*: Interrelation of RE and architectural design

In order to gain a rich, in-depth understanding of the subject of investigation, we conducted interviews with all study participants and, in addition, collected data by means of questionnaires.

The paper is structured as follows: first, we summarize the findings from previous studies and practice reports related to our research question (Section 2). Subsequently, we outline our study design (Section 3). Then, we present the results of our study for each topic of interest (Section 4) and draw conclusions for future RE research based on our findings (Section 6). We discuss the validity of our results in Section 6 and provide a summary and outlook in Section 7.

2   Related Work

The existing literature concerning the state of practice and industry needs in RE can be classified into two main categories: empirical studies and industrial case reports. Contributions in the first category include [7], [13], [14], [15], [16], and [25]. Contributions in the second category include [1], [5], [6], [8], [20], and [24]. In the following, we shortly summarize the related work with regard to the four topics of interest outlined in Section 1.

- *Natural language vs. requirements models*: Several studies have investigated the use of models in RE practice. The main results from these studies are that requirements are specified predominantly using natural language and that models are mainly used in an informal manner, e.g. to support elicitation and validation (see e.g. [8], [16], and [24]). However, previous studies have neither investigated whether a more intensive use of models is desired nor which factors inhibit a more intensive use. The paper at hand addresses these shortcomings.
- *Support for high system complexity in RE*: Challenges in RE practice related to high system complexity are reported, for instance, in [8], [13], [14], and [24]. According to [8], the separation of different aspects by means of views is successfully applied in practice to deal with high system complexity. Amongst others, [24] suggests structuring the specification of a complex software-intensive system by means of a hierarchy of abstraction layers. However, practitioners' needs regarding method and tool support for abstraction layers have not been investigated. This paper investigates this issue.
- *Requirements quality assurance*: Previous work such as [4], [7], [8], and [9] reports that major improvements are necessary with regard to the support for the validation and verification of requirements, particularly for high assurance systems. However, there are no definite results about what quality criteria for requirements are most challenging to fulfil in RE practice and hence require improved methodical support. These results are delivered herein.
- *Interrelation of RE and architectural design*: Several authors report a tight interrelation between RE and architectural design in industrial practice (see e.g. [1] and

[4]). Yet, practitioners' needs with regard to an improved support for tightly inter-related RE and design activities have not been investigated. We have investigated this issue and report on the results.

3 Study Design

The study was designed to allow for quantitative and qualitative data to be collected. Section 3.1 explains the study context in which the data was collected. Section 3.2 provides demographic data about the participating professionals. Section 3.3 outlines the investigative method.

3.1 Context of the Study

The study was conducted in 2009 with seven companies from five branches of the embedded systems domain: automation technology, automotive, avionics, medical technology, and energy technology. The companies were large, Germany-based, in-ternationally operating equipment manufacturers, as well as suppliers. Both bespoke as well as market-driven product development is performed by the participating com-panies. Products developed by the participating companies are mainly safety-critical, software-intensive embedded systems.

3.2 Study Participants

The study participants were selected within companies participating in the German Innovation Alliance SPES 2020 (Software Platform Embedded Systems, [10]), partly based on their company roles and partly by convenience sampling (see e.g. [3]). As the study required participants with a good overview of the needs related to RE and other development phases across different projects in their companies, only depart-ment leaders, research personnel, and project consultants were recruited to participate in the study. In total, 17 company representatives participated in the study. The par-ticipants were not balanced across companies. However, when multiple representa-tives from the same company participated, the representatives were recruited from different departments or branches.

3.3 Investigative Method

As the purpose of the study was to gain insight into essential industry needs and the-reby to identify novel research areas in the field of RE, the investigation was of quali-tative nature. However, it was the authors' aim to support the information elicited in the interviews with comparable data. Therefore, a combination of qualitative and quantitative techniques was used. Three data acquisition devices were used: a demo-graphic questionnaire, an interview, and a post-interview questionnaire. These devices are explained in more detail in the following sections. All four RE-related topics out-lined in Section 1 were addressed in the interviews as well as in the questionnaires. The study was conducted in German; the questionnaire and interview guide items have been translated for the purpose of this paper in such way that the emphasis of the individual statements is preserved.

Demographic questionnaire. This questionnaire consisted of 13 short questions about the industrial context and the individual participants' professional backgrounds such as their experience with RE. 60% of the participants' self-reported their experience with RE to be between 5 to 10 years, 20% reported more than 15 years of experience. 90% of the participants self-reported their level of experience in requirements engineering as advanced or expert. Because this study aims at revealing what fields of RE are most pertinent for industry practitioners instead of assessing a typical professional's knowledge about RE, we have chosen the participants' years of experience instead of "knowledge of RE" as the most suitable measure of the participants' qualification.

Interview. The goal of the interviews was to gain deep insight into each participant's views and opinions regarding current RE practice. The total time dedicated to each interview session was about two hours. During the interviews, an interview guide was used to lead the interviewer and interviewee through the conversation. Strict adherence to the interview guide was not enforced, as the interviewer should be allowed to flexibly react to the participants' answers and investigate issues emerging during the interview in more detail. Written protocols documented the participants' answers and were transcribed during the interviews. Each participant reviewed the protocol of his or her respective interview to ensure that the essence of the answers was gathered correctly and to clarify possible misunderstandings.

Post-interview questionnaire. The goal of this questionnaire was to gain quantitative data supplementing the qualitative data from the interviews in order to ease interpretation of the data. The questionnaire contained statements related to RE practice and industrial needs that have been identified through an extensive literature research and pre-study discussions with embedded systems professionals. The questionnaire consisted of about 60 items. About 45 of these items contained predefined statements to which the participants could express their approval or disapproval using five-point-scales ("1: applies never/strongly disagree", "2: applies rarely/disagree", "3: applies sometimes/indifferent", "4: applies often/agree", and "5: applies always/strongly agree"; multiple answers were discouraged). The remaining items were to be answered according to predetermined answer choices (multiple answers were allowed). We used adverbs such as "predominantly" or "often" in our questions to make clear that we were interested in the typical case and did not expect that an individual company representative can make a general statement that holds for the entire company. Thereby, we aimed to avoid mediocrity in the data.

From the 17 participants, 10 answered the questionnaires completely. The results from the all completed post-interview questionnaires are used in this paper to support our findings.

4   Key Results of the Study

This section reports on the findings of the investigation for each topic of interest as defined in Section 1. Section 5 draws conclusions for future research in RE resulting from our study.

4.1 Natural Language vs. Requirements Models

RE approaches investigated by researchers are mainly focused on model-based RE. In contrast, requirements are documented in practice predominantly using natural language. Therefore, a major question of the study was in how far practitioners regard model-based RE approaches as beneficial.

We checked our assumption regarding the use of natural language by means of a questionnaire item stating "requirements are available to us predominantly as text documents". As can be seen from Fig. 1 the participants mostly expressed agreement.

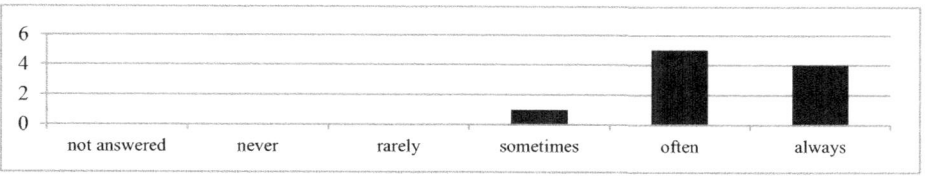

Fig. 1. Participants' answers for the statement "Requirements are available to us predominantly as text documents"

Despite natural language being the dominant documentation form for requirements, the study participants expressed dissatisfaction with the use of natural language. This is supported by Fig. 2. Half of the participants agreed with the statement that using natural language to document requirements is not satisfactory. Only one participant expressed disagreement.

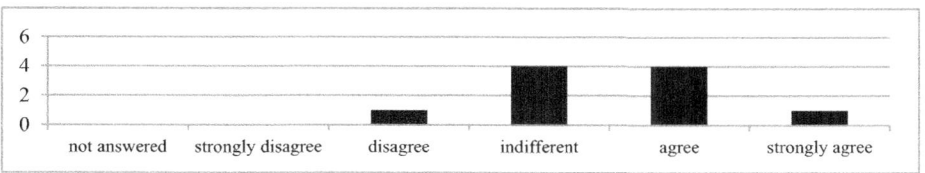

Fig. 2. Participants' answers for the statement "The specification of requirements by means of natural language is often not satisfying"

Concerning the use of models in current RE practice, most participants expressed a rather low intensity of model use in requirements specifications. This is supported by the participants' answers to the corresponding questionnaire item shown in Fig. 3, Graph a). The interviews revealed that models are typically not considered as an appropriate way of documenting legally binding requirements. Furthermore, the use of models in requirements specifications is not mandatory in most companies. Hence, they are not included in the final requirements documents that are provided, for instance, to suppliers.

However, the interviews revealed that models are frequently as a supportive means during RE. For instance, as depicted in Fig. 3, Graph b), most participants agree that models often or always help them understand complex requirements more easily. According to the interviews, domain-specific models of the product (such as a power

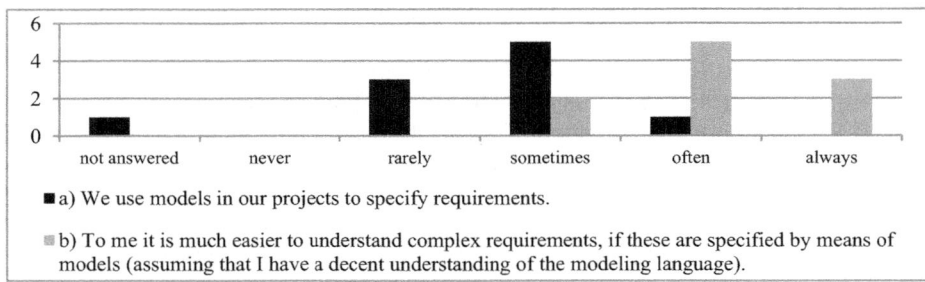

a) We use models in our projects to specify requirements.

b) To me it is much easier to understand complex requirements, if these are specified by means of models (assuming that I have a decent understanding of the modeling language).

Fig. 3. Participants' answers for two questionnaire items concerning the benefits of model use

plant or an airplane) as well as models of the structure, functions, and behavior (such as UML/SysML) of the embedded system are used to support RE activities.

In the questionnaire, the participants stated which models they regard as beneficial for RE. The results are shown in Fig. 4. Interestingly, while goal-oriented RE plays an important role in current research [23], goal modeling appears to be only of marginal importance in current practice.

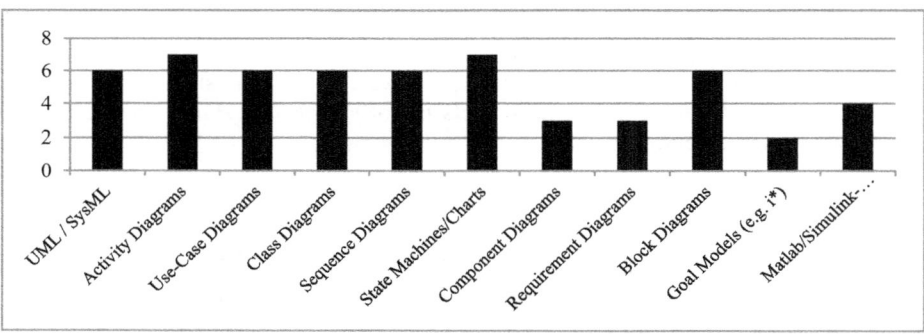

Fig. 4. Participants' answers for the questionnaire item "The following modeling languages and model types can be used gainfully in RE." Multiple answers per participant were possible.

Summarizing, models are regarded as a supportive means for communication, collaboration, and analysis, but are not used for specifying legally binding requirements.

Several participants stated that a major obstacle for using models more intensively in RE is the lack of appropriate method guidance and/or (commercial) tool support. The lack of method guidance leads to uncertainty about how models should be used in the RE process. In particular, participants proposed that especially uncertainties concerning the satisfaction of legal and contractual matters as well as safety standards (e.g. RTCA DO 178B [21]) impair more intensive model use. Furthermore, according to several participants, substantial confusion exists concerning the distinction between requirements and design models. The dissatisfaction with method and tool support for model use in RE is also confirmed by the questionnaire results depicted in Fig. 5, Graph a).

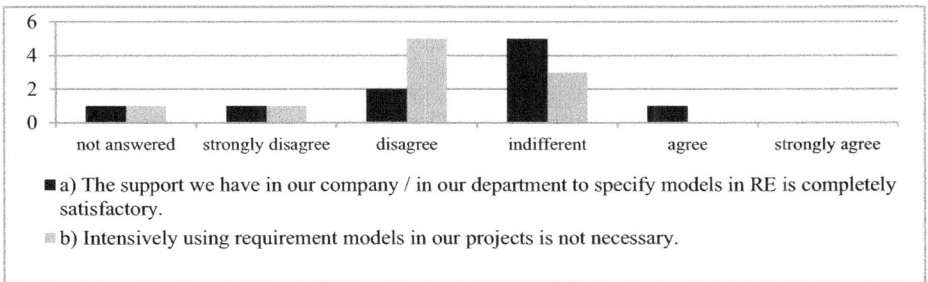

a) The support we have in our company / in our department to specify models in RE is completely satisfactory.

b) Intensively using requirement models in our projects is not necessary.

Fig. 5. Participants' answers for two questionnaire statements concerning the satisfaction with support for model use during RE and the need for more intensive model use in RE

Despite the identified difficulties, most study participants expressed a strong wish for using models more intensively in RE. More than half of the participants consider that an intensive use of requirements models is necessary for their projects (see Fig. 5, Graph b). Note, that since a negative formulation was used for the corresponding questionnaire item, the participants, who expressed (strong) disagreement, are in favor of intensive model use.

4.2 Support for High System Complexity

As depicted in Fig. 6, the study participants expressed a low satisfaction with the support of existing RE methods for developing complex systems.

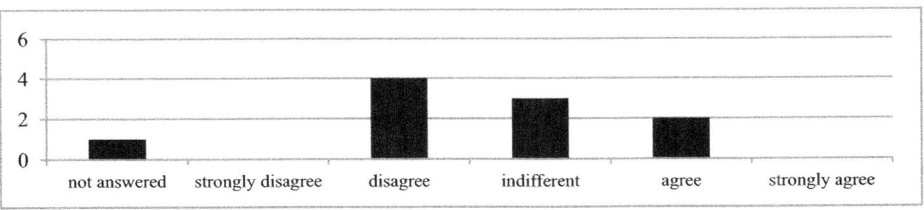

Fig. 6. Participants' answers for the statement "Existing requirements engineering methods are capable of dealing with the complexity of the systems we develop"

The lack of appropriate RE method support for complex systems leads, for instance, to an enormous effort needed to ensure requirements consistency across different engineering domains such as mechanics, electronics, software of a system or product.

In the study, the use of abstraction layers was identified as an important means for dealing with high system complexity in practice. In the questionnaire, six participants reported that their projects often or always involve the specification of requirements at different abstraction layers (Fig. 7). The number of abstraction layers that are used ranged from two to six. In some cases, the use of abstraction layers is formally imposed. For instance, standards such as [2] and [21] define several abstraction layers of requirements.

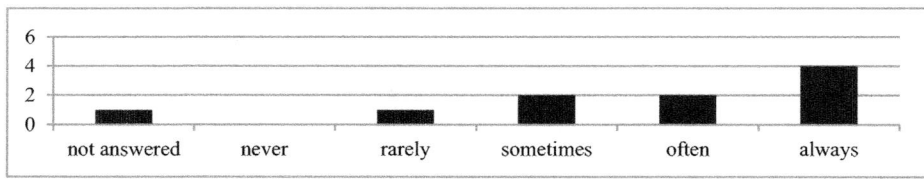

Fig. 7. Participants' answers for the statement "In our company/in our department, requirements are strictly managed on different abstraction layers (e.g. market/product requirements, system requirements, subsystem requirements, or hardware/software requirements)"

The use of abstraction layers and the satisfaction with the existing support for developing requirements across multiple abstraction layers were investigated in more detail in the study. The interviews revealed that despite abstraction layers being in use, there is a substantial confusion regarding what should and should not be contained in the requirements specification at the different abstraction layers. In addition, existing requirements management tools are considered unsatisfactory for dealing with requirements at different abstraction layers.

Nearly all participants expressed a strong need for methodical support for refining requirements across abstraction layers. This finding is also supported by the questionnaire results depicted in Fig. 8, Graph a).

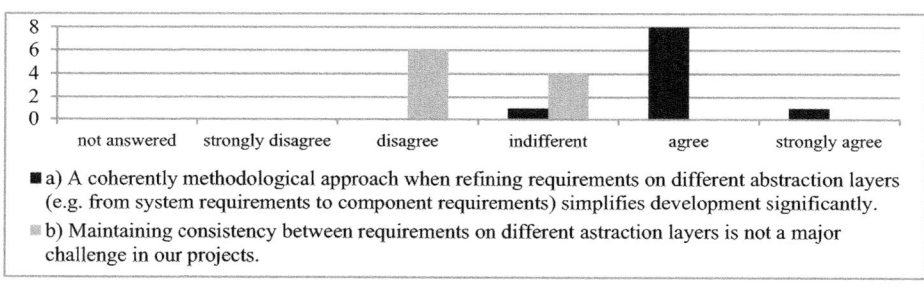

Fig. 8. Participants' answers for two questionnaire statements concerning the use of abstraction layers during RE

Furthermore, many participants consider requirements traceability and requirements consistency across abstraction layers as significant challenges. Fig. 8, Graph b), shows that the majority of participants consider that maintaining requirements consistency across multiple abstraction layers is difficult to accomplish (note the negative formulation of the questionnaire item). The need for improved methodical support for assuring requirements traceability and consistency, in general (i.e. not specifically related to different abstraction layers) is further discussed in Section 4.3.

In addition to the use of abstraction layers, the use of models (see Section 4.1) may be regarded as a means for coping with high system complexity, too (e.g. due to the improved structuring and the possibility of automation). However, Fig. 9 shows that only three participants indicated that models often or always help managing system complexity. Hence, these results show no conclusive indication that using models is or is not considered a feasible way to cope with high system complexity.

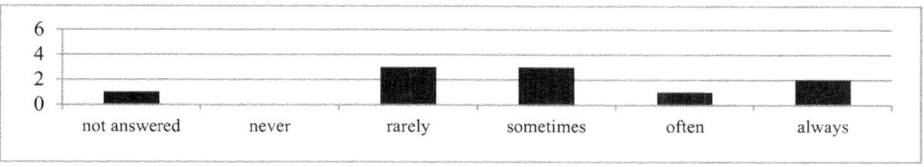

Fig. 9. Participants' answers for the statement "Without using models to specify system requirements, the complexity of the systems that are being developed cannot be handled"

4.3 Quality Assurance of Requirements

The study participants regarded high requirements quality as crucial since the systems in the considered domains are safety-critical in many cases. For these systems, the level of quality assurance to be achieved and, partly, the techniques to be applied are regulated by safety standards (e.g. ISO 26262 [11], RTCA DO 178B [21]).

However, still manual techniques were reported to be the dominant form of checking requirements quality. Nine out of ten participants reported that inspections are regularly conducted in their respective organization for checking requirements quality. In contrast, only one participant reported the use of automated consistency checking of requirements. As Fig. 10 shows the existing methodical support for requirements validation and verification was judged as only partly satisfactory by the participants.

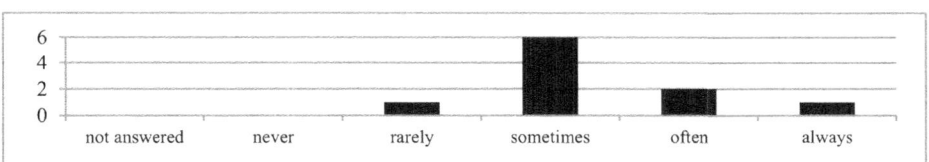

Fig. 10. Participants' answers for the statement "The method support we have for validation and verification of requirements is completely sufficient"

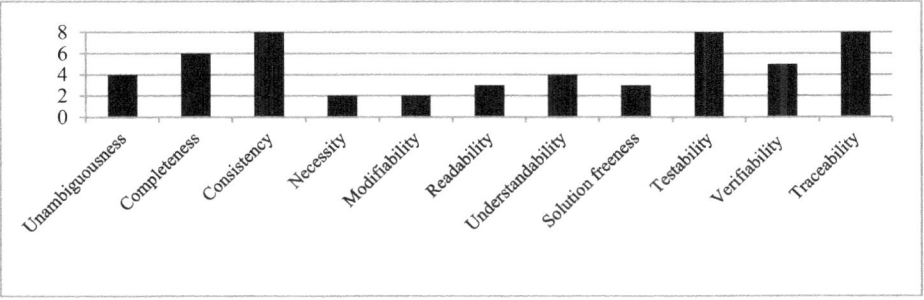

Fig. 11. Participants' answers for the question "For which requirement quality properties do you expect a significantly improved methodical/tool support?" Multiple answers per participant were possible

According to most participants, there is a strong need for improved methodical support with regard to the quality criteria consistency, testability, and traceability. These three criteria were stated by 80% to 100% of the participants. Other criteria were stated less frequently as can be seen by Fig. 11. In addition, many participants noted the high effort that must be spent in their projects for ensuring requirements traceability and consistency.

The use of models in RE is considered a promising approach to simplify quality assurance in RE. 70% of the participants agree that using models intensively during RE would simplify validation and verification of requirements tremendously, only 20% distinctively disagree. These results are visualized in Fig. 12.

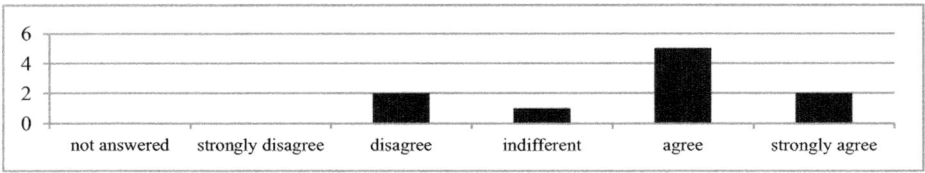

Fig. 12. Participants' answers for the statement "Using models during requirements engineering would significantly improve requirement validation and verification"

4.4   Interrelation of RE and Architectural Design

Many existing methods assume a clear separation between RE and design, i.e. RE activities and artifacts are clearly separated from design activities and artifacts. However, some authors have indicated a less clear separation between RE and design or even a close intertwining of RE and design in practice (e.g. [18] and [17]).

Our study provides further evidence for the somewhat blurry separation between RE and design in practice. Only two participants stated that a clear separation between RE and design is maintained often or always in their projects (Fig. 13). According to the interviews, practitioners conceive the separation between RE and design as a distinction between problem definition and solution finding. However, this separation strongly depends on the stakeholders' perspectives as explained in [19], pp. 24-26. Model-based development increases the confusion related to separating requirements from design artifacts because many model types can be used to specify requirements as well as design (see Section 4.1). This is supported by the fact that some of the interviewees expressed a strong need for workable rules on how to develop solution-free requirements models.

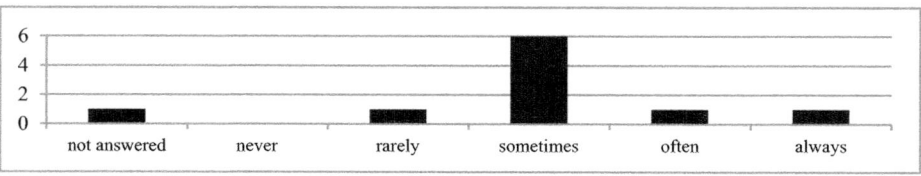

Fig. 13. Participants' answers for the statement "We clearly distinguish between RE and Architecture Design in our projects"

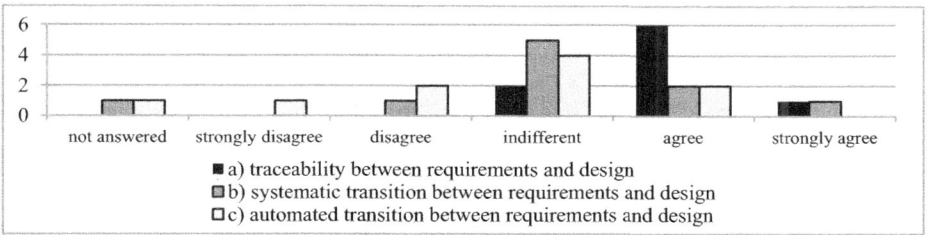

Fig. 14. Participants' answers for three questionnaire statements concerning the support for the transition between requirements and design

The transition from requirements to design has been an important research topic for the last decades. In our study, we investigated what kind of support practitioners seek for the transition from requirements to design. We differentiated the following three kinds of support:

- Traceability between requirements and design
- A systematic approach for the transition between requirements and design
- An automated transition from requirements to design

The strongest approval was expressed by the participants with regard to the systematic support for traceability between requirements and design (see Graph a) in Fig. 14). No consistent indication can be determined from the results with regard to improved systematic approaches for the transition between requirements and design (see Graph b) in Fig. 14). Also, no consistent opinion could be observed with regard to the automation of the transition between requirements and design (Graph c) in Fig. 14). Hence, only the support for traceability could be identified as an urgent need.

5 Conclusions for RE Research

In this section, we draw conclusions from our study results (see Section 4) regarding topics that RE research should address. Potential threats to the validity of our results and the conclusions outlined in this section are discussed in Section 6.

Support for Model-based RE
As indicated in Section 4.1, practitioners consider natural language as insufficient for specifying requirements for complex systems. For instance, checking a simple consistency rule causes an enormous effort when performed manually for a requirements specification with several thousands of requirements. The study participants expressed a strong interest in using requirements models more intensively which we partly attribute to the higher level of automation of RE tasks that models facilitate. However, practitioners must be provided appropriate guidance to overcome major issues that currently inhibit the use of models. This guidance must clarify how requirements models can be used when safety standards must be satisfied, a requirements document must be provided that is legally binding and must be passed on to a

supplier, and how to prevent specifying the design instead of the requirements when creating models.

A possible way of resolving part of the current issues could be a tighter integration of requirements models with textual requirements which allows switching more easily between these two representations.

Support for Abstraction Layers in RE

Requirements for complex systems are specified at different layers of abstraction. In a typical case, requirements need to be defined for the product (e.g. an airplane or a power plant), each individual system of this product, each system function, and each hardware and software component needed to implement the system functions. As the results presented in Section 4.2 indicate, RE methods need to support the development of requirements across such layers of abstraction in order to be applicable in the embedded systems domain. The methodical support should include at least refinement, traceability, and consistency checking across different abstraction layers. Therein, a tight integration between RE and architectural design is needed since, in a hierarchy of abstraction layers, the architecture defines the context and scope of each requirement (see e.g. [22]).

To provide practitioners with workable guidelines for developing requirements at different abstraction layers, the concept of abstraction layers itself needs further clarification. A possible way of clarifying the methodical issues is to provide reference models with clearly defined abstraction layers, rules stating what should and what should not be specified at each abstraction layer, and guidelines how requirements at different abstraction layers should relate to each other.

Support for Quality Assurance in RE

As stated in Section 4.3, existing quality assurance techniques for requirements are only partly satisfactory. Our results indicate that existing, general quality assurance techniques should be refined to provide workable guidelines for practitioners to systematically deal with specific requirements quality criteria such as consistency, traceability, or testability. In addition, sound evidence is needed which quality criteria are positively influenced by the use of requirements models.

Furthermore, a better methodical alignment of RE and safety engineering is necessary. RE methods should, for instance, support determining the type and extent of quality assurance based on the safety requirements resulting from safety analyses such as the required safety integrity level of a component or function.

Support for the Transition between RE and Design

Regarding the transition between RE and design, our results (Section 4.4) indicate that the conditions under which an automated transition from requirements to design is desirable and feasible in the industry should be carefully examined.

Industry has a strong need for systematic, workable approaches for traceability between requirements and design. Existing RE and design methods need to be better aligned and the typical use cases for traceability in the development process of embedded systems must be taken into account to provide such traceability support. In addition, a high level of automation is needed to reduce the effort for creating and maintaining traceability links.

6 Critical Evaluation

Although great care was exercised during the creation of the interview guide and during the design of the questionnaires, some investigative issues remain.

It could be objected that the purposefully introduced vagueness in questionnaire items (e.g. through the use of adverbs such as "predominantly") may have led to distortions in the measured data due to different interpretations of the questions by individual participants. However, this strategy contributed to avoid possible mediocrity in the data and allowed us to capture the trends in typical everyday cases in development projects.

Since our research focus is on model-based RE, researcher bias may have influenced the results concerning the participants' attitude with regard to using models in RE during the interviews. To reduce this threat to validity, we motivated the participants to express their true opinion and paid special attention to adequately honor any objections against the use of models in RE. In addition, the participants' expertise made them less susceptible to be influenced by the researchers' opinion. Furthermore, we specifically designed the questionnaires to counteract possible researcher bias by means of the Flip-Flop Technique [3] and counter-balanced question wording.

The participant population might not be representative for all companies in the embedded systems domain. Section 3.2 shows how this issue was reduced by involving companies from five different branches of the embedded systems domain with different roles in product development and by focusing on personnel with a good overview of RE-related issues. The participants' (albeit self-reported) many years of industrial experience further increases the trustworthiness of the obtained results.

Furthermore, the joint application of interview data and questionnaires helped reducing the risk of invalid results by cross-checking interview and survey data. The questionnaires were designed to complement the qualitative findings from the interviews (see Section 3.3). Note that the purpose of the questionnaires was not to allow statistical testing of hypotheses as this study is qualitative in nature.

7 Summary and Outlook

This paper reports on the results of an industrial survey in the embedded systems domain intended to reveal major needs of industry practitioners in the field of RE and thereby to indicate directions for future RE research. The study focused on four selected topics: use of natural language vs. requirements models, support for high system complexity, quality assurance of requirements, and interrelation of RE and design. Despite a number of industry surveys have been reported on in previous articles, these topics have thus far not been investigated, yet are imperative for RE research to develop industry-ready methodology.

The study was conducted in 2009 with seven large companies from five branches of the embedded systems domain (automation technology, automotive, avionics, medical technology, and energy technology). The data was gathered by means of interviews as well questionnaires in order to increase the confidence in the results. In total, 17 company representatives participated in the interviews, 10 of the representatives completed additional questionnaires.

From these results, we have derived conclusions indicating important threads of future research in RE (Section 5). An important result of the study is that practitioners advocate a more intensive use of models in RE, yet the use of models is currently impaired by uncertainties regarding the use of requirements models in legally binding requirements documents for safety-critical systems. Furthermore, methodical support for abstraction layers is of critical importance for the adoption of RE methods in industry. A strong need for workable solutions for assuring specific requirements quality criteria (consistency, traceability, and testability) has been revealed whereas an automated transition from requirements to design could not be identified as a prevalent need. The generalizability of these results is discussed in the paper along with other threats to validity.

In our future work we will exploit the study results to extend and enhance an existing RE method for embedded systems that was developed in our group in order to address urgent industrial needs to a larger extent. In addition, we believe that the results conveyed in this paper will contribute to developing RE methods that can be transferred more easily into embedded systems practice.

Acknowledgments. This paper was funded in part by the German Federal Ministry of Education and Research (BMBF) in the innovation alliance SPES 2020 (grant number 01 IS 08 045). We thank Dr. Kim Lauenroth for his support in conducting the study, Marian Daun, Sebastian Gabrisch, and Heiko Stallbaum for their help in evaluating the data, as well as our industry partners for participating in the study.

References

[1] Anderson, S., Felici, M.: Controlling Requirements Evolution - An Avionics Case Study. LNCS (2000)
[2] Automotive SIG: Automotive SPICE® - Process Assessment Model (PAM) v2.5., http://www.automotivespice.com (accessed October 2010)
[3] Corbin, J., Strauss, A.: Qualitative Research, 3rd edn. Sage Publications, California (2008)
[4] Curtis, B., Krasner, H., Iscoe, N.: A Field Study of the Software Design Process for Large Systems. Communications of ACM 31(11), 1268–1287 (1988)
[5] Cysneiros, J.M.: Requirements Engineering in the Health Care Domain. In: Proceedings of the IEEE Joint Intl. Conf. on Requirements Engineering (2002)
[6] Denger, C., Feldmann, R., Höst, M., Lindholm, C., Shull, F.: A Snapshot of the State of Practice in Software Development for Medical Devices. In: 1st First Intl. Symp. ESEM (2007)
[7] Emam, K., Madhavji, N.: A Field Study of Requirements Engineering Practices in Information Systems Development. In: Proc. 2nd IEEE Intl Symp. Requirements Engineering (1995)
[8] Graaf, B., Lormans, M., Toetenel, H.: Embedded Software Engineering: The State of the Practice. IEEE Software, 61–69 (2003)
[9] Grimm, K.: Software Technology in an Automotive Company – Major Challenges. In: Proc. Intl. Conf. on Software Engineering (2003)
[10] Innovation Alliance Software Plattform Embedded Systems 2020 research project, http://www.spes2020.de (accessed October 2010)

[11] ISO DIS 26262: Draft International Standard Road Vehicles – Functional Safety (2010)
[12] Juristo, N., Moreno, A., Silva, A.: Is the European Industry Moving toward Solving RE Problems? IEEE Software (2002)
[13] Karlsson, L., Dahlstedt, A., Dag, J.: Challenges in Market-Driven Requirements Engineering – Aan Industrial Review Study. In: Proc. 8th Intl. Workshop on Requirements Engineering (2002)
[14] Lubars, M., Potts, C., Richter, C.: A Review of the State of the Practice in Requirements Modeling. In: Proceedings of the IEEE Symp. on Requirements Engineering, pp. 2–14 (1993)
[15] McPhee, C., Eberlein, A.: Requirements Engineering for Time-to-Market Projects. In: Proceedings of the Ninth Annual IEEE Intl. Conf. and Workshop ECBS (2002)
[16] Neill, C., Laplante, P.: Requirements Engineering -: The State of the Practice. IEEE Software, 40–45 (2003)
[17] Nuseibeh, B.: Weaving Together Requirements and Architecture. IEEE Computer 34(3), 115–119 (2001)
[18] Nuseibeh, B., Kramer, J., Finkelstein, A.: A Framework for Expressing the Relationship between Multiple Views in Requirement Specification. IEEE TSE 2(10), 760–773 (1994)
[19] Pohl, K.: Requirements Engineering – Fundamentals, Principles, Techniques. Springer, Germany (2010)
[20] Pretschner, A., Broy, M., Krüger, I., Stauner, T.: Software Engineering for Automotive Systems: A Roadmap. In: Proceedings of FOSE (2007)
[21] RTCA: DO-178b – Software Considerations in Airborne Systems and Equipment Certification, 2nd Ed Radio Technical Commission for Aeronautics (1999)
[22] Sikora, E., Daun, M., Pohl, K.: Supporting the Consistent Specification of Scenarios across Multiple Abstraction Levels. In: Wieringa, R., Persson, A. (eds.) REFSQ 2010. LNCS, vol. 6182, pp. 45–59. Springer, Heidelberg (2010)
[23] Van Lamsweerde, A.: Requirements Engineering: From System Goals to UML Models to Spftware Specifications. Wiley, West Sussex (2009)
[24] Weber, M., Weisbrod, J.: Requirements Engineering in Automotive Development – Experiences and Challenges. IEEE Software, 16/22 (2003)
[25] Weidenhaupt, K., Pohl, K., Jarke, M., Haumer, P.: Scenarios in System Development: Current Practice. IEEE Software, 34–45 (1998)

Applying Restricted English Grammar on Automotive Requirements—Does it Work? A Case Study

Amalinda Post[1], Igor Menzel[1], and Andreas Podelski[2]

[1] Robert Bosch GmbH, Corporate Research, Stuttgart, Germany
{Amalinda.Post,Igor.Menzel}@de.bosch.com
[2] University of Freiburg, Department of Computer Science, Freiburg, Germany
podelski@informatik.uni-freiburg.de

Abstract. [**Context and motivation**] For an automatic consistency check on requirements the requirements have to be formalized first. However, logical formalisms are seldom accessible to stakeholders in the automotive context. Konrad and Cheng proposed a restricted English grammar that can be automatically translated to logics, but looks like natural language. [**Question/problem**] In this paper we investigate whether this grammar can be applied in the automotive domain, in the sense that it is expressive enough to specify automotive behavioral requirements. [**Principal ideas/results**] We did a case study over 289 informal behavioral requirements taken from the automotive context. We evaluated whether these requirements could be formulated in the grammar and whether the grammar has to be adapted to the automotive context. [**Contribution**] The case study strongly indicates that the grammar, extended with 3 further patterns, is suited to specify automotive behavioral requirements of BOSCH.

Keywords: automotive, requirements, formalization, real-time.

1 Introduction

In this work we investigate whether the restricted English grammar provided by Konrad and Cheng [1] suffices to express behavioral requirements taken from the automotive context. The grammar looks like natural language, however it allows an automatic translation into linear time logic (LTL)[2], computational tree logic (CTL)[2], graphical interval logic (GIL)[3], metric temporal logic (MTL)[4], timed computational tree logic (TCTL)[4], and real-time graphical interval logic (RTGIL)[5].

We are only interested in requirements specifying the *behavior* of the system, i.e., we do *not* consider any other kind of requirements. Thus, in the following, every time we speak of "requirements" we mean in fact *behavioral requirements* [6], i.e., requirements specifying the behavior of the system. We consider behavior without exact timing bounds (e.g., "*If the system is in diagnostic mode then previously the diagnostic request* DiagStart *held.*") and behavior with exact timing

D. Berry and X. Franch (Eds.): REFSQ 2011, LNCS 6606, pp. 166–180, 2011.

bounds (e.g., *"If the diagnostic request* IRTest *appears then the infrared lamps are turned off after at most 6 seconds"*). The case study is motivated from automotive development processes. In this context sets of requirements often comprise of several hundred pages. The requirements are mainly written in natural language. There are a lot of involved stakeholders, many of them spread over different companies [7]. Furthermore, requirements specifications are *manually* checked for errors, e.g., by peer reviews [8].

The problem addressed in this work is that such a manual check is a considerable effort since requirements affect each other and cannot be analyzed in isolation [9]. Therefore *automatic* checks are desirable already for small sets of requirements [10,11,12]. However, to allow automatic checks the requirements need to be available in a formal language, such as, e.g., a logic like LTL. In addition to that, the new functional safety standard for Automotive Electronic Systems ISO26262 (currently under development) states that for safety critical systems at least a semi formal specification of safety requirements is highly recommended [13]. Thus, in the automotive domain a need arises for methods developing semi formal or formal requirements.

Unfortunately such formalizations are rarely accessible to the stakeholders who need to read them [14,1]. Thus, before working with a formal specification all the stakeholders would need to be trained in the chosen logic, even beyond company boundaries. In practice this is clearly unrealistic. Another possibility is to develop both a formal and an informal requirements document. But this is double work and it will be difficult to hold both documents consistently over the development time of 2-5 years.

Thus, the idea is to use a language that retains the mathematical rigor but uses a vocabulary and syntax very close to natural English language. Such a language is provided by Konrad and Cheng [1]. They propose a restricted English grammar that represents a *specification pattern system* (SPS), such that every pattern looks like natural language but can be translated into a logical formula in LTL, CTL, TCTL, RTGIL or MTL. The drawback of this language is that it covers only a subset of the statements possible to express in the particular logic. For example the following requirement cannot be expressed in the SPS as the SPS provides no pattern that expresses such a behavior: *"For a codeword with 5 digits, the time between entering the first digit and the last one is less than 5 seconds"*. However, the SPS does not claim to be complete. Thus, the question is not whether *all* possible requirements can be expressed in this SPS but: *Does* in practice *the SPS suffice to express* automotive *requirements?*

If this would be true, then automotive requirements could be expressed in SPS, i.e., they would be still readable for all stakeholders (as they look like natural language) but could be automatically checked by a computer (as they can be automatically translated into logical formulas). To investigate that question, we did a case study over 289 requirements taken from five projects from the automotive domain. The requirements were given in informal prose. For the case study we checked for every requirement in this sample whether it could be reformulated in the SPS without loss of meaning.

2   Related Work

Various tabular notations aim to provide requirements that are both accessible and suitable for formal analysis. For example, Heitmeyer et al [11] have built a variety of tools for checking consistency, completeness, and safety properties of requirements expressed in the tabular SCR notation. In contrast to the tabular notation, formalisms like B or Z [15] aim to express requirements in a mathematical way. E.g., the formalism Z defines rigid notations for logical operations, quantifiers, sets, and functions. Whereas Z is strictly designed as a specification language, the goal of B is to use mathematical proofs to verify consistency between refinement levels and to enable an automatic transformation of requirements into some executable code. However neither B nor Z offer a natural language representation.

Some research, such as the Attempto Controlled English project [16] and the work of Han [17], attempt to construct formal specifications from natural language requirements. However, automatic interpretation of natural language is still error-prone, as natural language is often vague and the information is often implicitly stated. The use of natural language in the work described here is much less ambitious.

This work investigates whether the restricted English grammar proposed by Konrad and Cheng [1] can be applied to the automotive context. The grammar depicted in Table 1 represents a specification pattern system (SPS) [1] with 16 non-recursive patterns. Every pattern can be mapped to logical statements in, e.g., the logics MTL, TCTL and RTGIL. The patterns without exact timing bounds were originally proposed by Dwyer et al in [18]. Konrad and Cheng extend these patterns in their SPS .

The patterns consist of non-literal terminals (given in a sans serif font) and literal terminals (confined via quotation marks). For example, the *min duration* pattern consists of "it is always the case that once " P " becomes satisfied, it holds for at least "c "time units", with P, c as non-literal terminals and the rest as literal terminals. The non-literal terminal P denotes a boolean propositional formulae that describes properties of states and is used to capture properties of the system. The non-literal terminal c is instantiated with integer values.

Both Dwyer et al [18] and Konrad [19] evaluate their approach with a case study. However, Dwyer evaluates the applicability only for patterns without exact timing bounds, and Konrad only for patterns with exact timing bounds. To our knowledge there are no case studies that evaluate the applicability of the SPS for mixed requirements.

The work of Dwyer et al has been extended in a number of directions. Grunske extends the patterns to express also probabilistic quality properties [20]. This extension might be useful to express availability or reliability requirements, however in our case study we consider only behavioral requirements, thus we base our work on Konrad's SPS.

Cobleigh et al. developed the tool PROPEL (PROPerty ELucidator) that aims to guide users through the process of creating property specifications in supporting them in selecting a suited pattern and scope [21]. The tool provides

Table 1. Restricted English grammar given by Konrad and Cheng in [1]

Start	1: property	::=	*scope* "," *specification* "."
Scope	2: scope	::=	"Globally" | "Before" R | "After" Q | "Between" Q " and" R | "After" Q "until" R
General	3: specification	::=	*qualitative type* | *realtime type* | *invariant type*
Quali.	4: qualitative type	::=	*occurrence category* | *order category* | *possibility category*
	5: occurrence category	::=	*absence pattern* | *universality pattern* | *existence pattern* | *bounded existence*
	6: absence pattern	::=	"it is never the case that" P " holds"
	7: universality pattern	::=	"it is always the case that" P " holds"
	8: existence pattern	::=	P " eventually holds"
	9: bounded existence	::=	"transitions to states in which " P " holds occur at most twice"
	10: order category	::=	"it is always the case that if" (*precedence pattern* | *response pattern* | *precedence chain 1-2* | *precedence chain 2-1* | *response chain 1-2* | *constrained chain*)
	11: precedence pattern	::=	P "holds, then" S "previously held"
	12: precedence chain 1-2	::=	S "holds and is succeeded by" T ", then" P " previously held"
	13: precedence chain 2-1	::=	P "holds then " S " previously held and was preceded by " T
	14: response pattern	::=	P "holds then " S "eventually holds"
	15: response chain 1-2	::=	P " holds" then " T "eventually holds and is succeeded by" T
	16: response chain 2-1	::=	S "holds and is succeeded by " T ", then " P "eventually holds after " T
	17: constrained chain	::=	P "holds "then " S "eventually holds and is succeeded by" T ", where" Z "does not hold between" S "and" T
real time	18: real time type	::=	"it is always the case that" (*duration category* | *periodic category* | *RT Order category*) | *possible real time category*
	19: duration category	::=	"once" P " becomes satisfied, it holds for" (*min duration* | *max duration*)
	20: min duration	::=	"at least" c " time unit(s)"
	21: max duration	::=	"less than" c " time unit(s)"
	22: periodic category	::=	P " holds" *bounded recurrence*
	23: bounded recurrence	::=	" at least every" c "time unit(s)"
	24: RT Order category	::=	"if" P " holds, then" S "holds" (*bounded response* | *bounded invariance*)
	25: bounded response	::=	" after at most" c "time unit(s)"
	26: bounded invariance	::=	" for at least" c "time unit(s)"

both a finite-state automaton representation and a natural language representation. However, the tool currently only supports patterns without exact timing bounds.

3   Planning of the Case Study

3.1   Study Goals and Questions

In order to assess whether the SPS proposed by Konrad and Cheng can be suitably applied in the automotive domain two questions should be raised: first, is the SPS expressive enough to express automotive requirements? And, second, do developers, requirements engineers, and sub-suppliers accept the SPS, in the sense that they think it easy to use and useful?

In this case study we address only the first question. However, in order to ensure that BOSCH requirements engineers and developers can understand requirements formalized in SPS and can apply it to their requirements, we did an initial informal survey. We showed them requirements formalized in SPS, and asked them to explain their meaning to us and to apply the SPS on some of their behavioral requirements. The results indicate that requirements formalized in SPS are easy to understand and SPS is easy to apply. However, many experts asked for tool support. Therefore, we plan to develop a tool and do a further case study to address this question in a bigger context — presuming the present case study indicates the SPS is expressive enough.

Another property we investigate in this case study is the *pattern complexity*: every pattern in the SPS can be expressed in logic, but not every pattern can be expressed in every logic. We define *pattern complexity* as a function that maps a

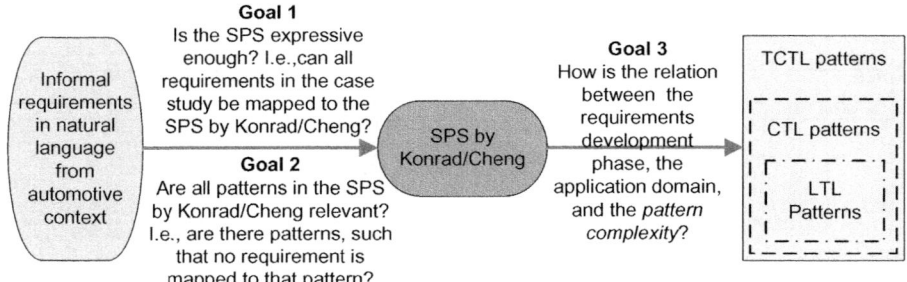

Fig. 1. In the case study we investigate the relation between requirements and SPS, and between requirements and pattern complexity

pattern to the least expressive logic of a given finite set of logics in which it can be expressed. We are interested whether our case study contains subsets with a small *pattern complexity*.

Therefore, we identified four subgoals of the case study:

Goal 1a. Is it possible to express all automotive requirements in the SPS by Konrad and Cheng?

Goal 1b. If there are automotive requirements, that cannot be expressed in the SPS, what is the reason? I.e. could such requirements be expressed in another formalism?

Goal 2. Are all patterns in the SPS by Konrad and Cheng relevant for the automotive domain? I.e. are there patterns that are never needed?

Goal 3. What is the relation between application domain (e.g., human machine interface, engine controller,...), the requirements development phase and the pattern complexity?

As depicted in Figure 1, the subgoals 1a, 1b, and 2 investigate the relation between requirements and SPS, whereas subgoal 3 relates requirements (via the SPS) with pattern complexity.

3.2   Selection of the Sample

Selection criteria for documents. In the first step we selected requirements documents from different BOSCH projects of the automotive domain. To get a representative sampling, we decided to apply stratified sampling over the automotive application domains car multimedia, driving assistance, engine controlling, powertrain development, and catalytic converter development. Moreover, we decided to use projects from different development stages, i.e. platform and customer projects [22] from concept phases to well-known development phases[1]. We then used convenience sampling to select a project out of every stratum.

---

[1] *Platform projects* develop a collection of reusable artifacts, such as requirements, software components, test plans etc. These artifacts are then reused in *customer projects* in order to build applications.

Each project had several requirements documents, some consisting of more than 100 pages. In order to get a representative sample we asked the corresponding requirements engineers to give us a requirements document such that, first, the document contained behavioral requirements, and, second, the document was representative for the application domain. This way we obtained the following five requirements documents: a document specifying a Human Machine Interface(HMI) D_1 (of a car multimedia project), a document specifying an error-handling concept D_2 (of a driving assistance project), one of a controller of a heater of an oxygen sensor D_3 (of a catalytic converter project), one of a powertrain controller D_4 (of a powertrain project), and one of an engine injection device D_5 (of an engine control project).

Selection criteria for requirements. Every document $D_1, \ldots, D_5$ consisted of several chapters. In the documents process requirements (e.g., *"The testing coverage shall be at least 99% over all code statements"*) or other nonfunctional requirements were mostly grouped together into chapters, thus separated from the behavioral requirements. In this work we are only interested in behavioral requirements. Therefore we scanned the chapters of the documents and made a list with the chapters containing such requirements. After that we randomly chose a chapter out of this list, and selected all requirements in the chapter. In this way we obtained the set of requirements R_1 out of $D_1, \ldots, R_5$ out of D_5. R, the union of these sets, consisted of 289 requirements. We randomly chose chapters instead of the requirements itself, as in our experience a requirement should not be interpreted out of its context.

After that we preprocessed the initial data set: we deleted 11 headings, and 22 statements, that were either mere descriptions but not real requirements (e.g., *"Most drivers prefer a smooth deceleration"*), or requirements that did not specify behavior (e.g., *"All failure thresholds shall be defined and documented by the developers."*). Furthermore we deleted 11 redundant requirements. In order to ensure that these redundant requirements, headings and statements could be safely deleted, we discussed every deletion with 2 further experts.

After that our sample consisted of 245 informal requirements in prose.

3.3 Case Study Design

The setting of the case study is depicted in Figure 2: As input we used 245 informal requirements. These are analyzed in a content analysis with the category system defined below.

The category system consists of three main groups: *phenomenon requirements, requirements expressible in SPS* and *requirements not expressible in SPS*. The category *requirements expressible in SPS* is further refined in the patterns defined in [1].

We defined a requirement as *phenomenon requirement* if it specified not behavior but data. An example for such a requirement is *"An error is built up as following: error name (2 Byte), error status (1Byte), odometer value when the error occurred (2Byte)"*. Note that a *phenomenon requirement* cannot be

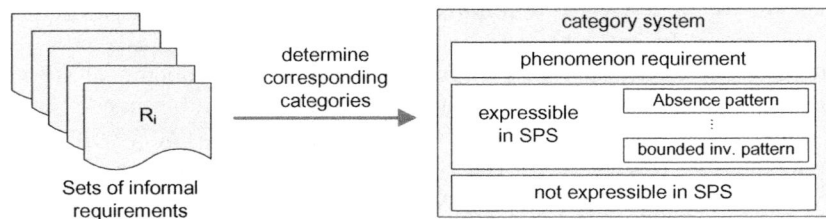

Fig. 2. case study design

mapped to a pattern, instead the data it specifies is mapped to non-literal terminals. Thus, *phenomenon requirements* are *indirectly* expressed in the SPS.

We defined a requirement as *expressible in SPS* if and only if the SPS provides one or more suitable patterns and there is an assignment to the non-literal terminals of these patterns, such that the conjunction of the instantiated patterns expresses the meaning of the requirement.

We defined a requirement as *not expressible in SPS*, if it was not a *phenomenon requirement* and could not be reformulated in the SPS without loss of meaning.

We then asked a requirements engineer to determine for every requirement in the sample whether it was a *phenomenon requirement*, a *requirement expressible in SPS* or a *requirement not expressible in SPS*. For *requirements expressible in SPS* the engineer should further give instantiated patterns expressing the meaning of the requirement.

The majority of the informal requirements could be reformulated into exactly one instantiated pattern. However, for some requirements a conjunction of multiple instantiated patterns was needed to express the meaning of the initial requirement. Thus, we obtained a set size for the resulting requirements *expressible in SPS, phenomena* and *not expressible in SPS* of 307. The following statistics concerning subgoal 1 and subgoal 2 relate to the initial number of requirements(245), the statistics for the subgoal 3 relates to the 307 SPS requirements.

4 Analysis of the Results

4.1 Goal 1: Expressivity of the SPS

In a first step we investigated whether it is possible to reformulate all requirements of the case study in SPS. Therefore we first measured how many requirements could be expressed in the SPS by Dwyer et al, which is limited to patterns without exact timing bounds. After that we compared these results with the measurements for the SPS by Konrad and Cheng. Figure 3 depicts the results.

The figure shows that for the requirements in the case study the extension of Konrad and Cheng strongly reduces the number of *not expressible* requirements. However, 39 requirements could not be reformulated. 25 of these requirements needed a branching time concept, not provided in the given patterns.

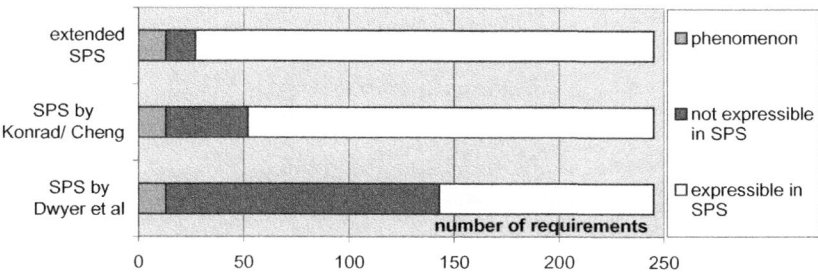

Fig. 3. The number of *not expressible* requirements is strongly reduced by Konrad and Chengs' patterns. It can be further reduced in extending the grammar with possibility patterns.

The branching concept was needed to allow the specification of *possible* behavior. Consider the requirement *If the gear is in P then it must be possible to start the engine.* In the later development phases this requirement will certainly be split into further more precise and deterministic requirements, e.g, *If the gear is in P and the ignition is turned on then the system starts the engine. If the gear is in P and the ignition is turned off, then the engine stays off....* However, in the early development phases it is desirable to allow also a less precise specification, as the information to specify the requirements in the deterministic way is probably not yet known. Thus, for early development phases we think that an extension with branching time concept patterns is needed.

Therefore, we propose to extend the grammar by Konrad and Cheng with *possibility patterns* depicted in Table 2. With the help of these patterns it is possible to reduce the number of *not expressible* requirements from 39 to 14, as depicted in Figure 3. Figure 4 depicts that in greater detail for $R_1, \ldots, R_5$: every bar represents the number of requirements, that were *not expressible* in the SPS by Konrad and Cheng. E.g., 25 requirements of R_4 were *not expressible*. The bars are further divided into two classes: the number of requirements that could be expressed by the new possibility patterns is depicted in light gray, the number of requirements that are still *not expressible* is depicted in dark gray. Note that in the case study the *possibility patterns* were especially needed for the requirements of the projects in an early development phase, particularly in R_4. This is plausible as in later development phases such requirements will be split into more precise requirements.

Table 2. Grammar of the extended patterns

possibility pattern ::=	"if" P "holds then there is at least one execution sequence such that" S "eventually holds"
possible bounded ::= response pattern	"if" P "holds then there is at least one execution sequence such that" S "holds after at most" c "time unit(s)"
possible bounded ::= invariance pattern	"if" P "holds then there is at least one execution sequence such that" S "holds for at least" c "time unit(s)"

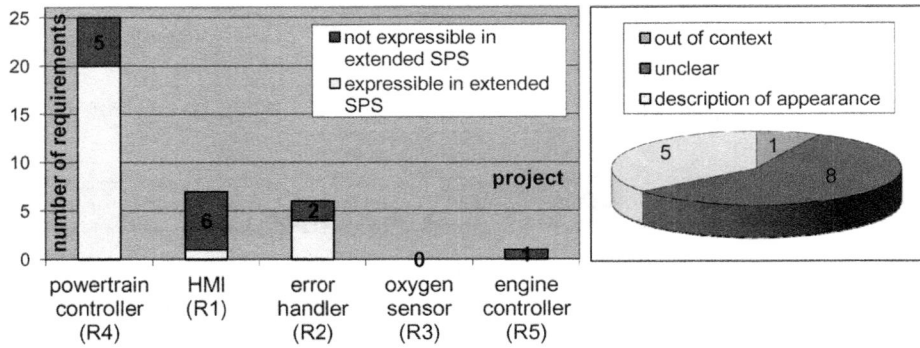

Fig. 4. The left Figure depicts the number of requirements *not expressible* in the language by Konrad/Cheng but expressible via extended patterns. On the right a further classification of requirements *not expressible in extended SPS*.

However, even with this extension it was not possible to find a reformulation in SPS for 14 requirements. Thus, we investigated what reasons made a requirement *not expressible*. We identified three reasons, depicted in Figure 4.

One *not expressible* requirement was only not expressible because it was out of the system context: *"If failures are detected in multiple electronic control units (ECUs) the same classification of faults shall be used in all ECUs"*. This requirement was given to a project developing a single ECU, but clearly this requirement cannot be solved on the ECU level as in this context it is not known what faults are detected by other ECUs. However, on the context level of the whole car the requirement could be expressed in SPS.

Five requirements could not be formalized as they did not specify any behavior. Instead they described the appearance of the product, e.g., *"the warning icon is an image of two cars with a star in between"*. As in this work we wanted to investigate only *behavioral* requirements, these requirements were wrongly selected into our sample. Thus, for the result of this case study (limited to behavioral requirements) these five requirements should be ignored.

Finally, the majority of requirements became *not expressible* because the meaning of the requirement was not clear or just too vague. Neither the requirements engineer who formalized the requirements in the first step, nor the evaluators understood what the requirement wanted to specify, thus, it was clearly impossible to formalize it. Examples for such requirements are *"The drag torque and the activation torque depend on the operating state."*(how?) and *"warning in central line of vision"*(how is the "line of vision" determined? E.g., adaptive to the size of the driver?). Thus, in these 8 cases, the problem was not that the SPS was not expressive enough but instead that the requirements were unclear. So, in fact the SPS helped to identify requirements that needed to be revised.

Thus, we come to the conclusion that the extended version of the SPS is well suited to express *behavioral* requirements from the automotive context. The majority of the behavioral requirements could be directly expressed in the SPS by [1]. With an extension of only three patterns, all behavioral requirements could be expressed as long as their meaning was clear. As only three further patterns were needed, the case study indicates that Dwyer et al may be right with their belief that *in practice* only some few patterns are needed to express requirements. The effort to extend the SPS was low, i.e., we had to add only three patterns with their formalization. Furthermore the SPS helped to identify requirements that needed to be revised. Thus it seems that for *behavioral* automotive requirements the SPS is well suited.

However, for requirements that are not behavioral requirements this claim does not hold. In fact the requirements specifying the appearance of the product were nearly impossible to formalize *in any formalism*. Thus, we think this is an indication that not all kind of requirements can be formalized. It seems that *behavioral* requirements are suitable for formalization, but for the other kinds of requirements this needs to be investigated. I.e., methods are needed that separate between requirements that can be formalized and requirements that need to be validated via other methods.

4.2   Goal 2: Pattern Relevance

Next, we evaluated whether all patterns in the SPS by Konrad and Cheng are relevant for the automotive application domain. This question needs to be asked to find a minimal pattern set. We assume that a less complex SPS with fewer patterns is easier and faster to use for developers than one with many patterns. However, we still want to express all automotive requirements. Thus, we evaluated whether the SPS by Konrad and Cheng contains patterns that were never needed in the case study.

We identified six patterns that were not needed to express any requirement in the case study: the *bounded existence, precedence chain 1-2, precedence chain 2-1, response chain 1-2, response chain 2-1* and *constrained chain* pattern. Thus, the case study indicates that for the system level in the automotive application domain these patterns might be omitted.

4.3   Goal 3: Pattern Complexity versus Application Domain

The SPS by Konrad and Cheng (and also the extended version) can be automatically transformed to the logics LTL, CTL, GIL, MTL, TCTL, and RTGIL. However, not every pattern can be translated into every logic. All provided patterns can be translated into TCTL. But, e.g., only the patterns without any reference to quantitative time or *possible* behavior can be expressed in LTL.

For LTL, CTL and TCTL tool support is available [23,24], therefore we focus in the following work on these logics. However, even for this subset of logics, there is a trade off between expressivity of the logic and its computational class. E.g., a consistency check for a set of requirements can be transformed into the satisfiability problem. However, the satisfiability problem is undecidable for TCTL [4], while decidable for LTL and CTL. Thus we are interested in the *pattern complexity* and its relation to the application domain (e.g., human machine interface, engine controller,...), and the requirements development phase. We define pattern complexity as a function that maps a pattern to the least expressive logic

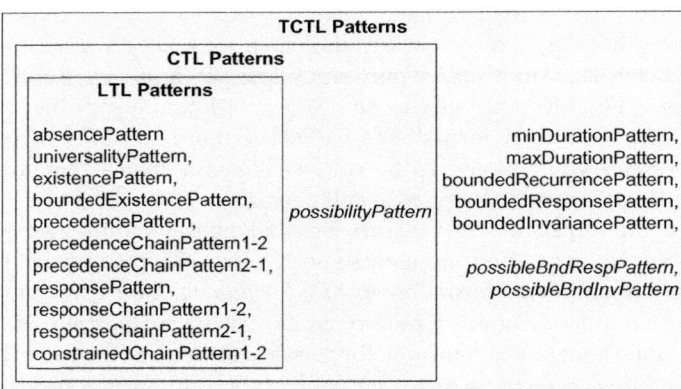

Fig. 5. The patterns are classified according to the least expressive logic they can be expressed in. The extended patterns are depicted in italic font.

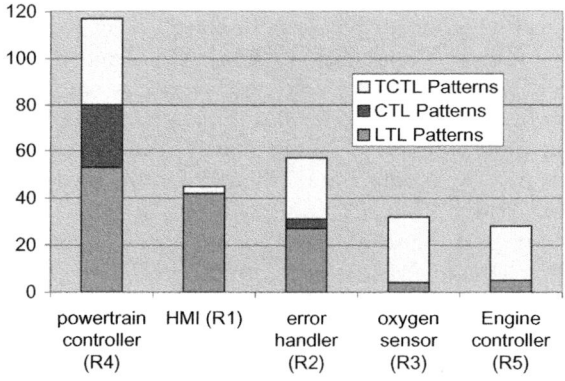

Fig. 6. TCTL-Patterns were needed in every project

$\in \{$LTL, CTL, TCTL$\}$ in which it can be expressed. The result of the mapping is depicted in Figure 5.

Note that all LTL Patterns can be expressed in CTL as well, and both CTL and LTL Patterns can be also expressed in TCTL. Generally, LTL is no subset of CTL. However, in this case all patterns that can be expressed in LTL can be expressed in CTL as well. We counted for every set of requirements $R_1, ..., R_5$ the number of LTL, CTL and TCTL Patterns.

As visible in Figure 6, TCTL Patterns were needed in every project. Only in the set of requirements of the earliest development phase the number of TCTL Patterns was negligible. This indicates that for the specification of the whole system functionality the need for TCTL Patterns is inevitable. However, it might be the case that individual components of the system could be solely expressed in less complex patterns. Further investigations are needed to prove or refute that thesis.

5   Threats to Validity

In this section, we analyze threats to validity defined in Neuendorf [25], Krippendorff [26], and Wohlin [27].

5.1   External Validity

Sampling validity   [25]. This threat arises if the sample is not representative for the requirements. In order to minimize this threat we used the selection procedure described in Section 3.2, thus getting representative requirements of every application domain. A limitation of the case study is that we only used requirements of BOSCH projects. Thus we cannot extend our results to the whole automotive domain but only for BOSCH's automotive domain.

Interaction of selection and treatment   [27]. This threat arises if the requirements engineer in this study (see Section 3.3) is not representative for BOSCH requirements engineers. However, the reliability analysis in Section 5.4 suggests that the application of the patterns is sufficiently independent of the evaluator.

5.2   Internal Validity

Selection   [27]. This threat arises due to natural variation in human performance. The requirements engineer in this study (see Section 3.3) could have been especially good in formalization. The reliability analysis in Section 5.4 suggests that the application of the patterns is sufficiently independent of the evaluator. Thus variation in human performance is probably not an issue.

5.3   Construct Validity

Experimenter expectancies   [27]. Expectations of an outcome may inadvertently cause the evaluators to view data in a different way. However, the evaluators have no benefit from a good or bad outcome for the applicability of the SPS as they did not invent it. Thus, such psychological effects probably did not affect the evaluators.

Semantic validity   [26]. This threat arises if the analytical categories of texts do not correspond to the meaning these texts have for particular readers. In the case study the categories are clearly defined in Section 3.3 and through the patterns in the SPS [1]. However, when reformulating an informal requirement in SPS there are several possibilities to instantiate a pattern with a phenomenon that shall correspond to the description in the text. Thus, in the formalization the requirements engineer might invent phenomena without clearly defining their meaning. Discussion with experts showed that a data dictionary is a potential candidate to minimize this threat.

Face validity   [25]. Face validity is the extent to which a measure addresses the desired concept, i.e. the question whether it measures what it is supposed to measure. In order to ensure face validity we discussed with experts, without mention of the case study, whether the instantiated patterns are a good representation of their concept of behavioral requirements. The discussion indicated that the patterns seem to capture typical behavioral requirements.

5.4   Conclusion Validity

Intercoder reliability   [25]. Unreliable coding limits the chance to make valid conclusions based on the results. In order to minimize this threat, especially for evaluators with varying backgrounds, we asked a requirements engineer with high experience in the application domain as well as an individual with low experience in the application domain and external to the project to code a set of 30 requirements. The requirements were randomly chosen out of the sample defined in Section 3.2. In order to minimize the threat of different interpretations of the phenomena we gave both evaluators a data dictionary. The results yielded a reliability of 0.86/0.86 according to Cohen's Kappa/Scott's pi. In consequence the measure seems to be very reliable.

Even though the reliability is good we were interested in the reasons for different codings. We identified that the requirements engineer tended to use his domain knowledge when formalizing the requirements. E.g, consider the following informal requirement: *"If the locally measured voltage is not available, the voltage value as received from the bus shall be used."*. Using the phenomena *localVoltageNotAvailable, busVoltage* and *internalVoltage* with their obvious meanings, the evaluator with low experience in the application domain expressed the requirement as following *"Globally, it is always the case that if* localVoltageNotAvailable *holds, then* internalVoltage == busVoltage *holds as well"*. However, the requirements engineer specified instead *"Globally, it is always the case that if* localVoltageNotAvailable & errorGetsActive & ¬ busOff *holds, then* errorVoltage == busVoltage *holds as well"*. The engineer used the additional system knowledge, that (first) the locally measured voltage is only needed to be stored if an error appears, and (secondly) that if the bus is off, then this requirement does not apply.

Thus, differing knowledge of the system context might lead to unreliable results. We believe that this threat can be further minimized if the coders discuss their interpretation of the informal requirements prior to the formalization.

6   Conclusion

This case study investigates the question whether in practice the SPS suffices to express automotive behavioral requirements. Based on the results of Section 4.1 we think that at least for automotive requirements of BOSCH this question can be answered with yes.

The belief of Dwyer et al is that some few patterns suffice to express the majority of the properties of a system. This is only a belief and cannot be proven. Nevertheless, we think that Dwyer et als', Konrad's and our case study confirm that belief: in every case study the majority of requirements could be reformulated in the SPS. Furthermore, the distribution of the patterns indicates the same: some few patterns are extensively used whereas a lot of patterns are only sparsely used. Thus, it seems that in practice some few patterns suffice to express automotive behavioral requirements of BOSCH. However, further studies with requirements of other automotive suppliers are needed to refute or strengthen that belief for the whole automotive domain.

Furthermore the case study indicates that for BOSCH the SPS may be even reduced, as six patterns were not needed. It might be beneficent to investigate whether developers can apply such a less complex SPS even faster.

Moreover the case study shows that the SPS can be easily adapted to a certain application domain. The adaptation to the BOSCH automotive domain required the addition of three further patterns to the SPS and their translation to the logical formalisms. This effort stays reasonable as only few further patterns are needed. Last, regarding the pattern complexity, it seems that on system level there are always requirements that can be solely expressed in TCTL Patterns. It would be interesting to investigate whether this is also true on component level.

Concluding, the results indicate that it will be worth developing tool support to allow the next stage of evaluation. In the next stage it should be evaluated whether *in practice* automotive requirements engineers accept the strictures of SPS and how strong they rate the benefit of formal reasoning.

References

1. Konrad, S., Cheng, B.H.C.: Real-time specification patterns. In: ICSE 2005: Proc. 27th Int. Conf. Softw. Eng., pp. 372–381. ACM, New York (2005)
2. Emerson, E.A.: Temporal and modal logic. In: Handbook of Theoretical Computer Science, vol. B, pp. 995–1072. Elsevier Science Publishers, Amsterdam (1990)
3. Ramakrishna, Y.S., Melliar-Smith, P.M., Moser, L.E., Dillon, L.K., Kutty, G.: Interval logics and their decision procedures. TCS 170(1-2), 1–46 (1996)
4. Alur, R.: Techniques for automatic verification of real-time systems. PhD thesis, Stanford University, Stanford, CA, USA (1992)
5. Moser, L.E., Ramakrishna, Y.S., Kutty, G., Melliar-Smith, P.M., Dillon, L.K.: A graphical environment for the design of concurrent real-time systems. ACM Trans. Softw. Eng. Methodol. 6(1), 31–79 (1997)
6. Davis, A.M.: Software requirements: objects, functions, and states. Prentice-Hall, Inc., Upper Saddle River (1993)
7. Heumesser, N., Houdek, F.: Experiences in managing an automotive requirements engineering process. In: RE, pp. 322–327. IEEE Computer Society, Los Alamitos (2004)
8. Walia, G.S., Carver, J.C.: A systematic literature review to identify and classify software requirement errors. Inf. Softw. Technol. 51(7), 1087–1109 (2009)
9. Dahlstedt, A.G., Persson, A.: Requirements interdependencies - moulding the state of research into a research agenda. In: REFSQ, pp. 71–80 (2003)
10. Heimdahl, M.P.E., Leveson, N.G.: Completeness and consistency analysis of state-based requirements. In: IEEE Trans. on SW Engineering, pp. 3–14 (1995)
11. Heitmeyer, C.L., Jeffords, R.D., Labaw, B.G.: Automated consistency checking of requirements specifications. ACM Transactions on Software Engineering and Methodology 5(3), 231–261 (1996)

12. Yu, L., Su, S., Luo, S., Su, Y.: Completeness and consistency analysis on requirements of distributed event-driven systems. In: TASE, Washington, pp. 241–244 (2008)
13. ISO26262: Road vehicles - Functional safety, Part 8, Baseline 17 (2010)
14. Hall, A.: Realising the benefits of formal methods. Journal of Universal Computer Science (J. UCS) 13(5), 669–678 (2007)
15. Abrial, J.R.: Formal methods in industry: achievements, problems, future. In: ICSE, pp. 761–768. ACM, New York (2006)
16. Kuhn, T.: AceRules: Executing rules in controlled natural language. In: Marchiori, M., Pan, J.Z., de Sainte Marie, C. (eds.) RR 2007. LNCS, vol. 4524, pp. 299–308. Springer, Heidelberg (2007)
17. Han, B., Gates, D., Levin, L.: From language to time: A temporal expression anchorer. In: TIME, pp. 196–203 (June 2006)
18. Dwyer, M.B., Avrunin, G.S., Corbett, J.C.: Patterns in property specifications for finite-state verification. In: ICSE, pp. 411–420. ACM, New York (1999)
19. Konrad, S.: Model-driven Development and Analysis of High Assurance Systems. PhD thesis, Michigan State University, East Lansing, MI (October 2006)
20. Grunske, L.: Specification patterns for probabilistic quality properties. In: ICSE, pp. 31–40. ACM, New York (2008)
21. Cobleigh, R.L., Avrunin, G.S., Clarke, L.A.: User guidance for creating precise and accessible property specifications. In: FSE, pp. 208–218. ACM, New York (2006)
22. Pohl, K., Böckle, G., Linden, F.J.v.d.: Software Product Line Engineering: Foundations, Principles and Techniques. Springer, USA (2005)
23. Behrmann, G., David, A., Larsen, K.G.: A tutorial on uppaal, pp. 200–236 (2004)
24. Cimatti, A., Clarke, E., Giunchiglia, E., Giunchiglia, F., Pistore, M., Roveri, M., Sebastiani, R., Tacchella, A.: NuSMV 2: An OpenSource Tool for Symbolic Model Checking. In: Brinksma, E., Larsen, K.G. (eds.) CAV 2002. LNCS, vol. 2404, p. 359. Springer, Heidelberg (2002)
25. Neuendorf, K.A.: Content Analysis Guidebook. Sage Publications, Thousand Oaks (2002)
26. Krippendorff, K.H.: Content Analysis: An Introduction to Its Methodology, 2nd edn. Sage Publications, Inc., Thousand Oaks (2003)
27. Wohlin, C., Runeson, P., Höst, M., Ohlsson, M.C., Regnell, B., Wesslén, A.: Experimentation in software engineering: an introduction. Kluwer Academic Publishers, Norwell (2000)

Agile Requirements Prioritization: What Happens in Practice and What Is Described in Literature

Zornitza Bakalova[1], Maya Daneva[2], Andrea Herrmann[3], and Roel Wieringa[4]

[1,2,4] University of Twente, Computer Science Department, PO Box 217, 7500 AE, Enschede,
The Netherlands
[3] Axivion GmbH, Stuttgart, Germany
`{z.bakalova,m.daneva,.r.j.wieringa}@utwente.nl,`
`herrmann@axivion.com`

Abstract. [**Context & motivation**] Requirements (re)prioritization is an essential mechanism of agile development approaches to maximize the value for the clients and to accommodate changing requirements. Yet, in the agile Requirements Engineering (RE) literature, very little is known about how agile (re)prioritization happens in practice. [**Question/problem**] To gain better understanding of prioritization practices, we analyzed the real-life processes as well as the guidance that the literature provides. We compare the results of a literature research with the results of a multiple case study that we used to create a conceptual model of the prioritization process. We set out to answer the research question: "Which concepts of agile prioritization are shared in practice and in literature and how they are used to provide guidance for prioritization." [**Results**] The case study yielded a conceptual model of the inter-iteration prioritization process. Further, we achieved a mapping between the concepts from the model and the existing prioritization techniques, described by several authors. [**Contribution**] The model contributes to the body of knowledge in agile RE. It makes explicit the concepts that practitioners tacitly use in the agile prioritization process. We use this for structuring the mapping study with the literature and plan to use it for analyzing, supporting, and improving the process in agile projects. The mapping gives us a clear understanding of the 'deviation' between the existing methods as prescribed in literature and the processes we observe in real life. It helps to identify which of the concepts are used explicitly by other authors/ methods.

Keywords: agile development, requirements prioritization, conceptual model.

1 Introduction

In recent years, the agile methods enjoyed broad popularity and captured the attention of both the practitioners and the research community. Two of the key merits of these methods are the fast and early creation of value for the clients and the reduction of risk. This is ensured by practices that are specific attributes of the agile methods only, in particular the short iterations and the frequent respond to changes and learning during the project. The agile methods allow for frequent decisions about the

D. Berry and X. Franch (Eds.): REFSQ 2011, LNCS 6606, pp. 181–195, 2011.

requirements that will be considered for implementation at each iteration and in practice this is implemented by the process of requirements re-prioritization. As Gottesdiener [11] puts it: "Each release represents the culmination of a series of requirements
decisions." The highest priority features (i.e. requirements in agile terminology) get
implemented early so that most business value gets realized, while exposing the project to as low a risk as possible. As the agile literature agrees upon, e.g. [3],[6],[13], a
key tenet of agile processes is that the requirements are prioritized by a customer,
customer team, or 'product owner' acting as a proxy for the end users of the intended
system. The rationale behind this is that the client is the one who can make a judgment about the value of each requirement. Nevertheless, researchers [5], [16] in agile
RE case studies found that the creation of software product value through requirements prioritization decision-making is only partly understood.

This paper presents a piece of work that is part of a series of studies about agile requirements prioritization. It builds upon our earlier publications [18],[20] in which we
investigated the agile requirements prioritization (RP) process as described in literature [18], and as it happens in real-life projects [20]. This research now compares
literature to practice and investigates and compares how complete and how detailed
agile software engineering literature describes requirements reprioritization. This is a
knowledge problem [26] aimed to identify the gap between practice and literature. We
make the note that the key differences between our earlier work [18], [20] and this
one consists in establishing the explicit mapping between the literature and the practice and in reasoning about its implications for research and practice.

This paper sets out to answer the following research question (**RQ**): "Which concepts of agile prioritization are shared in practice and in literature and how they are
used to provide guidance for prioritization." We answer it by mapping existing agile
prioritization techniques to findings from a case study. In this paper we (i) first
present a generic model derived from the case study and describe the conceptual categories that appear in it, and (ii) perform the mapping between these categories and
existing techniques from literature, which is the main contribution of the paper.

This research represents a further step to contribute to the understanding of agile
requirements reprioritization at inter-iteration time, and to assess the guidance the
different RP methods provide. As per Alenljung and Person [2], a decision-making
situation is "a contextual whole of related aspects that concerns a decision-maker",
that is – in our case, the client or the product owner in an agile project.

The paper is structured as follows: Sect. 2 presents our motivation, Sect. 3 introduces
the research method and Sect. 4 describes the results of its application. Sect. 5 discusses
the results, Sect. 6 is dedicated to validity threats, and Sect.7 concludes the paper.

2   Motivation

The practices of regular RP, with strong client participation, are a relatively recent
phenomenon. In turn, they are only partially understood. Furthermore, the RP is an
essential mechanism to maximize the business value (BV) for the clients and to accommodate changing requirements. We make the note that our previous study on BV
creation brought us to think that we can not expect one universal definition of BV. In
contrast, the notion of BV varies across projects and organizations, depending on

(i) the different project-specific settings, (ii) the specific needs of the client (for example, the need to have highly reusable or highly scalable software), and (iii) the market position of the client's organization. It comes out of a human judgment that is based on competencies and deep knowledge of the client's domain and needs. For this reason, for the purpose of this study under BV we understand the client's perceived value of a requirement.

The reasoning in the previous paragraph motivated us for studying the agile RP process as it happens in real life and as described in literature. Moreover, we also made the observation that the agile literature [12],[13],[22] provides rather coarse-grained descriptions of the agile reprioritization process only [20], the literature is not complete and the RP methods are not described in such detail that a practicing software engineer can take them and immediately use them in his/her work. For example, we searched literature for specific information on how the process of value creation takes place in an agile project [17] and we could find no source that indicates how exactly this happens. In this work we investigate the guidance that the different RP methods described in literature provide to the decision-makers, by comparing literature sources with each other. We do this by using the concepts of our conceptual model as the common ground for our comparison. From this mapping and comparison, we can learn how complete and detailed is the published guidance.

Agile literature sources suggest, e.g. in [4], that never before in the software engineering history the customer has been that actively involved in the requirements reprioritization as he/she is in agile. However, our case study [19] indicates that in many cases the developers or their representative (e.g. a product owner), are actively involved and more often than not are leading the inter-iteration decision-making process, keeping in mind the value-creation for the clients. That's why we felt motivated to study the decision-making - as perceived by the developers, with client's goals in mind. Given this backdrop, we think that more clarity is needed in respect to: What do the decision-makers need to consider in order to create more value for the clients / stakeholders? Thus, a decision-maker would profit from a clear model of the prioritization process available to him/her. We think that a conceptual model can help the decision-maker (e.g. the client) in at least three ways: (i) to navigate through the agile process of delivering business value; (ii) to make explicit the tacit assumptions in different RP methods; (iii) to identify those possible pieces/sources of information important to the outcome of the prioritization and, consequently, to the project.

We also think that our model would help those RE researchers who are interested in carrying out empirical research to investigate how agile requirements decision-making happens in practice, to structure research questions and empirical data. The goal of this study is to identify which concepts of agile prioritization are shared in practice and in literature, and to understand if there is a gap between the guidance for prioritization that literature provides to practitioners, and the prioritization process as observed in a case study. This result is meant to help to: (i) map different techniques and concepts to each other; (ii) analyze the level of guidance the different method descriptions provide to practitioners (in terms of those concepts that are explicitly used). (iii) be used as a framework for structuring the discussion about requirement priorities in an agile project and thus lead to explicit and better motivated requirements choices.

3   The Research Method

In this section we provide a description of the case study that yielded the conceptual model. First, we conducted an explorative multiple-case study, applying the Yin's guidelines [27]. It included semi-structured open-end in-depth interviews with practitioners from 8 agile software development organizations. Second, we mapped the existing prioritization techniques to the categories identified in the case study.

3.1   The Case Study Process and Participants

Our case study is performed in the following steps: (1) Compose a questionnaire; (2) Validate the questionnaire through an experienced researcher; (3) Implement changes in the questionnaire based on the feedback; (4) Do a pilot interview to check the applicability of the questionnaire to real-life context; (5) Carry out semi-structured interviews with practitioners according to the finalized questionnaire; (6) Sample and follow-up with those participants that possess deeper knowledge or a specific perspective.

The case companies characterized themselves as organizations that follow agile methodologies. Some of them did strictly follow Scrum principles such as daily stand–up meetings and release retrospective. Most of them, though, applied a combination of agile practices without sticking precisely to a specific agile software development or project management approach.

Each interview lasted 60 to 90 minutes. Each interviewee was provided beforehand with information on the research purpose and the research process. At the interview meeting, the researcher and the interviewee walked through the questionnaire which served to guide the interviews. The questionnaire consisted of three parts: (i) questions referring to the prioritization practice in one concrete project; (ii) questions about the general prioritization practice in the company, based on the interviewees' experience; and (iii) questions about the role of value-consideration for (re)prioritization. Examples of the questions asked are: "Who performs the prioritization?", "What criteria do you consider?". The study included 11 practitioners who described a total of ten projects (two practitioners worked on the same project holding different roles). The application domains for which these practitioners developed software solutions represent a rich mix of fields including banking, health care management, automotive industry, content management, online municipality services, and ERP for small businesses. The information about the participating companies and specialists is summarized below:

- 1 middle size company in the Netherlands (2 cases, 3 participants)
- 2 small companies in the Netherlands (3 cases, 3 participants)
- 1 small company in Bulgaria (1 participant)
- 1 middle size company in Bulgaria (1 participant)
- 1 German university (1 student project)
- 1 large consultancy in Italy (1 participant)
- 1 IT department in a large governmental organization in Turkey (1 participant)

Table 1 explains the primary role the case-study participants had in the studied projects.

Table 1. Table 1. Participants in the Interviews

Interviewee's primary role	Number of interviewees
Project Manager	5
Developer	3
Product Owner	1
Client	1
Scrum Master	1
Total Number of Interviewees	**11**

3.2   The Data Analysis Strategy

In our case study, the data analysis was guided by the Grounded Theory (GT) method according to Charmaz [7]. It is a qualitative approach applied broadly in social sciences to construct general propositions (called a "theory" in this approach) from verbal data. GT is exploratory and well suited for situations where the researcher does not have pre-conceived ideas, and instead is driven by the desire to capture all facets of the collected data and to allow the theory to emerge from the data. In essence, this was a process of making analytic sense of the interview data by means of coding and constant comparison of pieces of data that were collected in the case study. Constant comparison means that the data from an interview is constantly compared to the data already collected from previously held interviews, until a point of saturation is reached, i.e., where new sources of data don't lead to a change in the emerging theory (or conceptual model).

We first read the interview transcripts and attached a coding word to a portion of the text – a phrase or a paragraph. The 'codes' were selected to reflect the meaning of the respective portion of the interview text to a specific part of the RQ. This could be a concept (e.g. 'value', 'method'), or an activity (e.g. 'estimation'). We clustered all pieces of text that relate to the same code in order to analyze it in a consistent and systematic way. The results of the data analysis are presented in Fig. 1 and discussed in Section 5.

4   Results

4.1   The Conceptual Model

This section builds upon our previous work [18], where a preliminary result of our GT process has been presented. Here, we draw on this early result, extend it, elaborate - more in detail, the concepts involved, and discuss how we use the conceptual model to analyze the prioritization methods (Sect. 5.2).

Our multiple iterations of coding, constant comparing of information from the interviews, and conceptual modeling in our GT process yielded the model presented in Fig 1. Its purpose is to explicate and bring insights into the decision-making, which is the core of the RP process. The model takes the perspective of the client, unlike other RP authors [4],[9],[12] adopting the perspective of the developers. This model is to help clients 'zoom-in' into the prioritization process and see those concepts which are important to consider in RP at inter-iteration time, including context. It describes what happens in all those RP processes about which we learnt from the participants in the case study. In the model we take a generic perspective of RP, that is, it abstracts from the use of a specific RP approach.

Our case study results suggest that there is a consensus among the practitioners that there are seven aspects that the clients consider when making decisions on requirements priorities: Project Context, *Prioritization criteria, Effort Estimation/ Size Measurement, Learning Experience, Input from the developers, Dependencies* and *External Change.* Iteration planning additionally considers *Project Constraints.* Below we explain each of these conceptual categories, and their impact on the RP process.

1. During the case study, we observed that the prioritization process itself varies significantly in terms of participants involved, prioritization criteria applied, purpose and frequency of the prioritization. The interviewees shared that, in their view, the variation depends to large extent on the context of the project. We represented this variability in the model by the concept **'*Project Context*'**. It includes those project settings such as 'size of the project' or 'size of the client's organization', and is used to explicate the impact of these settings on the prioritization process. In the projects of our practitioners, the concrete instantiations of the prioritization processes were deemed to be linked with these contextual settings. For example, our interviewees observed that in projects with similar contexts, the instantiated prioritization processes are similar in respect to who are the *decision-makers* and the *amount of participation of the different* parties in the process.

2. All interviewees agreed on that the *project context* has a significant impact on the **'*Prioritization Criteria*'**. We observed also that they all consider the **Business Value** the dominating RP criterion, whereby *Business Value* is estimated by the customer alone. In some projects we observed one recurring question being asked at requirements reprioritization time: *"Is a requirement absolutely necessary to support the main usage scenario?"* This question implies a notion of 'damage to the client' or 'negative value to the client' in the case the requirement is not implemented. We termed this criterion **'*Negative value*'**. One study participant said: *"All features that belong to the main usage scenario were considered mandatory and needed to be included in the product. This drove the decision-making process."* In addition to Business Value, the client in some projects considers the **Risk** caused by a requirement's implementation.

3. In the experience of the interviewees, the client considers **'*Estimated Size*'** based on functional size when making decisions on priorities. The estimation of *Size/ Effort* impacts the value estimation as well. For example, a participant put it this way *"If we give a high estimation for certain requirement (in terms of time /cost), it happens that the client starts considering this requirement as less important as previously thought."* We make the note that size, effort, cost and risk are estimated by the developers and provided to the clients for their decision-making. From the client's perspective, size is a given – though potentially uncertain – input.

4. Another 'building block' in the RP process appeared to be *the developer's perspective* (box '**Input from the Developer**' in Fig. 1). While the literature [3] deems the role of the developers for the RP process secondary, the case study revealed a different situation. In the majority of the cases the developers were the more influential party, providing advice and alternative solutions, but also taking into considerations

the interests of their own organization (such as 'possible reuse of the requirement', 'importance of the project for the organization', 'available resources at the moment').

5. The conceptual category **'External Change'** stands for those events that happen during the project and impact the company, the business environment or the product under development. Such changes can impact the value of requirements. The interviewees deemed the external changes be one of the reasons for clients' requirements change requests.

6. The category **'Learning Experiences'** represents new insights acquired by both the clients and the developers during the project, such as new knowledge about technical solutions, or new insights about the desired functionality of the product under development. They impact the value estimation, the prioritization decisions and the size estimation. For example, while working in a project that we investigated, the developer learned about the exact functionality of open-source software that he intended to use. This new insight triggered changes in the initial estimations and thus in the priorities of the requirements. Learning is an in-built principle in agile development. Harris and Cohn [13] advise *"Incorporate new learning often, in order to decide what to do next"*.

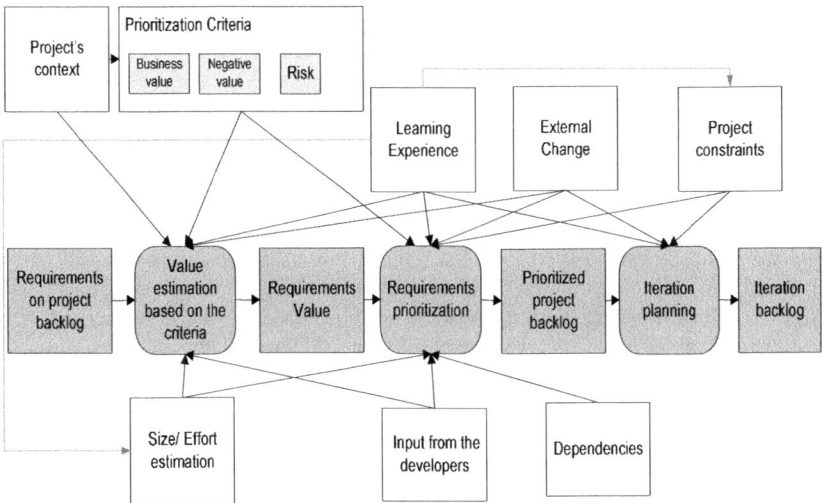

Fig. 1. Conceptual model of the agile prioritization process

7. The **'Project Constraints'** such as duration, release date, budget, velocity and available resources, impact both the prioritization decisions and the iteration planning.

8. **'Dependencies'** between requirements can be of different nature – e.g. chronological or architectural dependencies. Both clients and developers express the dependencies that have to be considered, from their perspective.

9. The **'Project Backlog'** means the list with requirements for the projects. Prioritized Project Backlog is the ordered list of requirements, and a sub-set of it (called iteration, and in some agile methods - sprint backlog) is to be implemented in the next iteration.

'Prioritized' means to assign a requirement a priority, which during iteration planning translates into an order of implementation: i.e. starting with the requirements with the highest priority, so many requirements are chosen for the iteration backlog as can be implemented within the next iteration and project constraints.

We make the following notes: First, we note that the iteration planning and the backlog of the follow-up iteration (i.e. the sprint backlog in the terms of some agile approaches), is out of the scope of this paper and is shown on the model for sake of completeness only. Second, we also note that in Fig 1, arrows reflect relationships between the concepts. For example, the 'learning experience' impacts the size/effort estimation. This is so because with the progress of a project the developers learn to better estimate both the amount of work they are able to perform in one iteration, as well the concrete effort (in hours), or the size of a requirement (e.g. in story points). The learning also is about the mapping factor of story points to effort in hours/ days. This leads to more correct estimations for the following iterations. We make the note, however, that the discussion on the nature of the relationships and the completeness of the set of relationships is outside the scope of this paper. Third, we traced the concepts back to the interview questions that we asked and the interview answers we collected. Because of space limitation, we do not provide information on this in this paper. However, we provide an illustration of this process by using the concept 'Negative value'. This concept originated from two questions: "Which factors played a role during the decision making?" and "Do you use explicit criteria for the prioritization?" The concept was derived based on the following statements of our interviewees "We considered how big the damage will be if a requirement is not implemented. We call this 'negative value', "Is a requirement absolutely necessary to support the main usage scenario?", and "How angry will the client be if certain feature is missing."

As indicated earlier, the resulting model is compatible with any RP technique. It does not prescribe any process or propose a new technique, but instead just describes what we found in the case study. This means that a decision-maker could use this conceptual model as a framework for reasoning about his/her RP process independently of his/her concrete context. Clearly, not all of the elements in the model are necessarily present in each RP process – i.e. some of them depend on the project context. For example, one can use the concepts of the model to depict a specific client's RP situation in a specific project, in a specific organization and, thus, take into account the topics important for clients to consider in RP at inter-iteration time. The model's completeness still should be validated empirically, e.g. by new case studies.

4.2 Mapping of the Existing Agile Prioritization Methods on the Model

In our previous work [20] we identified from the literature 22 prioritization techniques that are being used in agile context. Here we don't provide motivation for the choice of the literature and references to the sources where the techniques are described, as this has been already discussed in [20]. We, therefore, suggest interested readers either look into the [20], or contact the authors for receiving the complete list with references.

In this section we perform a mapping between the conceptual categories of the model in Fig. 1, and their presence in the existing prioritization methods. By means of this mapping, we will see which of the conceptual categories (that we discerned in the case study and that constitute the model) are in fact used by other authors and techniques. The mapping is performed by reading the descriptions of the methods and identifying those concepts that correspond to the ones in our model (Fig. 1). The result is presented in Table 2. Therein, the first column presents the 22 RP techniques. The other columns are named after the categories in the conceptual model in Fig. 1. A row in the table is to indicate those concepts that a particular technique supports and does this up to a certain extent, i.e. the concept appears explicitly in the description of the technique. In the table, we populate the cells with the symbols 'y' to mean those RP method in the description of which we observe that the corresponding concept has been stated and used explicitly. Furthermore, in addition to the concepts that appear in the model, we have added an additional column S in Table 2 to acknowledge that a description of a method indicates the use of tacit knowledge in the requirements prioritization. In this column, we place in the symbol 'x' to mean those methods where we identified that the decisions are made based on implicit, subjective opinion of the decision-maker ("intuitive prioritization"). We make the note that the empty cells in Table 2 mean that we could not find explicit indication about the use of the concept. For example, the second row is about the method *Ping Pong Balls*. From the description we discern that this technique uses value and risk as prioritization criteria ('y' in the first cell), the context of suitability of the methods is described ('y' in the second cell), and cost is considered as well. We proceeded analogically with all methods and concepts. We make the note that most of the techniques are not described in the literature in great detail. Further, they don't discuss explicitly what concepts drive the prioritization decision. For example, the 'Round-the-group' prioritization, and the 'Ping Pong Balls', take the subjective judgment of each participant as an input into the decision-making process, without discussing why each participant estimates one requirement (or feature) to be of higher priority than another. The majority of the descriptions of the techniques are focused on the steps that transform an initial list of requirements into a prioritized list, i.e. in which order they shall be executed, and say almost nothing about the considerations used to determine the priority order itself. For example, Gottesdiener [12] says about the Pair-wise analysis: *"You successively rank requirements by comparing them in pairs until the top requirements emerge at the top of the stack."*

However, we found that there are almost no methods, described in the literature, that explicitly state the criteria on which the decisions are based and the influence of the context. Nor there is indication about who is or should be involved in the decision-making process. We think that a possible reason for this finding could be the nature of the agile decision-making itself, where the team is empowered and self-organized and where team members' tacit knowledge plays a significant role. Further, our observations indicate that some of the methods don't strive for perfection in the sense that their authors mean them to be universally useful. Instead, these methods are just 'good enough' for certain application contexts. Wiegers [25] is one of the very few who explicitly states the criteria used and that these criteria he uses in his approach are not the only one that play a role during prioritization. For this reason he warns practitioners that the scheme he proposes should not be considered as the only method to set priorities. Moreover, he advises to use this approach to decide about 'negotiable' features only, i.e. the ones that are not in the top-priority category. The core features shall be included anyway.

Another reason for the low level of detail of the methods described in literature might be that the practitioners who are authors of the compared methods consider that it requires only common sense to execute the prioritization, and they trust the team to do it right without much guidance.

Furthermore, in Table 2 we observe that:

1. Learning is treated explicitly only by Extreme Programming (XP). This observation is surprising, given the fact that many authors deem the explicit use of learning between two iterations the main advantage of the agile paradigm [9],[13] we assume this is incorporated rather implicitly in the methods, by means of their iterative nature and frequent decision-making cycles.

2. External change – although an important aspect in agile development, is not mentioned even once. It seems that the published methods do not discuss how external changes influence reprioritization. Our gut feeling is that it is included implicitly in the implementation of the processes because in the case study we found that this is a tacit consideration which the developers do take into account.

5   Discussion

Our observations in Table 2 confirm the finding discussed in our previously published paper [20], namely that the descriptions of RP techniques from the agile RE literature use mainly coarse-grained concepts. This becomes obvious when looking at Table 2, as it was possible to populate only part of the cells in the table. This means that our conceptual model is at a finer level of detail compared to the levels that the authors of the 22 techniques considered when describing their approaches. Moreover, our conceptual model reveals that in practice there are many more concepts that impact the prioritization decisions than those concepts that literature describes. Also, only few methods among the 22 that we investigated and that were described in literature, explicitly take the client's perspective – those are the Kano model and the QFD. In fact, literature treats requirements reprioritization very superficially and often does not give a complete cook book recipe. For example, although it is always emphasized that learning and context are important [13] in agile process, no method describes how they should be considered. McDaniels and Small [15] plead for consensus-building that would lead to making decisions on requirements priorities. As per [15], a deliberative process rests on a common understanding of the issues based on the joint learning experience of the decision makers with respect to systematic (e.g. explicit) and anecdotal (e.g. tacit) knowledge. Example of such a process is the communicative process that promotes rational value disputes [21]. The decision-making on priorities is governed by establishing rules of a rational discourse, a specific form of a dialogue in which the stakeholders that make the decisions have equal rights and duties to present their claims and test their validity. These rules also define the role and relevance of both systematic and anecdotal knowledge for making choices.

Table 2 represents: (i) a new knowledge as it makes explicit the gap between the descriptions in the literature and the process as experienced by practitioners in real life projects; (ii) it can be eventually used as a framework to structure a deliberate decision-making process by providing the concepts that can be used to frame the discussions. The concepts of our model can serve as objects of the decisions to be made and could be the topic of a meeting. As per [24], 'deliberation' implies equality

Table 2. Mapping between the concepts from the model in Fig. 1 and the prioritization methods

Concept → Prioritization method	Intuitive prioritization	Prioritization criteria, e.g. value, risk	Project context	Size/effort estimation	Input from developers	learning	external changes	Project constraints	Dependencies	Project backlog	value of requirement	Prioritized project backlog	Iteration/Sprint backlog
Round-the-group prioritization	x		y						y				
Ping Pong Balls	x		y										
$100 allocation		y		y									
Multi-voting system cumulative voting			y										
MoSCoW	x	y											
Pair-wise analysis	x	y								y			
Weighted criteria analysis		y											
Analytic Hierarchy Process (AHP)		y		y									
Dot voting	x	y								y			
Binary Search Tree		y											
Ranking based on product definition		y			y					y	y		y
XP: Planning Game/ Poker		y		y	y	y		y		y	y		y
Quality function deployment (QFD)		y	y							y	y	y	y
Wieger's matrix approach		y	y	y	y			y		y	y		
Mathematical programming techniques		y		y				y			y		y
Technique of bucketing requirements	x	y											y
Kano Model		y											
Eclipse Process Framework		y								y			y
Relative weighting		y											
Larman [9]		y											
Theme screening / scoring		y		y								y	
FDD		y								y			

among the participants, and an orientation towards resolving conflicts in consensual way. In its core, this is the nature and the goal of the agile prioritization.

The implication for the practice is that the mapping between the methods and the concepts allow for a better-motivated and explicit rational-discourse-based process, that includes the concepts from the model.

The implications for the research community is that more research is needed in order to understand: (i) do the practitioners need more detailed guidance about the decision-making process, and if so – for which methods / decision-makers, and project contexts, and (ii) how the assumptions behind the RP techniques (quantitative and discourse-based) shape the outcomes of the decision-making and which technique is better in which agile context.

6   Threats to Validity

We make the note that in this paper we propose a conceptual model. This model, as suggested by GT methodologists [7],[8], is not supposed to be validated against the data that has been used for the development of the model. According to GT methodologists [10],[23], we can *only* evaluate the resulting model against the three evaluation criteria of GT: (i) adequacy, (ii) fitness (or relevance) and (iii) modifiability. We ensured adequacy of the result of the GT process by applying the set of techniques and analytical procedures in the GT. We adhered as closely as possible to the GT processes, coded the data independently by each researcher before re-coding them in joint work discussions. To ensure that the conceptual model makes sense to both researchers and practitioners, i.e. its fitness, we searched and included the so-called 'in-vivo' codes, as recommended in [7]. These are special terms from the world of the practitioners in the studied context, which are assumed that everyone "knows and shares" them. In our case, examples of in-vivo codes, associated to clients in agile RE, are "negative value" (meaning the damage in case the requirement is not implemented), "project backlog", "iteration backlog". Next, the modifiability of an emerging theory is ensured by the level of granularity that we chose for the model. We made a conscious effort to maintain a balance between keeping the concepts abstract enough - so that the theory can serve as a general explanation, and making sure the concepts do not get too abstract as to lose their sensitizing characteristics. The mapping of the conceptual categories with the existing prioritization methods used in practice shows that both the concepts themselves, as well as the level of granularity, are appropriate, as such mapping was possible and yielded meaningful results.

To minimize potential bias of the researcher, we considered also construct validity of our study. We followed Yin's [27] recommendations in this respect, by establishing a chain of evidence. First, the reports of the case study (e.g. partially published in [19]) showed clear links to the data, as well as reflected the link between the questions posed in the study protocol and the results. Second, we had a draft case study report reviewed by one key informant - one of the participants in the case study, who read and re-read multiple versions of the case study results. The third recommendation – using multiple sources of evidence, could not be implemented in the scope of our study, as interviews were the only source we consulted.

Furthermore, we make the note that we wanted to create a conceptual model about prioritization from the perspective of creating business value for the client, yet the majority of our interviewees were from development teams (e.g. we had only one client and one product owner who explicitly served as clients' proxy). We asked these professionals to put themselves 'in the shoes of the clients' when we discussed how agile prioritization creates clients' value. Nevertheless, we are conscious about that we obtained developers' perceptions only regarding the concept of clients' business value. It might be, therefore, well possible that if we had interviewed clients exclusively, we could have obtained some other categories in addition to those that we already have in the model. We consider this is an interesting study that concerns the expendability of our conceptual model and we plan it as research for the future.

The choice of the companies participating in the study could represent a threat to the validity of the results in a number of respects:

(i)   As we are interested in the phenomenon 'agile prioritization', we want to be sure that this indeed is the context of the studied companies. We relied on the information provided by the companies' representatives and on our own observations, and 'mapped' them to the principles stated in the Agile Manifesto [1] in order to identify the agility of a company. The companies varied in respect to size, level of organizational rigor and hierarchy, and thus – in level of agility.

(ii) The choice of the companies was not motivated by any other criteria except the one – to be agile. The authors relied on their professional and personal network to establish contacts with the companies.

(iii) The studied projects are not representative for all the possible ways in which prioritization is performed in agile organizations. We, however, consider that our findings can be observable in companies and projects that have similar contexts to those included in our study only.

We make the note that while the conceptual model considers the perspective of the client, the analyzed literature treats prioritization from the development team's perspective. We, however, think that this does not pose an issue because we are aware that we investigate the client's perspective as it is seen with the developers´ eyes, because in our case study, the 10 out of 11 interviews were made with representatives of the development team.

Last, we make the note that although this study used the model produced by our previous study [18][20], we do not think that this represents a major threat to validity . The initial model was based on literature sources, authored by agile experts. For this reason we expected to find the same concepts in the interviews. We can expect that practitioners, who say they follow an agile methodology, are familiar with the literature and try to work in a way which is consistent with it and with the underlying concepts. Thus, the initial model cannot be regarded as preconceived ideas in the sense of the GT.

7   Summary and Outlook

This paper made two contributions: first it investigated the concepts that are important to consider when practitioners work on (re)prioritizing agile requirements at inter-iteration time, and second, it mapped these concepts against 22 agile RP techniques described in literature. The results of our effort are, respectively: (1) a refined conceptual model which describes on an abstract, generic level, the concepts that seem to impact the agile prioritization process, and (2) a table with mappings between the concepts of the model and the methods as described in literature.

Our conceptual model was created by applying GT. The model explicates the RP in agile projects. It presents the state of the practice described by concepts that we discerned from interviews with 11 practitioners. The model provides a generic framework for describing the decision-making situation while prioritizing the requirements. We used it to map different literature sources, methods and terminologies to each other, by identifying the use of the concepts from the model in the methods from literature. The mapping table that we obtained gives us a clear understanding of the 'deviation' between the existing methods as prescribed in literature and the process we observe in real life. It helps to identify which of the concepts that we identified are used explicitly by other authors/ methods. Furthermore, we identified clusters of methods and make a suggestion to use a discursive approach for those methods that rely on implicit, tacit knowledge.

We think that the results can be of value in at least two ways: (1) to serve as a roadmap for further empirical research to investigate the level of literature guidance on the decision-making, needed in different contexts, and (2) it can be used as a framework to provide better guidance to practitioners and allow for better motivated, discourse-based process.

Acknowledgments. We are indebted to the anonymous reviewers for their detailed and constructive comments that added to the improved quality of this paper. This research has been funded by the Netherland's NWO under the QUADREAD project.

References

1. Agile Manifesto, http://agilemanifesto.org/principles.html
2. Alenljung, B., Person, A.: Portraying the Practice of Decision-making in Requirements Engineering: a Case Study of large Scale Bespoke Development. Requirements Engineering Journal 13, 257–279 (2008)
3. Ambler, S.W.: Agile Modeling - Effective Practices for eXtreme Programming and the Unified Process. Wiley, New York (2002)
4. Augustine, S.: Managing Agile Projects. Prentice-Hall, Englewood Cliffs (2005)
5. Barney, S., Aurum, A., Wohlin, C.: A Product Management Challenge: Creating Software Product Value through Requirements Selection. Journal of Software Architecture 54, 576–593 (2008)
6. Beck, K.: eXtreme Programming Explained: Embrace Change. Addison-Wesley, Reading (2000)
7. Charmaz, K.: Constructing Grounded Theory: a Practical Guide through Qualitative Research. Sage, Thousand Oaks (2007)
8. Clarke, A.: Situational Analysis: Grounded Theory after the Postmodern Turn. Sage, Thousand Oaks (2005)
9. Cohn, M.: Agile Estimating and Planning. Prentice-Hall, Englewood Cliffs (2005)

10. Glaser, B.G.: Basics of Grounded Theory Analysis: Emergence vs Forcing. Sociology Press Mill Valley (1992)
11. Gottesdiener, AView To Agile Requirements, E EBG Consulting, Inc., http://www.ebgconsulting.com, http://ebgconsulting.com/Pubs/Articles/AViewToAgileRequirements-gottesdiener.pdf
12. Gottesdiener, E., At a Glance: Other Prioritization Methods, EBG Consulting, Inc., http://www.ebgconsulting.com, http://www.ebgconsulting.com/Pubs/Articles/At%20a%20Glance-Other%20Prioritization%20Methods-supplement-EBG%20Consulting.pdf
13. Harris, R.S., Cohn, M.: Incorporating Learning and Expected Cost of Change in Prioritizing Features on Agile Projects. In: Abrahamsson, P., Marchesi, M., Succi, G. (eds.) XP 2006. LNCS, vol. 4044, pp. 175–180. Springer, Heidelberg (2006)
14. McDaniels, T., Small, M.J.: Rsk Analysis and Society: an Interdisciplinary Characterization of the Field. Cambridge University Press, Cambridge (2004)
15. McDaniels, T., Small, M.J.: Risk analysis and society: an interdisciplinary characterization of the field, Timothy. Cambridge University Press, Cambridge (2003)
16. Petersen, K., Wohlin, C.: A Comparison of Issues and Advantages in Agile and Incremental development between State of the Art and an Industrial Case. Journal of Systems and Software 82, 1479–1490 (2009)
17. Racheva, Z., Daneva, M., Sikkel, K.: Value creation by agile projects: Methodology or mystery? In: Bomarius, F., Oivo, M., Jaring, P., Abrahamsson, P. (eds.) PROFES 2009. LNBIP, vol. 32, pp. 141–155. Springer, Heidelberg (2009)
18. Racheva, Z., Daneva, M., Herrmann, A.: A Conceptual Model of Client-driven Agile Requirements Prioritization: Results of a Case Study. In: IEEE International Symposium on Empirical Software Engineering and Measurement (ESEM), Bolzanao, Italy (September 2010)
19. Racheva, Z., Daneva, M., Sikkel, K., Herrmann, A., Wieringa, R.: Do we Know Enough about Requirements Prioritization in Agile Projects: Insights from a Case Study. In: The Proceedings of Requirements Engeneering 2010, Australia (2010)
20. Racheva, Z., Daneva, M., Herrmann, A., Wieringa, R.: A conceptual model and process for client-driven agile requirements prioritization. In: The Proc. of 4th International Conference on Research challenges in Information Science (RCIS), Nice, France. IEEE, Los Alamitos (2010)
21. Rippe, S.: Demokracy and Environmental Decision-making. Environmental Values 8, 75–98 (1999)
22. Schwaber, K.: Agile Project Management with SCRUM. Microsoft Press (2004)
23. Strauss, A.L., Corbin, J.M.: Basics of Qualitative Research - Grounded Theory Procedures and Techniques. Sage, Newbury Park (1991)
24. Webler, T.: "Right" discourse in citizen participation. An evaluative yardstick. In: Renn, Webler, Wiedemann (eds.) Fairness and competence in citizen participation. Evaluating new models for environmental discourse, pp. 35–86. Kluwer, Boston (1995)
25. Wiegers, K.: First Things First: Prioritizing Requirements. Software Development 7(9) (1999)
26. Wieringa, R.J.: Relevance and problem choice in design science. In: Winter, R., Zhao, J.L., Aier, S. (eds.) DESRIST 2010. LNCS, vol. 6105, pp. 61–76. Springer, Heidelberg (2010)
27. Yin, R.K.: Case Study Research: Design and Methods, Thousand Oaks (1984)

Mining Requirements Links

Vincenzo Gervasi[1,2] and Didar Zowghi[2]

[1] Dipartimento di Informatica, University of Pisa, Italy
[2] School of Software, University of Technology, Sydney, Australia

Abstract. **[Context & motivation]** Obtaining traceability among requirements and between requirements and other artifacts is an extremely important activity in practice, an interesting area for theoretical study, and a major hurdle in common industrial experience. Substantial effort is spent on establishing and updating such links in any large project – even more so when requirements refer to a product family. **[Question/problem]** While most research is concerned with ways to reduce the effort needed to establish and maintain traceability links, a different question can also be asked: how is it possible to harness the vast amount of implicit (and tacit) knowledge embedded in already-established links? Is there something to be learned about a specific problem or domain, or about the humans who establish traces, by studying such traces?

[Principal ideas/results] In this paper, we present preliminary results from a study applying different machine learning techniques to an industrial case study, and test to what degree common hypothesis hold in our case. **[Contribution]** Reshaping traceability data into knowledge can contribute to more effective automatic tools to suggest candidates for linking, to inform improvements in writing style, and at the same time provide some insight into both the domain of interest and the actual implementation techniques.

Keywords: traceability, machine learning, knowledge mining.

1 Introduction

A famous definition of *Traceability* in requirements is provided in [4]:

> "Requirements traceability refers to the ability to describe and follow the life of a requirement, in both a forwards and backwards direction (i.e., from its origins, through its development and specification, to its subsequent deployment and use, and through periods of on-going refinement and iteration in any of these phases)."

This definition places particular emphasis on the ability to *follow* the life of requirements, or in other words, on following the *links* established between requirements and other artifacts, or among requirements (which, in turn, can include requirements at different stages of evolution, or business requirements to requirements specifications, or various requirements in a single requirements document which taken together describe a single feature, etc.).

The major hurdle to ensure traceability is the effort needed to establish and maintain the links between all those artifacts, while the artifacts themselves undergo their evolution. It is not surprising then that most research in the area has aimed at facilitating

D. Berry and X. Franch (Eds.): REFSQ 2011, LNCS 6606, pp. 196–201, 2011.

the establishment of links, typically by providing semi-automatic tools to that end. In the most common approach, Information Retrieval techniques such as the Vector Space Model (VSM) or Latent Semantic Indexing (LSI), are used to identify a set of candidate requirements to be linked, based on the similarity of terms they contain [2,6,5].

In this paper we take the dual approach: instead of asking ourselves how to suggest traceability links, we investigate what can be learned from links that are already established. The situation where a set of links is already established is in fact common in industrial practice, especially in large or long-lived projects. In that context, other factors compound the problem: for example, changing teams means that links established at different times follow different conventions for what is relevant; requirements databases being exchanged between organizations (e.g., from a contractor to the main company, or when actual programming is outsourced outside of the main company) means that a full set of requirements and links, established according to unfamiliar or inconsistent principles, are acquired together.

2 Case Study and Experiments

We used a publicly-available dataset of requirements with traceability information, originally based on the CM-1 project by the NASA Metrics Data Program [1]. The dataset comprises 235 high-level SRS (software requirements specification) which are refined to 220 low-level SDS (software design specification) for the same DPU (data processing unit); 361 manually-verified links relate the two sets and, so to say, "tell the story" of the refinement. Notice the 361 links constitute just the 0.7% of all possible pairwise[1] links between SRS and SDS, so the linking relationship in the dataset is very selective. On this dataset we ran two series of experiment, described in the following.

2.1 Using Machine Learning to Infer Traces

Most approaches to semi-automatic tracing are based on the assumption that the occurrence of similar terms in two requirements increases the likelihood of them being related by a link (with [3] and [7] being recent exceptions). This likelihood is estimated with techniques such as VSM based on *tf-idf* (term frequency-inverse document frequency), where very common terms contribute less to the similarity score than highly-specialized ones that only appear in few places. Normally, this hypothesis is tested by verifying how many suggested links above a certain likelihood threshold are correct, thus giving rise to the two usual metrics of *precision* (which percentage of the suggested links are correct) and *recall* (which percentage of the correct links were suggested).

We set instead to verify if the hypothesis itself (i.e., that the occurrence of the same terms in two requirements implies greater link affinity) could be mined from the available set of correct links. This was obtained through the following procedure:

---

[1] In theory traceability should be $n:m$, i.e. a set of elements to another set of elements, but in practice most industrial tools have them as 1:1 relations, and their possible grouping is left to the interpretation of the reader. We will submit to the common usage here.

1. All requirements were tokenized[2] and stemmed; stopwords where then removed, thus obtaining a set of 1785 terms that constitute the domain vocabulary employed in our requirements (only 268 of these appeared in both SRS and SDS).
2. From each term t in the vocabulary, two features were derived, one for the occurrence of t in a high-level requirement (named t_H) and one for the similar occurrence in a low-level requirement (named t_L), giving in total 3570 features.
3. Each requirement was then transformed into a vector of features, with each feature having the tf-idf value of the corresponding term. Higher values indicate higher significance, with 0 indicating a non-occurring term.
4. From these vectors was derived a set of *classification cases* by joining one high-level requirement and one low-level requirement, and adding a classification of `link` or `nolink` based on whether that particular pair was a true link in the original dataset, or not. To facilitate application of the machine learning algorithms, the set was composed of 722 classification cases, half each for `link` and `nolink`. Notice that this alters the statistical features of the set (we have 50% links compared to 0.7% in the original dataset); this issue will be discussed later.
5. Finally, the dataset was used to train and test two different classifiers from the WEKA [8] collection, a Naive Bayesian classifier and the J48 decision-tree classifier (based on the C4.5 algorithm), in a standard 10-fold cross-validation scheme, and both the structure of the classifiers obtained, and the evaluation of their performances, were analyzed.

2.2 Using Traces to Infer Domain Thesaurus

In the second experiment, we considered whether the existing traces could suggest stronger affinity between different terms, and weaker affinity between the same terms, compared to the basic hypothesis of VSM that affinity coincides with identity (i.e., only the occurrence of the same term contributes to estimating the probability of a link).

To this end, we derived an affinity score a for each pair of terms (p_H, q_L) as follows:

$$a(p_H, q_L) = \sum_{P,Q} s(P,Q) \cdot (t(p_H, P) + t(q_L, Q))$$

where P is a high-level requirement, Q is a low-level requirement, $s(P,Q)$ is $+1$ if P and Q are linked or -1 otherwise, and $t(r, R)$ is the tf-idf value for term r in requirement R. For the purpose of this particular experiment, we do not concern ourselves with scaling the values based on document size, since we are considering a single dataset.

With the formula above, terms that occur particularly often in linked requirements pairs, and not commonly in unlinked requirements, would have positive affinity; neutral terms would have an affinity close to 0; negative affinity indicates that those terms tend to appear more frequently in unlinked requirements.

The null hypothesis is that pairs (t_H, t_L) should have high affinity, meaning that the occurrence of the same term in a high-level and a low-level requirement is an indication

---

[2] A purely alphabetic tokenizer was used; this simplistic choice caused the breaking up of acronyms such as "DPU-1553", "DPU-BOOT", "BIT_DRAM" which could be considered a single term. On the other hand, cases such as "write/read/compare" were correctly split.

that they should be linked. In contrast, pairs (p_H, q_L) with high affinity, where $p \neq q$, indicate that p and q are strictly related terms, despite being different.

3 Results and Discussion

The Naive Bayes classifier obtained 60.5% precision and 60.1% recall, whereas the J48 one obtained 67.6% for both, which in the given conditions is a 17.6% improvement over the 50% a trivial classifier would obtain (e.g., one that classifies all pairs as `link`, or as `nolink`, or at random). This figure should be compared with the one obtained by traditional VSM, which for our case is 86.5% at a threshold of 0.04 (see Figure 1). Notice again that these figures are somewhat artificial, in that in common practice, the number of non-links is often a hundredfold greater than the number of links, whereas in our sample they were forcibly set equal[3].

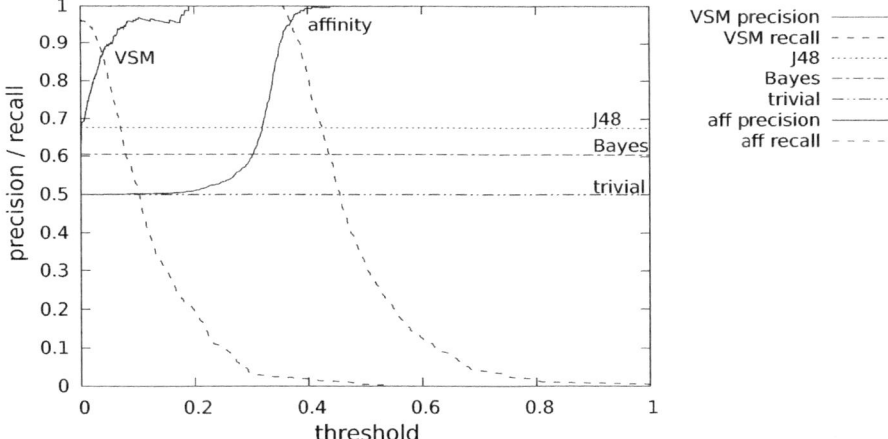

Fig. 1. Compared performances of VSM, J48, Naive Bayesian, trivial and affinity classifiers on predicting links for the CM-1 case study

As Figure 1 shows, VSM is a clear winner over both Naive Bayesian and J48. However, the 17.6% improvement the latter has over the trivial classifier was obtained *without* recourse to the VSM hypothesis that occurrence of the same terms in two requirements imply greater link affinity. In fact, direct inspection of the decision tree learned by the J48 classifier shows very few instances in which the appearance of the same term in both high-level and low-level requirements is a crucial factor for the classification decision. This observation suggests that further improvements over VSM can be obtained by harnessing the models mined by training the classifiers.

The good performance of VSM can also be described via the affinity scores of identical pairs, e.g. $a(t_H, t_L)$. Indeed, based on the results of our second experiment

---

[3] If we had used the natural distribution, a trivial classifier always answering `nolink` would have scored 99.3%, making any relative improvement very difficult to measure.

Table 1. Distribution of affinity for identical pairs and for all pairs

$a(p_H, q_L)$	> 0	$= 0$	< 0	N
identical pairs	89%	4%	7%	268
all pairs	45%	6%	48%	134531

Table 2. Best and worst affinity scores for identical and non-identical pairs of terms

$a(t_H, t_L)$			$a(p_H, q_L)$ with $p \neq q$		
90.620	bit_H	bit_L	124.779	$boot_H$	$dram_L$
84.640	ssi_H	ssi_L	114.231	$boot_H$	bit_L
77.838	ccm_H	ccm_L	113.881	$boot_H$	$bootstrap_L$
73.437	$dram_H$	$dram_L$	112.550	csc_H	$dram_L$
71.521	icu_H	icu_L	97.982	$boot_H$	$eeprom_L$
59.682	$error_H$	$error_L$	97.419	$boot_H$	$test_L$
...			...		
-6.962	$allocate_H$	$allocate_L$	-54.900	dpu_H	$data_L$
-7.360	$software_H$	$software_L$	-57.036	dpu_H	dpa_L
-28.600	csc_H	csc_L	-60.287	$boot_H$	$data_L$

(see Table 1), almost 90% of the terms had a positive affinity with themselves. It is thus clear that VSM, where it is assumed that all terms have positive affinity with themselves, provides a good approximation of the real traces.

Still, better can be done by mining the affinity scores from trace data, and using those to refine the results of VSM. In fact, not only 11% of the terms did not satisfy VSM's underlying assumption (and their use in predicting traces was thus detrimental), but a large number of non-identical pairs had even higher affinity scores than the identical pairs. For example, Table 2 lists the highest and lowest affinity scores in our case. On one side, it is interesting to note how most terms shown are domain-specific acronyms; these tend to characterize most strongly the subject of a requirement. In contrast, most common terms (e.g., state, command, application, routine, etc.) tend to have neutral affinity scores (i.e., closer to 0). On the other side, it can be observed how the affinity of certain non-identical pairs (e.g., $boot_H$ with $DRAM_L$, bit_L, $bootstrap_L$, $EEPROM_L$) is higher than that of identical pairs. It turns out that using affinity scores instead of cosine similarity on the tf-idf vectors, in our case we have a remarkable maximum of 95.7% simultaneous precision and recall, vs. 86.5% for VSM (Figure 1).

Another interesting observation is that from affinity data we can obtain some insight into the domain. For example, CSC_H and CSC_L have negative affinity (Table 2); investigation in the domain reveals that "CSC" is a generic term from "(sub)system", hence it is not surprising that different occurences of "CSC" refer to different things, and do not imply a relationship between requirements. On the contrary, $boot_H$ and $bootstrap_L$ have high affinity, for obvious linguistic reasons that would be missed by VSM. More interestingly, $boot_H$ and $dram_L$ also have high affinity: something that is explained only when realizing that, in the implementation, the DRAM of the system is initialized from stored values at boot time.

4 Conclusions

In this preliminary study, we have identified some of the information that can be mined from requirements traces, showing that "there is life beyond VSM". In our case study, we harnessed two such sources of information: (i) the decision tree generated by the J48 machine-learning algorithm, and (ii) the affinity measure we defined above. In both cases, the additional knowledge gained could be used to help familiarize with an unknown domain, to shed some light on refinement decisions, to understand linking policies, or – in the end – to obtain a more accurate semi-automatic linking of new or changed requirements based on previous history.

In further pursuing this line of research, we will investigate how the various techniques we employed behave on data with a more realistic distribution (namely, with less than 1% of all possible pairs of requirements linked instead of 50% as in this preview), a study which is rendered difficult by the substantial computational power needed to process large datasets. We will also test how to best integrate the affinity measures we mined from the data, in order to improve the results from well-established techniques.

We will also extend the analysis to more datasets, to assess how generalizable the finding from the CM-1 case study are, and explore how data mined from existing links can be best visualized and exploited for other tasks, e.g. to infer a domain glossary.

Acknowledgements. The authors would like to thank Jane Hayes for her help in accessing the data and inspiration with this work. This material is based upon work supported by the National Science Foundation under Grant No. 0811140.

References

1. Center of excellence for software traceability,
   http://www.traceabilitycenter.org/
2. Cleland-Huang, J., Berenbach, B., Clark, S., Settimi, R., Romanova, E.: Best practices of automated traceability. IEEE Computer 40(6) (June 2007)
3. Cleland-Huang, J., Czauderna, A., Gibiec, M., Emenecker, J.: A machine learning approach for tracing regulatory codes to product specific requirements. In: Proc. of the 32nd Int. Conf. on Software Engineering, pp. 155–164. ACM, New York (2010)
4. Gotel, O., Finkelstein, A.: An analysis of the requirements traceability problem. In: Proc. of the First Int. Conf. on Requirements Engineering, pp. 94–101. IEEE CS Press, Los Alamitos (1994)
5. Marcus, A., Maletic, J.I.: Recovering documentation-to-source-code traceability links using latent semantic indexing. In: Proc. of the 25th Int. Conf. on Software Engineering, pp. 125–137 (2003)
6. Nattoch Dag, J., Gervasi, V., Brinkkemper, S., Regnell, B.: Speeding up requirements management in a product software company: Linking customer wishes to product requirements through linguistic engineering. In: Proc. of the 12th IEEE Int. Requirements Engineering Conf., IEEE CS Press, Los Alamitos (2004)
7. Sultanov, H., Hayes, J.H.: Application of swarm techniques to requirements engineering: Requirements tracing. In: Proc. of the 18th IEEE Int. Requirements Engineering Conf., pp. 211–220. IEEE CS Press, Los Alamitos (2010)
8. Weka 3: Data mining software in Java, http://www.cs.waikato.ac.nz/ml/weka/

Clustering Stakeholders for Requirements Decision Making

Varsha Veerappa and Emmanuel Letier

University College London, Gower Street, London WC1E 6BT, United Kingdom
{v.veerappa,e.letier}@cs.ucl.ac.uk

Abstract. [**Context and motivation**] Novel web-based requirements elicitation tools offer the possibility to collect requirements preferences from large number of stakeholders. Such tools have the potential to provide useful data for requirements prioritization and selection. [**Question/problem**] However, existing requirements prioritization and selection techniques do not work in this context because they assume requirements ratings from a small number of stakeholders groups, rather than from a large number of individuals. They also assume that the relevant groups of stakeholders have been identified a priori, and that all stakeholders within a group have the same preferences. [**Principal ideas/results**] This paper aims at addressing these problems by applying cluster analysis techniques used in the area of market segmentation for identifying relevant groups of stakeholders to be used for requirements decision making. [**Contribution**] We describe a clustering analysis technique that can be used in this context and evaluate its adequacy on a pilot case study.

Keywords: Stakeholder segmentation, cluster analysis, web-based requirements elicitation, requirements prioritization and selection.

1 Introduction

There is a trend towards using web-based application such as forums, wikis, and recommender systems to elicit and prioritizing requirements from very large number of stakeholders [1], [2]. For example, StakeSource is a web-based requirements elicitation tool that allows stakeholders to recommend other stakeholders, submit requirements, and rate each other's requirements [3]. Such systems help collecting large amount of data that can be used for understanding stakeholders' preferences, identifying conflicts, and guiding requirements selection and prioritization.

There exists a wide range of qualitative and quantitative techniques for identifying the best tradeoffs among the preferences of multiple stakeholders [4]. Cost-value based requirements prioritization techniques rely on eliciting the relative costs and value of each requirements for each stakeholders group [5]. By assigning weights to the groups, one can compute the overall value of a requirement as the weighted sum of its value for each stakeholders group, and rank the set of requirements accordingly. Different variants of this approach are used in practice [6], [7], [8]. However, generating a full ranking of requirements based on a single numerical value hides conflicts between stakeholders instead of exposing them. More recent requirements selection

D. Berry and X. Franch (Eds.): REFSQ 2011, LNCS 6606, pp. 202–208, 2011.

techniques have therefore looked at the problem as a multi-criteria decision problem and developed support for exploring the space of optimal solutions and reasoning about the fairness of the requirements selection [9], [10], [11].

All these techniques have been developed in a context where requirements values are elicited for a small number of stakeholders groups only. They do not scale to the context of online requirements elicitation tools where values are elicited from a large number of *individual* stakeholders (for example, hundreds of individuals instead of five groups, which is roughly the number of groups that can be handled by multi-objective group decision-making techniques [11]). Furthermore, they assume that homogenous groups of stakeholders can be identified a priori, and that all stake-holders within a group agree on the value to be given to each requirement. An additional difficulty specific to online elicitation tools is that some groups of stakeholders are likely to be under-represented or over-represented in the collected ratings. For example, stakeholders who have more time to express their preferences online are likely to be over-represented compared to more busy stakeholders whose opinion may be no less important to the project success.

The objective of our work is to study the application of clustering techniques for identifying homogenous groups of stakeholders that can be used as input to existing requirements selection and prioritization techniques.

Our technique takes as input individual stakeholders' values for a set of requirements to be evaluated, and generates as output a set of stakeholders groups together with the value assigned to each requirement by each group. These group values can then be used by existing decision-making techniques to rank the requirements or generate a Pareto front and fairness diagram. A good grouping is one where all groups are composed of stakeholders with similar ratings so that the group values for each requirement are close to the ratings of its group members. Using group values that are close to the individual ratings as input to the decision-making techniques will result in decisions that better reflect the collected individual preferences than if the values used as input are further from the individual ratings. As a simple example, if a requirement is given very high rating by half the stakeholders and very low by the other half, splitting the stakeholders into two groups with a very high and very low group value for the requirement for each is better than having a single group where the requirement is given a medium group value. In the latter case, the group value fails to represent any-one's preference accurately and the result of decision-making techniques using this value will possibly satisfy no one. When generating groups, there is a conflict between minimizing the number of groups and maximizing their homogeneity. An extreme situation in which each stakeholder forms a single group would be very homogenous but would not help decision making.

Our approach relies on clustering techniques used in market segmentation for product development and marketing [12]. In this area, one distinguishes between a customer's characteristics that are product-independent such as his age, location and revenue, characteristics that are product-dependent such as his perceptions, benefits and loyalty for the product. Our approach groups stakeholders based their ratings which are product-dependent characteristics, instead of grouping them according to product-independent characteristics such as their job title or age.

This paper describes our approach and illustrates its use on a pilot case study conducted at UCL where we explore the impact of using different group size and compare clustering approaches.

2 Using Cluster Analysis to Group Stakeholders: An Example

Similarity between stakeholders' ratings is determined by their Euclidian distance. Given two stakeholders S_i, S_j and their ratings r_i, r_j for n requirements, the distance between their ratings is given by

$$d(ri, rj) = \sqrt{[(r_{1i} - r_{1j})^2 + (r_{2i} - r_{2j})^2 + \dots + (r_{ni} - r_{nj})^2]}$$

where r_{ki}, r_{kj} denote the ratings of S_i and S_j for requirement k, respectively. We generate stakeholders groups using the weighted average linkage clustering algorithm [12], [13]. This agglomerative hierarchical clustering algorithm allows one to form group hierarchies where small, highly homogenous groups at the bottom of the hierarchy are incrementally merged to form larger groups. This clustering algorithm has other properties that are highly desirable in our context: it is deterministic, not prone to reversal and chaining problems and it considers the size of the clusters when merging them [13].

To test our approach, we have carried out a survey at UCL asking 50 potential stakeholders to rate 5 requirements R1, R2, R3, R4 and R5 for an online calendar on a 10 point scale. We obtained responses from 47 stakeholders, labeled S1 to S47. Our product-specific characteristics are the values of each requirement to the stakeholders. We have also gathered a few product-independent characteristics related to the stakeholders like their position at UCL, number of years at UCL, and average number of hours spent online per day. Table 1 shows a sample of the data collected.

Table 1. Sample data collected from survey carried out at UCL

Stakeholder	Position	Time spent on internet daily (hrs)	No. of years at UCL	Ratings				
				R1	R2	R3	R4	R5
S1	Admin	6	4	5	3	10	10	10
S2	Research	10	7	3	10	3	3	3
..	....	.....	....	....	....	....	....	....
S9	Postgraduate	8	1	1	2	3	4	8
..	....	.....	....	....	....	....	....	....
S47	Academic	4	3	4	4	9	4	2

Figure 1 shows the dendrogram representing the clusters generated by the weighted average linkage clustering algorithm on these ratings. A dendrogram is a two-dimensional diagram that depicts how the agglomeration or division are done at the different stages of the cluster analysis [13]. The Y-axis depicts the distance among the ratings while the X-axis lists the stakeholders. At the topmost level of the hierarchy at cut off 10, we have a single cluster with all 47 stakeholders. When we move to the next level at a cut off 9 we have 3 clusters. The first one consists of stakeholders S26 to S31 in the dendrogram, the second one consists of stakeholders S2 to S34 and the third one consists only of stakeholder S9. As we decrease the distance along the Y-axis i.e. increase similarity, we have an increasing number of clusters which are smaller in size. We can see that in some cases, individual stakeholders are added to a

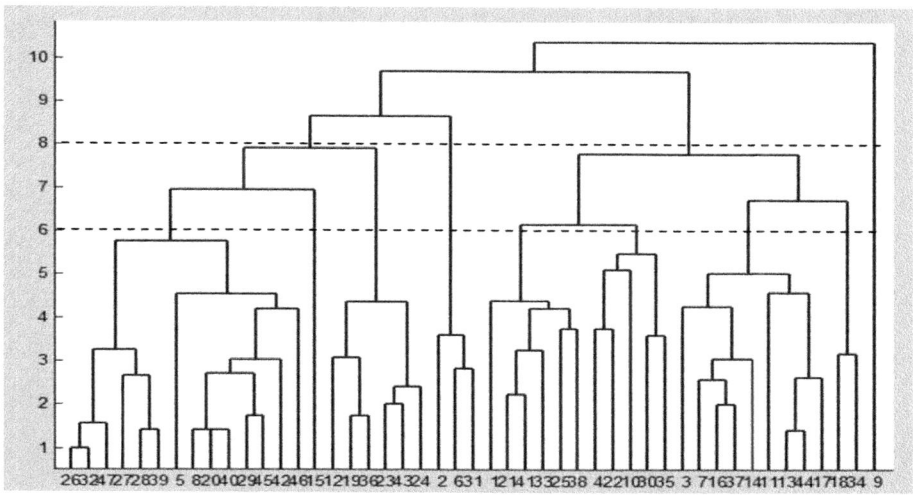

Fig. 1. Dendrogram for cluster analysis using weighted average linkage

cluster very late (at a greater distance) and these are outliers whose ratings could either be discarded or investigated in more depth depending on the importance and expertise of the particular stakeholder. One such example is stakeholder S9.

When using our technique, requirements engineers need to define where they want to cut off the hierarchy to get the optimal clusters in their context. To explore the impact of such decisions, we have decided to cut off the dendrogram at two places, that is, at distance 8 and 6. At cut off 8 we have 4 clusters and at cut off 6 we have 9 clusters. In each group, the value given to a requirement is taken to be the median value for all stakeholders in the group.

To assess the quality of the generated groups and their associated requirements value, we compare for each stakeholder the distance between the requirement values for the group to which the stakeholders belong and the actual values given by the stakeholder. For comparison purposes, we will also compute the distance of the actual ratings from the median of ratings with no clustering (i.e. all stakeholders are put in a single group) and when the stakeholders are grouped by their position at UCL. The results of this comparison are shown in Figure 2 for stakeholders S1 to S20 (the others are not shown to save space). The figure shows that the median values used to represent the stakeholders with no clustering and grouping by role are generally farther from the actual ratings of the stakeholders than when clustering is used at all. With clustering, it can be seen that with a cut off at a lower difference results in a median value closer to the actual rating of the stakeholder. Stakeholder S9 is an outlier as it is a cluster on its own and the median values with clustering will be the actual ratings of the stakeholder.

To further demonstrate how the overall decision process is improved, we fed the median for the clusters (labeled G1 to G3) at cut off 8 into the Volere prioritization template [6] giving equal weight to all of the clusters. We have dropped the ratings of outlier S9, so we are left with 3 groups each having a weight of 33%.

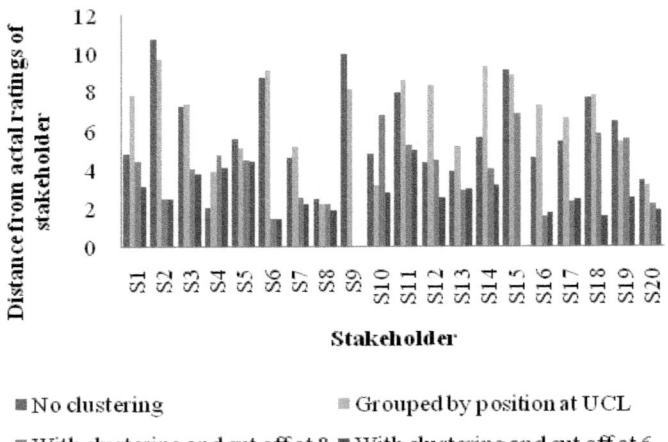

Fig. 2. Distance between the actual ratings of stakeholders and the median ratings for their group using different cluster sizes and approaches

The critical question of how to determine the weight of each group is currently left to the decision makers. The simple approach of estimating these weights by counting the number of stakeholders in each group will generally not be the best approach as some important stakeholders' views may be under-represented in the collected ratings and some important requirements such as legal or security requirements may be given low values by everyone except a few individuals who are experts in that area. Clustering stakeholders according to their ratings can mitigate these problems by highlighting these situations and allowing decision-makers to adjust the group weights or decide that some requirements must be implemented independently from the ratings. Standard prioritization techniques like AHP can also be used to help determining the group weights.

Figure 3 shows the requirements ranks after running Volere prioritization using median ratings with and without clustering. The requirements values and rankings are different in the two approaches. For example, when stakeholders are first grouped in clusters, requirement R2 moves above R1 and R5 in the ranking order. As we have shown in Figure 2, this ranking is obtained by using median requirements values for

Without Clustering

	Requirements Value	Rank
R1.	6	3
R2.	5	5
R3.	9	1
R4.	9	1
R5.	6	3

With Clustering at cut off 8

	G1 0.33	G2 0.33	G3 0.33	Weighted Sum Value	Rank
R1.	7	3	5	4.95	4
R2.	4	9	7	6.6	3
R3.	9	4	8.5	7.095	1
R4.	7	5	9.5	7.095	1
R5.	3	3	9	4.95	4

Fig. 3. Extract from results of Volere Prioritization with and without clustering

each cluster that are closer to the actual values given by each stakeholder than the overall median value when no clustering technique is used. Thus, assuming the weights given to the groups are valid, we can claim that moving R1 from 3rd to 4th better reflects the choice of the stakeholders because it relies on using requirements values that are globally closer to the individual ratings than if all stakeholders are viewed as forming a single group. Furthermore, grouping stakeholders as we have done also opens up the possibility of applying more elaborate group decision-making techniques based on multi-objective optimization and fairness analysis [11].

3 Conclusion

Identifying stakeholders groups is essential for applying requirements prioritization and selection techniques when requirements values are collected from large number of individual stakeholders. Our approach consists in forming such groups from stakeholder's ratings using a hierarchical clustering analysis technique. We have applied our technique on a pilot case study at UCL for which we have shown that there is an improvement in overall closeness of the ratings used to make decisions when using cluster analysis. Our future work includes implementing a tool to enable requirements engineers to use this technique. We aim to enhance the technique with methods to describe the profiles of stakeholders belonging to a group and help decision makers assessing the weight to be assigned to each group. Divergences among stakeholders rating within a group might also be used to detect ambiguous requirements. Our immediate future plan is to test our technique on large independent data sets collected using StakeSource [3].

References

1. Laurent, P., Cleland-Huang, J.: Lessons learned from open source projects for facilitating online requirements processes. In: Glinz, M., Heymans, P. (eds.) REFSQ 2009. LNCS, vol. 5512, pp. 240–255. Springer, Heidelberg (2009)
2. Lim, S.L., Quercia, D., Finkelstein, A.: StakeNet: using social networks to analyse the stakeholders of large-scale software projects. In: Proc. ICSE 2010, pp. 295–304 (2010)
3. Lim, S.L.: Social Networks and Collaborative Filtering for Large-Scale Requirements Elicitation. PhD Thesis. School of Computer Science and Engineering, University of New South Wales (2010)
4. van Lamsweerde, A.: Reasoning About Alternative Requirements Options. In: Mylopoulos, J., Borgida, A., et al. (eds.) Conceptual Modeling: Foundations and Applications. LNCS, vol. 5600, pp. 380–397. Springer, Heidelberg (2009)
5. Karlsson, J., Ryan, K.: A cost-value approach for prioritizing requirements. IEEE Software 14, 67–74 (1997)
6. Robertson, S., Robertson, J.C.: Mastering the Requirements Process. Addison-Wesley, Reading (2006)
7. Karl Wiegers, E.: First things first: Prioritizing requirements. Software Development 7(10), 24–30 (1999)
8. IBM - Project, product and portfolio management software - Rational Focal Point - Software, http://www-01.ibm.com/software/rational/

9. Zhang, Y., Harman, M., Mansouri, S.A.: The multi-objective next release problem. In: Proc. GECCO 2009, pp. 1129–1137 (2009)
10. Finkelstein, A., Harman, M., Mansouri, S.A., Ren, J., Zhang, Y.: Fairness Analysis in Requirements Assignments. In: Proc. RE 2008, pp. 115–124 (2008)
11. Zhang, Y.: Multi-Objective Search-based Requirements Selection and Optimisation. PhD Thesis. Department of Computer Science, King's College London (2010)
12. Wedel, M., Kamakura, W.A.: Market segmentation: conceptual and methodological foundations. Springer, Heidelberg (2000)
13. Everitt, B.S., Landau, S., Leese, M.: Cluster Analysis, Hodder Arnold (2001)

Author Index